Unaccompanied Children in America

Recent Titles in the
CONTEMPORARY WORLD ISSUES
Series

Remote Learning and Distance Education
William H. Pruden III

Religious Belief and Science
Glenn H. Utter

Child Welfare in America
Yvonne Vissing

Water in the West
Jacqueline Vaughn

Teen Runaways in America
Michele Wakin

Electronic Waste
Josh Lepawsky

Youth Activism
Hava Rachel Gordon

Extreme Weather and Climate Change
Mariangelica Groves

Black Lives Matter
Shaonta' Allen, Simone N. Durham, and Angela Jones

Human Rights around the World
Yvonne Vissing

Political Representation in America
Lori Cox Han and Caroline Heldman

Paying College Athletes
Jimmy Sanderson, Editor

Privilege in America
Kelly L. McFaden and Sheri C. Hardee

Mass Incarceration in America
Rachel M. Durso

Unaccompanied Children in America

A Reference Handbook

Robert G. Hasson III

BLOOMSBURY ACADEMIC
NEW YORK • LONDON • OXFORD • NEW DELHI • SYDNEY

BLOOMSBURY ACADEMIC
Bloomsbury Publishing Inc, 1359 Broadway, New York, NY 10018, USA
Bloomsbury Publishing Plc, 50 Bedford Square, London, WC1B 3DP, UK
Bloomsbury Publishing Ireland, 29 Earlsfort Terrace, Dublin, 2, D02 AY28, Ireland

First published in the United States of America 2026

Cover image: John Moore / Staff / Getty Images

Library of Congress Control Number: 2025951056

ISBN: HB: 978-1-4408-8076-6
ePDF: 978-1-4408-8077-3
eBook: 979-8-7651-1661-6

Series: Contemporary World Issues

Typeset by Integra Software Services Pvt. Ltd.
Printed and bound in the United States of America

For product safety related questions contact productsafety@bloomsbury.com.

Contents

Preface

This book focuses on a uniquely vulnerable and growing population of immigrants. It sheds light on the background, experiences, challenges, and opportunities unaccompanied children encounter as they arrive in the United States and begin navigating a complex and unforgiving immigration system. The book begins with key historical contexts, including landmark federal legislation that directly impacts the lives and well-being of unaccompanied children. It also covers the migration journeys unaccompanied children experience and the placement pathways they navigate, while paying special attention to the distinct federal programs that are designed to support unaccompanied children.

Chapter 2 focuses on the problems, controversies, and solutions that relate to unaccompanied children in the United States, including analysis of the reasons that contribute to migration to the United States, the migration journey itself, key features of border encounters and apprehension, the role and impact of immigrant detention for unaccompanied children, and the different contexts of placement processes unaccompanied children must navigate as they resettle in the United States. Chapter 2 concludes with an analysis of the integration experience of unaccompanied children and explores key questions regarding health, mental health, education, neighborhoods, and legal status, and how these domains influence unaccompanied children's integration.

Chapter 3 offers compelling accounts from experts who work directly with unaccompanied children in various settings, as well as policy and academic experts who contribute to the growing knowledge base on unaccompanied children. Chapter 4 profiles the various federal agencies and nonprofit organizations that directly interact with unaccompanied children as well as individuals who are leaders of organizations that advocate for and provide services for unaccompanied children. Chapter 5 presents key documents that add context to the analysis provided in other chapters. Chapter 6 offers a review of the various resources that can deepen understanding of unaccompanied children, including the books, articles and reports, journals and magazines, and films that focus on unaccompanied children. Chapter 7 provides a chronology of events related to the subject of unaccompanied children. The book concludes with a glossary of key terms and an index.

Acknowledgments

This book is based on research across almost ten years, and it was made possible due to the support of many different individuals. My parents, Bob and Sue Hasson, have supported and encouraged my work from the beginning. I don't think I would have been able to write a book without my parents reading me so many books in my childhood and showing me the magic that stories and writing can give us.

My colleagues in the Department of Social Work at Providence College have encouraged my growth as a professor and social worker, and I am especially grateful for Susan Grossman, Michael Hayes, Katie Kranz, Kendra Marasco, Molly Driessen, Jordyn Hagar, Sara Melucci, and Mel Wathen. My colleague, Bob Hackey, connected me with ABC-CLIO. Our friendly hallway chats have been immensely helpful for me as I grow as a faculty member. Will Toner, Director of the Writing Center at Providence College, provided space and valued encouragement during faculty writing groups.

My colleagues at the Center for Immigration and Child Welfare have been valued thought partners throughout my career as a social work professor. Tom Crea has offered generous mentorship beyond my years as a PhD student, and I appreciate his guidance and encouragement. I am particularly grateful for my colleagues who contributed essays for the book, including Kerri Evans, Zayna Lyon, Maryam Rafieifar, and Silvia Melgar.

Among the most joyful collaborations for me have been with student researchers, some of whom contributed to research that is included in this book, including Bianca LaBella, Clara Oliva, Marifer Sanchez Gaspar, Salam Makram, and Gabriela Muniz Gonzalez.

This book received a lot of support from colleagues at ABC-CLIO, especially Kevin Hillstrom and Nicole Azze. I am thankful for their helpful encouragement and generous editorial insights.

Much of the research outlined in this book was possible due to collaborations with different organizations. Dorcas International Institute of Rhode Island has been a supportive partner in building the knowledge base on unaccompanied children and developing supports to help their integration in the United States.

I am especially grateful for the staff and unaccompanied children who met with me throughout the course of this book project.

I am grateful for various funders of the research in this book, including the Providence College Department of Social Work, The Providence College School of Education and Social Work, and The Rhode Island IDeA Network of Biomedical Research Excellence (RI-INBRE) program.

This book was encouraged and championed by my closest friend and love of my life, my wife, Caitlin Fairfield Hasson. She is the most thoughtful reader and most brilliant writer I know, and her feedback and encouragement throughout this book project was an enormous inspiration.

Pan Am
Pan Am

1

Background and History

The waiting room at the nonprofit is usually bustling. Several people—individuals, couples, or families—are seated in the room, meeting with a staff person or waiting to do so. On the wall are multiple clocks set to time zones around the world, providing a connection between the United States and the family, friends, and other loved ones still in their home countries. Around the room are posters announcing upcoming English-language classes, employment training opportunities, an advertisement for a local farmers market, and information regarding legal rights. Not unlike the bustling rows of benches and long lines at Ellis Island in a previous century, the activity in the small waiting room of this nonprofit continues the time-honored tradition of helping immigrants from around the world begin their new journey in the United States.

The waiting room is a constant din of case managers speaking with clients, clients speaking with one another, and clients speaking into their cell phones. Any language imaginable can be heard throughout the room. The conversations range from learning how to read a rental agreement with a landlord to how to apply for a job to how to enroll in school. The people in the waiting room represent all manner of those who migrate to the United States, including refugees and asylum seekers. They arrive as individuals, as couples, or as families. But some arrive as young people, completely alone and without family or caregivers. These young people migrate to the United States seeking safety and opportunity. In the waiting room, they may be with their sponsor, a family member, or another adult sponsor who serves as their guardian. The story of their migration journey to the United States is a unique one and includes vulnerability and risks that are

---

South Vietnamese children on board a Pan Am flight to San Francisco during Operation Babylift, April 5, 1975. The month-long US government initiative focused on evacuating children displaced by the Vietnam War and resulted in more than 3,000 children being airlifted out of the country. (US National Archives)

distinct for children. This book is about these young people—unaccompanied children—and the experiences they have before they migrate to the United States, during their journey, and after they arrive at a US border. The book unpacks the complexities of the US immigration system that unaccompanied children must navigate and sheds light on the hopes, dreams, and ambitions that unaccompanied children bring with them.

Overview

Throughout history, the United States has been the destination for millions of immigrants who come from all corners of the world to pursue opportunity, seek refuge, and build new lives. According to the Migration Policy Institute, the number of legal permanent residents (LPR) steadily increased beginning in 1820, with 1,285,349 arriving in 1907. The number of LPR plummeted to 23,068 in 1933 as the United States navigated the challenges of the First World War and was later on the cusp of the Second World War. After the Second World War and throughout the remainder of the twentieth century, however, the number of people arriving in the United States steadily grew, with 1,826,595 arriving in 1991, which was the largest number in a single year since 1820 (Migration Policy Institute 2022). Between 1991 and 2023, the pattern of high numbers of immigrants arriving in the United States continued, with an average of 968,263 arrivals per year. These immigrants constituted individuals, couples, and families, all arriving in the United States seeking what is spelled out clearly at the base of the Statue of Liberty—a "yearning to breathe free" (Lazarus n.d.).

In more recent decades, particularly since the end of the Vietnam War, new types of child immigrants began arriving in the United States to escape war, avoid destitution, and pursue freedom and opportunity. However, unlike the millions of immigrants throughout US history who have arrived as individual adults, adults in families, or children in families, these immigrants are unique in that they are alone and under age eighteen. Classified by the US government as "unaccompanied alien children," these young people enter the US immigration system without caregiver support, which is among the most important protective factors for the healthy development of children. For example, caregivers can prevent children from directly experiencing harm, mitigate risk when children do experience harm, and buffer the effects of adversity by physically and emotionally soothing children to promote strong attachments (Masten

2014). Furthermore, psychologist Ann Masten explains that "among the most devastating dangers faced by children are circumstances that destroy or damage the availability or function of families" (Masten 2014, 217). Given the wide body of research that demonstrates the critical role parents and caregivers play in ensuring the health and well-being of children, it is clear that unaccompanied children—immigrants who are apprehended at the US border without a parent or caregiver, are under eighteen years old, and do not have legal status in the United States—are an especially vulnerable group of immigrants.

Historical Contexts of Unaccompanied Children in the United States

Unaccompanied children have migrated to the United States in unprecedented numbers since 2014; however, there is a much longer history of unaccompanied children arriving at the US border. According to historian Ivón Padilla-Rodríguez (2020), unaccompanied children have been migrating to the United States since the nineteenth century. Between 1892 and 1924, a time of record immigration, 2.78 million children entered the country. Children migrated to the United States during this time to escape violence from war, to seek family reunification, and to pursue education opportunities—all reasons that mirror the reasons unaccompanied children migrate to the United States nearly 100 years later in the twenty-first century.

In the early part of the twentieth century, children from different parts of the world faced unique challenges to immigration. Children from Asia were at risk of deportation due to the Chinese Exclusion Act of 1882, as well as the *Takao Ozawa v. United States* Supreme Court decision, in which a Japanese immigrant was denied naturalization despite having lived in the United States for twenty years. Migration from Mexico in the early twentieth century was largely unencumbered, due to the border being largely unguarded. However, children migrating to the United States from Mexico faced stricter border control and increased risk of deportation with the 1924 Immigration Act. After the Second World War, children migrating from Mexico also faced increased racial discrimination, which complicated their migration to the United States (Padilla-Rodríguez 2020). Unaccompanied children were admitted to the United States in small numbers post-Second World War, with approximately 33,000 children arriving through twelve different immigration programs. These twelve programs were not designed specifically for unaccompanied children; rather, they formed a patchwork of policies to address the needs of unaccompanied children in the context of broader immigration trends in the United States as well as growing crises (Steinbock 1989, 140). Other programs aimed at specifically addressing the needs of unaccompanied children followed.

The Wagner-Rogers Children's Bill of 1939 would have admitted 20,000 unaccompanied children, primarily Jewish, from Germany in response to the rise of Nazi race laws that endangered the lives of Jewish children and families, among other marginalized groups in Germany. The Wagner-Rogers Children's Bill was never adopted, and opposition was fierce and wide-ranging. The wide range of opposition to the bill included disagreement regarding the circumstances requiring the children's removal and concern that the bill would complicate existing quota systems in immigration laws. However, there were also criticisms of the bill that echoed nationalist political ideology, including the belief that aid in the bill should be redirected to American children suffering from poverty, the concern that the German children would later take employment opportunities from American adults, and that admitting unaccompanied German children would lead to later pressure to admit other family members. In addition, anti-Semitism drove opposition to the bill, as opposition was based in part on the belief that the majority of children being resettled would be Jewish, even though the bill was not explicitly limited to Jewish children. As is discussed later in this book, these concerns in the 1930s serve as a prelude to later opposition for unaccompanied children from other parts of the world, including recent arrivals from Central America (Steinbock 1989, 147).

Programs in subsequent years that aimed to support unaccompanied children by facilitating admission to the United States included the Evacuation of British Children Program of 1940 (1,311 children), Child Refugees on the Continent in 1942 (110 children), Truman Doctrine of 1945 (1,275 children), the Displaced Persons Act of 1948 (3,037 children), the Refugee Relief Act of 1953 (4,000 children), the Refugee Escape Act of 1957 (2,500 children), the Hungarian Refugee Program in 1956–7, and the Cuban Refugee Program in 1960–2 (8,000 children) (Steinbock 1989, 141). However, it was not until the Refugee Act of 1980 that the United States formalized an approach to meet the needs of unaccompanied children. Prior to this, as legal scholar Daniel Steinbock (1989) explains, a variety of creative legal maneuvers were used to influence unaccompanied children's admission to the United States in the responses to crises, such as the Second World War. The legal mechanisms sometimes focused on admitting unaccompanied children as part of national quotas in existing immigration law and policy.

Operation Pedro Pan

The Cuban Refugee Program was in response to the Cuban Revolution (1953–9), where thousands of people were displaced as a result of fleeing government repression. Within this program was the largest migration of unaccompanied children to the United States. Known as Operation Pedro Pan and facilitated in part by the US government, the operation differed from previous migration experiences in Europe that were public and in response to growing fascism and the rise of Nazi rule in Germany. As journalist Yvonne Conde (1999) explains, "In contrast to these European exoduses, the political exodus of 14,048 Cuban children to the United States in the early 1960s is the only such event in the Western Hemisphere. Not an organized mass departure and more covert than the European exoduses, the children's departures were a cautious trickling out of Cuba, on commercial airplanes, on a daily basis" (xii).

In a wide-ranging book on Operation Pedro Pan, Conde (1999) details the life experiences of children who experienced the migration from Cuba to the United States. Research on mental health outcomes of this population of child migrants shows that children who migrated to the United States from Cuba as part of Operation Pedro Pan exhibited resilience that was best explained by their anticipation of family members later joining them. However, a more nuanced look at the life experiences of these children shows the toll that migration-related stress and trauma can have on children's well-being: "This life-altering trauma left each and every Pedro Pan child changed. It left each child wise beyond his or her years. It enlivened a survival instinct that children rarely need to rely on to survive their childhood. Without a doubt, the impact of the separation is still a vital part of the adult children" (Conde 1999, 207).

Operation Babylift

After Operation Pedro Pan, the next major migration of unaccompanied children to the United States occurred in the context of war. Like the Second World War, the Vietnam War resulted in conditions that placed children and families at risk and in need of safe haven from the trauma of war. This resulted in thousands of unaccompanied children being admitted to the United States through a variety of programs, including Operation Babylift in 1975.

Operation Babylift was a US government-sponsored program that lasted the month of April in 1975 and focused on evacuating Vietnamese children who were displaced as a result of the Vietnam War. The initiative resulted in more than 3,000 children being airlifted from Vietnam and was the cause of some controversy. For example, some in the United States viewed the effort as an attempt by the US government to gain support for the war, which at the time was unpopular among large portions of the US population. In addition, some questioned whether or not the Vietnamese children were unaccompanied at all, or if their parents and caregivers remained in Vietnam. After the operation, lawsuits in the United States attempted to use the court system to force the reunification of the children with their parents; however, these efforts largely failed, and only twelve children, of the more than 3,000, were eventually reunified with their parents. The chaotic nature of war limited the ability of the US and Vietnamese governments to keep accurate records of the children and their parents, which hampered later efforts at reunification. Although lasting only a month, Operation Babylift was a catalyst for future efforts to support children displaced because of the Vietnam War. These efforts included the Indochina Refugee Program (800 children), the Indochinese Refugee Program (8,000 children), and the Amerasians Program (300 children), which began in 1982.

US Refugee Act of 1980

It was not until the 1980 Refugee Act that official policy was implemented that guided the care, custody, and protection of unaccompanied children in the United States. The importance of the 1980 Refugee Act as it related to the care of unaccompanied children is hard to overstate, as Steinbock (1989) details: "The Refugee Act of 1980 and the regulations and policies developed for its administration have resolved many of the most serious recurring problems in supporting, supervising, and placing unaccompanied children admitted to the United States" (154). One of the major policy challenges prior to the 1980 Refugee Act was coordinating funds for foster care and health services for unaccompanied children upon their arrival in the United States. A dramatic influx of unaccompanied children from Cuba between 1960 and 1962 overwhelmed the capacity of nongovernmental agencies to provide these key services for unaccompanied children, which prompted a more concerted effort to coordinate resources. Policy development during this time period was reactionary and implemented only after unexpected arrivals of unaccompanied children resettled in the United States. Government financial assistance for unaccompanied children resettled in the 1970s was implemented under the Indochinese Refugee Assistance Program; however, this program was expected to expire at the end of 1979 (Steinbock 1989).

The passage of the 1980 Refugee Act formalized a series of supports and resources for unaccompanied refugee children in the United States. In particular, the law gave authority and responsibility to the US Office of Refugee Resettlement (ORR), which is directed under the auspices of the US Department of Health and Human Services, for "the care and supervision of and legal responsibility for unaccompanied refugee children in the State" (Office of Refugee Resettlement [ORR] 2012). The law also explains that ORR, in coordination with state child welfare authorities, is responsible for placement of the unaccompanied refugee child before or shortly after their arrival in the United States. Furthermore, the law specifies that unaccompanied refugee children are provided care until one month after they turn eighteen, or a higher age if allowed under the State's child welfare laws and implementation of part B of title IV of the Social Security Act (ORR 2012). One gap in the US Refugee Act of 1980 is a lack of language that specifies the length of time an unaccompanied child can remain in a detention-style facility. This gap was addressed in 1985 in response to a class action lawsuit filed against the US government for its long detentions of immigrant children and their families.

Flores Settlement Agreement

The Flores Settlement Agreement is the result of a class action lawsuit, *Flores v. Reno*, a 1985 California case. The class action was in response to the detention of immigrant families and children and specifically challenged the constitutionality of the US government's practices and policies related to the apprehension and detention of immigrant children. Immigrant advocates recognized concerning conditions regarding the facilities children were held in, as well as the timeline of their detention.

The certified class in the lawsuit extended beyond unaccompanied children and included "all minors who are detained in the custody of the INS." At the time of the lawsuit, unaccompanied minors in US custody were under the care of

Immigration and Naturalization Service (INS). The lawsuit included more than a decade of litigation and resulted in a consent decree in 1997 that established standards for where unaccompanied children are housed while in the United States. The consent decree begins by establishing context and emphasizing the special care required for immigrant children in detention. Specifically, the consent decree required INS to treat "all minors in its custody with dignity, respect and special concern for their particular vulnerability as minors." In addition, immigrant minors in US custody must be placed in the least restrictive setting available that is appropriate for their age and any special needs they present. INS is also not required to release children to "any person or agency" who is believed to be a risk for harming or neglecting the child or fails to appear with the child in immigration court.

The Flores Settlement Agreement consent decree includes specific instructions that aim to ensure the health and safety of immigrant children who are detained by immigration authorities. The consent decree explains: "Whenever the INS takes a minor into custody, it shall expeditiously process the minor and shall provide the minor with a notice of rights, including the right to a bond redetermination hearing if applicable." Facilities where children are detained must also have resources to meet basic human needs, including: "Access to toilets and sinks, drinking water and food as appropriate, medical assistance if the minor is in need of emergency services, adequate temperature control and ventilation, adequate supervision to protect minors from others, and contact with family members who were arrested with the minor."

The Flores Settlement Agreement specifies the steps necessary for placing children in the least restrictive setting possible. Within three to five days of apprehension and detention, the government must follow one of two paths to placement: "(1) release the minor to a parent, legal guardian, adult relative, or other 'capable and willing' designated adult or entity; or (2) place the minor in a nonsecure facility licensed by an appropriate State agency to provide residential, group, or foster care services for dependent children." The settlement agreement specifies that unaccompanied children are to be separated from unrelated adults, and if separation is not possible, children cannot be detained with an unrelated adult for longer than twenty-four hours. Along with specifying the placement setting, the Flores Settlement Agreement limits the time unaccompanied children spend in detention upon their apprehension at the US border. Given how detrimental incarceration is on children, the Flores Settlement Agreement provides important guardrails for unaccompanied children who do not readily have parents or relatives to provide care in the United States. Importantly, the timeline of three to five days for placement in the least restrictive setting possible can be relaxed during emergencies or a substantial increase in unaccompanied children apprehended at the US border. In these circumstances, federal officials are tasked with placement of unaccompanied children in nonsecure licensed facilities "as expeditiously as possible" (Congressional Research Service 2021).

The Flores Settlement Agreement also identifies an order of preference for releasing children from detention. The order of preference includes a parent, legal guardian, or an adult relative such as a sibling, aunt, or uncle. An unrelated adult may take custody of the child, so long as an immigration official witnesses the signing of a declaration that details the relationship between the child and the adult. Additional placement types include licensed programs, such as a residential treatment center.

Individuals who take custody of an unaccompanied child must agree to a set of stipulations outlined in the Flores Settlement Agreement, including agreeing to meet the child's physical, emotional, and financial needs and ensuring the child will attend all future immigration court proceedings. The adult also must agree to notify the US government within five days of changing address, or if the adult leaves the United States or is otherwise unable to meet the physical, emotional, or financial needs of the child. The US government can also require a home study to assess the adult's capacity to meet the child's immediate needs. If the child is unable to be placed with a parent, legal guardian, or other sponsor type, they will remain in the custody of the US government and will reside in a licensed program until placement in a less restrictive setting is available.

Since the consent decree was established in 1997, federal officials have based immigration policy for unaccompanied children in compliance with the Flores Settlement Agreement. However, President Donald Trump's first administration was the first known presidential administration to actively attempt to avoid aspects of the consent decree. Among the most direct attempts by the administration to undermine the Flores Settlement Agreement was the 2017 Zero-Tolerance Policy. As legal scholar Richard Vadasy (2021) outlines, this policy required immigration officials to arrest anyone attempting to cross a US border and detain them during their immigration proceeding. Many families crossing the border at this time were seeking asylum. Given the lengthy timeline for asylum cases to be heard in immigration court, this meant children would be detained long past the maximum twenty days allowed under the Flores Settlement Agreement. Furthermore, the Zero-Tolerance Policy required the forced separation of children from their parents, which led to adult migrants being detained and children being transferred to the care and custody of the ORR. As Zero Tolerance resulted in the forced separation of children from their parents, there was growing concern in the legal community that central tenets of the Flores Settlement Agreement were being overlooked or ignored. This resulted in various lawsuits on behalf of children who were detained beyond the length of time allowed by the agreement.

First, a lawsuit in 2018, *Ms. L. v. U.S. Immigration and Customs Enforcement* resulted in the US District Court for the Southern District of California ruling in favor of migrant families, with the court finding that "the family separation policy was in violation of the Due Process Clause because children were being removed from their parents without the parents first being deemed unfit" (Vadasy 2021, 85). Immediately after this lawsuit, the Trump administration filed a court motion asking that the Flores Settlement Agreement be amended "to allow maximum flexibility for handling family units," which would result in lengthy detention of unaccompanied children. While this was initially overruled by a federal judge, it was later upheld in January 2020 by the US District Court of the Southern District of California, which ruled that the Trump administration was implementing immigration policy that was in accordance with the law. This resulted in continued detention of parents, under the guise that their arrest for crossing the US border deemed them unfit for parenting.

Finally, the Trump administration challenged the Flores Settlement Agreement altogether during the lawsuit *Flores v. Barr.* In September 2019, a federal judge ruled in favor of preserving the Flores Settlement Agreement. President Trump's proposal, it was ruled, would place unaccompanied children further at risk by substantially altering their living conditions and the parameters of their detainment. For example, the proposal would remove the twenty-day limit on detention for immigrant children and would also change family detention licensing standards from state-based to meeting standards outlined by Immigration and Customs Enforcement (ICE).

Homeland Security Act of 2002

The Department of Homeland Security (DHS) was formed in response to the 9/11 terrorist attacks in New York, Washington, DC, and Pennsylvania. Eleven days after the 9/11 attacks, the White House formed the Office of Homeland Security to coordinate safety and national security responses at the federal level

(US Department of Homeland Security 2023). There are several components to the primary mission of DHS, including preventing terrorist attacks in the United States and minimizing any damage from terrorist attacks that occur. The Homeland Security Act of 2002 also led to landmark changes to how immigration enforcement is organized at the federal level.

Prior to the Homeland Security Act of 2002, immigration matters were managed by the INS. However, with the passing of the Homeland Security Act of 2002, all immigration matters were transferred to DHS, INS closed, and the newly formed US Citizenship and Immigration Services department was established. These changes included moving all border patrol functions under the purview of DHS.

The Homeland Security Act of 2002 specified that unaccompanied children apprehended by DHS officials, including Border Patrol, would be transferred to the ORR, which is under the US Department of Health and Human Services. This important shift was an attempt to ensure that the best interests of children would be prioritized. Under the auspices of the Director of ORR, various responsibilities outlined in the Homeland Security Act of 2002 included "coordinating and implementing the care and placement of unaccompanied alien children who are in Federal custody by reason of their immigration status." By law, the act also specified that officials collect an array of biographic data, including an unaccompanied child's name, date of birth, country of birth, date of arrival in the United States, and information regarding placement in shelters upon arrival in the United States. The Homeland Security Act of 2002 is among the most recent pieces of federal legislation that outlines specific responsibilities for caring for unaccompanied children who are transferred from DHS to the Department of Health and Human Services, of which ORR is part.

Unaccompanied Alien Child Protection Act of 2005

After the Homeland Security Act of 2002 reorganized immigration enforcement at the federal level, additional laws were passed to address the specific needs of unaccompanied children. Congress passed the Unaccompanied Alien Child Protection Act of 2005, which aims to strengthen the supports for unaccompanied children in US custody. Originally introduced in the 108th Congress as H.R. 3361, the Unaccompanied Alien Child Protection Act of 2003, the bill identifies "procedures for immigration officers who find an unaccompanied alien child at a U.S. land border or point of entry who is a national or habitual resident of a contiguous country." Much of the bill aims to incorporate child welfare best practices to ensure the health and well-being of unaccompanied children. For example, the bill prioritizes family reunification and prohibits detention of unaccompanied children in adult facilities. Other aspects of the bill acknowledge the complex intersection of child welfare and immigration needs that are unique to unaccompanied children. For example, the bill prohibits the federal government from repatriating unaccompanied children back to countries of origin that may pose threats to their safety and also shields unaccompanied children from certain deportation pathways. The bill also authorizes unaccompanied children to have access to legal counsel and a guardian *ad litem* to ensure their best interests are identified and advocated for. Finally, the bill outlines documentation and training requirements, such as including data on human trafficking in annual reports and providing training on the needs of unaccompanied children for immigration officials (H.R.3361, 108th Congress 2003).

Trafficking Victims Protection Reauthorization Act of 2008

The Trafficking Victims Protection Reauthorization Act (TVPRA) of 2008 is an amendment of the Trafficking Victims Protection Act of 2000 that aims to prevent and mitigate the harms caused by human trafficking. Along with various procedures for caring for unaccompanied children, TVPRA broadly calls for coordinated efforts between the Secretary of Homeland Security, the Secretary of State, the Attorney General, and the Secretary of Health and Human Services to facilitate the safe repatriation of unaccompanied children to their country of origin. It also outlines an array of special considerations for unaccompanied children who are nationals or are a "habitual resident of a country that is contiguous with the United States." This essentially means that TVPRA outlines special considerations for unaccompanied children from Canada or Mexico.

The chief consideration is determining an unaccompanied child's ability to remain in the United States. TVPRA explains that immigration officers can determine an unaccompanied child as inadmissible under three different conditions: (1) if the child has not been the victim of human trafficking and there is no known fear of trafficking if the child is returned to their country of origin, (2) there is no known fear that the child is at risk of persecution if returned to their country of origin, and (3) "the child is able to make an independent decision to withdraw the child's application for admission to the United States" (H.R.7311, 110th Congress 2008, 122 STAT. 5075).

TVPRA also explains conditions that must be met in the event an unaccompanied child from a contiguous country is apprehended at the US border and determined ineligible for admission. Led by the Secretary of State, TVPRA requires that the United States have ongoing agreements with countries contiguous to the United States so unaccompanied children are safely returned to their country of origin. This includes coordinating with border officials in the country of origin, collaborating with child welfare workers, returning children at "reasonable business hours," and ensuring that border officials of contiguous countries have training on the unique needs of unaccompanied children.

Unaccompanied children are screened within forty-eight hours of apprehension by border officials to determine if they meet criteria for repatriation as described by TVPRA. In the event they do not meet criteria for repatriation and are eligible to remain in the United States, they are transferred to the care of the Department of Health and Human Services, specifically the ORR. TVPRA also required the Secretaries of State, Health and Human Services, and Homeland Security to create a pilot program for facilitating the safe return of unaccompanied children from contiguous countries. In addition, the law requires assessment of country conditions to ensure children are not returned to unsafe environments.

TVPRA also requires annual reporting on the numbers of unaccompanied children ordered removed from the United States and the number returned to their country of origin. This annual report also includes an array of demographic data, including the nationalities, ages, and genders of the unaccompanied children. The report also requires data on the type of immigration relief unaccompanied children attempted to receive and were subsequently denied.

Unaccompanied Children Today

An unaccompanied child is defined as: "a child who has no lawful immigration status in the United States; has not attained 18 years of age; and, with respect to whom, there is no parent or legal guardian in the United States, or no parent or legal guardian in the United States available to provide care and physical custody" (Administration for Children and Families 2024). Unaccompanied children migrated to the United States in increasing numbers beginning in 2012. In FY2012, 13,625 unaccompanied children were apprehended and referred to the ORR. This number nearly doubled in FY2013, to 24,668 unaccompanied children. The trend of dramatic increases in unaccompanied children arriving in the United States continued, with 57,496 arrivals in FY2014, 33,726 arrivals in FY2015, 59,170 arrivals in FY2016, 40,810 arrivals in FY2017, 49,100 arrivals in FY2018, and 69,488 arrivals in FY2019. There was a dramatic decrease in the number of unaccompanied children arriving in FY2020, to 15,381, as a result of the global Covid-19 pandemic. However, a record number of unaccompanied children—122,731—arrived in FY2021, followed by another record number of arrivals in FY2022, 128,904. FY2023 included a slight decrease to 118,938 unaccompanied children apprehended and transferred to ORR; however, this number is several times the number of arrivals just a decade earlier (ORR 2024a).

While unaccompanied children migrate to the United States from around the world, the overwhelming majority migrate from three Central American countries—El Salvador, Guatemala, and Honduras. Data from the ORR indicates that in FY2023, nearly half of all unaccompanied children who were referred to ORR migrated from Guatemala (42 percent), followed by children from Honduras (28 percent), and children from El Salvador (9 percent). Children from Mexico comprised 8 percent of arrivals, and all other countries comprised 13 percent of arrivals in FY2023. FY2023 is not a standout year—previous years reveal a similar pattern, with Guatemala comprising the majority of arrivals between FY2015 and FY2023 (ORR 2024a).

There is also a stark difference by gender for unaccompanied children arriving in the United States. Historically, the majority of unaccompanied children arriving in the United States identify as male. In FY2023, 61 percent of unaccompanied children identified as male, and 39 percent identified as female. This trend of substantial gender differences is similar between FY2012 and FY2023.

Most unaccompanied children who migrate to the United States are between fifteen and seventeen years old. In FY2023, 35 percent of arrivals were 17 years old, 34 percent were 15–16 years old, 19 percent were 0–12 years old, and 12 percent were 13–14 years old. One explanation for most arrivals being older adolescents is the various hazards that are part of the migration journey, including human trafficking and sexual and economic exploitation. However, substantial numbers of children are much younger, indicating that various supports are needed to meet different developmental needs.

Before the migration journey to the United States, unaccompanied children and their families face seemingly impossible decisions. Migration journeys are influenced by a need to escape violence or poverty or to pursue education or economic opportunities. Sometimes, children migrate to reunify with a parent they have not seen in years. In other circumstances, parents face an anguished decision to send their child to the United States to escape community violence and live with a family member, such as an aunt, uncle, or cousin.

The duration of migration journeys varies and can be affected by delays in crossing the borders of countries on the way to the US border. Unaccompanied children who migrate to the United States typically travel using a variety of methods, including walking, buses, cars, rafts, and trains. Children may travel alone or with siblings, but many migrants from Central America are escorted to the United States with the assistance of a smuggler, known as a *coyote*. Unaccompanied children forced to flee violence and deep poverty face a migration journey that contains shifting and unpredictable conditions that threaten their health and well-being. The challenges and risks unaccompanied children face while migrating to the United States are explored in more detail in Chapter 2.

Unaccompanied Children and the US Immigration System

The US immigration system is a vast bureaucratic network that manages the flow of millions of people who arrive in the United States each year. This includes managing various types of visas for students, workers, and individuals reunifying with family who have resettled in the United States, as well as welcoming refugees escaping war or persecution in their native countries. The US immigration system also includes monitoring and securing thousands of miles of land and water borders. Managing US borders includes preventing unauthorized border crossings, as well as apprehending and processing individuals who migrate to the United States to file a claim of asylum. Unaccompanied children are among the most vulnerable immigrants of the hundreds of thousands of immigrants who are apprehended at the US border each year.

Unaccompanied children are typically apprehended at the US border by US Border Patrol and are transferred to the care and custody of the ORR. ORR is part of the US Department of Health and Human Services and is responsible for the care of unaccompanied children, including placing them in the least restrictive setting that aligns with their developmental and safety needs. The transfer from US Border Patrol to ORR is a result of changes in US law. Prior to the 2002 Homeland Security Act, unaccompanied children were cared for by INS. However, the 2002 Homeland Security Act included the change that unaccompanied children should be cared for by ORR, in an attempt to move away from immigration detention practices typically used with adults. Since this time, ORR has cared for more than 700,000 unaccompanied children, including finding placements and connecting the children with sponsors in the United States (Administration for Children and Families 2024).

Data shows that unaccompanied children, after apprehension at the US border, remain in ORR custody for varying lengths of time before being placed with a sponsor. Since 2015, the shortest average length of time an unaccompanied child was in ORR custody was twenty-seven days in 2023. The longest average length of time in ORR custody was sixty-nine days in 2020. This number corresponds with the lowest number of unaccompanied children referred to ORR in ten years, likely due to complications from the Covid-19 pandemic. Along with lower referrals to ORR, unaccompanied children remained in ORR custody for longer periods of time, likely due to complications with the sponsor placement process caused by the pandemic.

The remainder of this chapter describes the contexts and the processes involved with apprehending unaccompanied children at the US border as well as the various placement pathways unaccompanied children navigate from their apprehension at the border to their eventual placement with a foster care provider or a sponsor.

Apprehension and Processing at the Border

According to the US Census, the US-Mexico border spans 1,933 miles between San Diego, California, and Brownsville, Texas. Most of the border, 1,241 miles, is in Texas. Along the border and within the four border states (California, Arizona, New Mexico, and Texas) are sixty-five different official ports of entry. Most of these ports of entry—thirty-two—are in Texas (US Customs and Border Patrol 2023). A port of entry is an official crossing, where people and goods are transferred between the United States and Mexico while being monitored by US Customs and Border Patrol in the United States and Border Patrol in Mexico. Many unaccompanied children who migrate to the United States are apprehended between official ports of entry and must cross natural barriers, such as the Rio Grande River, or, at nearly 700 miles of the border, a physical border wall rising 30 feet above the ground. Some unaccompanied children seek out US Border Patrol, typically at an official port of entry, to begin the process of reunifying with family or caregivers who are in the United States. Many unaccompanied children arrive in the United States seeking asylum, which means the experience of crossing the border differs from the process other immigrants navigate as they arrive.

Unaccompanied children are processed by two different parts of US Customs and Border Protection: the Office of Border Patrol (OBP) and the Office of Field Operations (OFO). OBP officials are responsible for securing the border to prevent the unauthorized entry of any individuals or illegal substances, such as drugs, from entering the United States. OFO officials are responsible for processing individuals and goods that enter or leave the United States at official ports of entry. The main difference between OBP and OFO is where they encounter unaccompanied children. OBP officials patrol areas near the border that are between official ports of entry, whereas OFO officials are stationed at official ports of entry.

Once apprehended by US Customs and Border Patrol, unaccompanied children are processed to determine basic background information and evaluate next steps in their care. The processing of unaccompanied children differs for OBP and OFO officers. If a child is apprehended by an OBP official, they are initially transported to a border patrol station and placed in a juvenile hold room. A hold room is defined as "detention cells or search or interview rooms where individuals are temporarily detained pending processing or transfer" (US Department of Homeland Security Office of Inspector General 2010, 4). Next, OBP officials collect biometric and biographical information from the child to determine name, age, and citizenship. The child's home country consulate is notified, and officials will check immigration and criminal databases to assess if the child has a legal right to remain in the United States, as well as if the child has committed any crimes in the United States.

If the child is encountered at an official port of entry, they are processed by OFO officers. This process is similar to the process followed by OBP officials; however, the main difference is the child is not transported to a separate station, as official ports of entry already have facilities to process unaccompanied children and other immigrants. Children at official ports of entry are initially moved to a secondary screening area. Hold rooms at official ports of entry are defined as "areas at ports of entry where detained individuals may be temporarily held pending secondary processing, which involves verifying documents and conducting interviews" (US Department of Homeland Security Office of Inspector General 2010, 4).

Children are screened to determine if they are victims of human trafficking or are at risk of persecution if returned to their country of origin. Unaccompanied children from contiguous countries (Mexico) are most often voluntarily returned to their country of origin within forty-eight hours of apprehension. Within seventy-two hours, children from noncontiguous countries, including El Salvador, Guatemala, and Honduras, are transferred from US Border Patrol via ICE to the ORR, which is part of the US Department of Health and Human Services. ORR then has custody and placement responsibilities for unaccompanied children, who are initially placed in shelters operated by contracted nonprofit organizations. This initial placement is under the guidance outlined in the Flores Settlement Agreement, which stipulates the conditions in which unaccompanied children are detained and the length of time they can be legally detained in restrictive settings. Prior to the 2002 Homeland Security Act, the custody of unaccompanied children was managed by INS. Since the passage of that Act, unaccompanied children have been placed by ORR. There are two distinct US government programs within ORR that provide services and support for unaccompanied children: the Unaccompanied Children Program and the Unaccompanied Refugee Minors (URM) Program.

Unaccompanied Children Program

The unaccompanied children program is overseen by ORR and includes an array of services provided by local organizations throughout the United States that receive ORR funding to deliver services. ORR and local organizations collaborate to ensure funding is allocated and specific program requirements are met to ensure unaccompanied children's needs are met. One of the first steps in the unaccompanied children program is determining where a child will initially live after transferring from border patrol to the custody of ORR.

There are a variety of settings where unaccompanied children are placed. Each setting differs in terms of available supports, and all placements are designed to meet any special needs unaccompanied children may have—such as health or mental health needs—while also being in the least restrictive setting possible. Placement locations include shelter facilities, foster care, group homes, staff-secure or secure care facilities, or residential treatment centers. While in ORR custody, there are two placement decisions that can affect an unaccompanied child: "(1) the initial placement into a care provider facility or setting and (2) transfer placement between care providers" (ORR 2024b). Throughout the placement process, ORR uses child welfare principles to ensure the health and safety of unaccompanied children.

ORR accounts for several aspects that concern unaccompanied children when making placement decisions, including age, gender, if the child has siblings, and if there are specific sponsor options available to the child. ORR also accounts for the location at which the child was apprehended. In addition, ORR accounts for special needs related to language, health, or mental health, or youth who are pregnant or are with a child. ORR also assesses various risks that may impact placement, including the child's behavior, any history of abuse or victimization, criminal history, suicidal ideation, and if the child identifies as a sexual minority (e.g., gay, lesbian, bisexual, transgender, or nonbinary). ORR makes special placement considerations for unaccompanied children who are younger than thirteen, siblings where one child is less than thirteen, youth who are pregnant or parenting, and children with other special or complex health needs (ORR 2024b).

There are times when special safety concerns arise that inform the placement decisions ORR makes for unaccompanied children. For example, special care is taken when children report fear of others in the context of human trafficking or exploitation (e.g., smugglers, drug cartel members, etc.), or if the child was a witness to any crimes. In these cases, ORR collaborates with local law enforcement agencies to ensure unaccompanied children are placed in safe locations that will not place additional risk on their safety.

Staff Secure and Secure Placements

Although ORR aims to place unaccompanied children in the least restrictive setting possible, there are times when restrictive settings are required to ensure the safety of the child and the safety of others. If there is clear evidence that a child poses a risk to their own safety or the safety of others, ORR may place a child in two different types of restrictive settings: staff secure and secure. Staff secure facilities are not locked but rather include "heightened level of staff supervision, increased communication, and services to control problem behavior and prevent escape" (ORR 2024b). Secure facilities, on the other hand, are typically locked and "have a secure perimeter, major restraining construction inside the facility, and procedures typically associated with correctional facilities" (ORR 2024b).

There are clearly outlined processes that ORR must follow when placing a child in a restrictive setting, whether it is staff secure or secure. ORR must provide the child written notice of their placement in a restrictive setting within 48 hours of placement, as well as every thirty days the child is in a restrictive placement. This documentation is communicated with unaccompanied children in a manner that aligns with their language skills and developmental stage. For unaccompanied children with major mental illness, ORR may place a child in a therapeutic restrictive setting, such as a residential treatment center. The documentation requirements for this process are the same as other placements in restrictive settings; however, special care is taken to communicate the reasons for placement with the child (ORR 2024b).

There are a variety of considerations ORR accounts for when deciding to place a child in a staff secure facility. These include assessing the degree of behavioral disruption a child demonstrates in a regular shelter setting or if they exhibit risk of running away from placement. If unaccompanied children have a history of nonviolent criminal behavior, they may be placed in a staff secure facility for increased monitoring and supervision. Finally, children who are placed in secure settings may transition to staff secure if they demonstrate improvement with behavior or stabilized mental health symptoms.

Placement considerations for secure facilities include a variety of criminal-activity-related criteria. For example, ORR assesses if the child has been charged with a crime, convicted of a crime, or is deemed "chargeable" with a crime. In addition, children who self-disclose committing violent crime, or who have committed sexual abuse may be placed in a secure facility (ORR 2024b).

Unification and Reunification

After apprehension by Customs and Border Protection and transfer to the ORR, a primary goal is to achieve placement stability for unaccompanied children. While pathways from apprehension to placement may differ for unaccompanied children, placement stability often means unification or reunification with family members. Unification refers to unaccompanied children being placed with family the child has not lived with before. This could be an uncle, aunt, or older cousin who moved to the United States when the child was younger, or even before the child was born. Reunification refers to unaccompanied children being placed with a family member they have not lived with since being in their home country. One example is a child's father moving to the United States, and the child migrating to the United States years later to reunify.

The process of reunification can be a stressful experience for unaccompanied children. Unaccompanied children need to manage feelings of uncertainty and anxiety related to joining a new community. Learning how to navigate the neighborhood, meeting new friends, joining a new school, and constantly confronting language barriers are all stressors children encounter after migrating to the United States. Along with these stressors, unaccompanied children must navigate more nuanced challenges within family systems. Research shows that unaccompanied children may struggle when reunifying with parents who they had not lived with in several years. For example, qualitative research has found that unaccompanied children in their adolescent years reunified with parents who they had not lived with since early childhood. Family turmoil emerged when unaccompanied children struggled to meet expectations that were not aligned with their current developmental stage. Furthermore, this turmoil sometimes resulted in the need for family stabilization services (Hasson et al. 2024).

Initial Placement by ORR

ORR receives referrals for services from a variety of sources, and an intake team operates on a 24/7 basis to identify the immediate needs of unaccompanied children and determine the placement setting that is the least restrictive while meeting any immediate needs. A comprehensive initial assessment identifies health-related information, such as major physical or mental health needs, as well as if the child is pregnant or parenting. Basic background information is also collected, including name, age, gender, country of birth, date of apprehension in the United States, location of apprehension, and assessment of any concern regarding human trafficking. ORR will also assess family history to identify possible sponsor options for the unaccompanied child. The assessment will also cover histories of violence, mental health issues that may result in danger to self or others, gang involvement, as well as runaway risk.

ORR uses the initial assessment to identify an appropriate care provider as an initial placement. Care providers include "Any physical site, including an individual family home, that houses one or more unaccompanied alien children in ORR custody and is operated by an ORR-funded program that provides residential services for unaccompanied alien children. Out-of-network placements are not included within this definition" (ORR 2024c). There are times when referring agencies, such as Border Patrol, will communicate with ORR ahead of transferring a minor to ORR care to notify them that the child is unaccompanied. This can help facilitate the placement and reunification process for the child and limit the time they are away from family or sponsors. This happens before the child is in ORR and federal custody, before ORR receives a written referral, and before the child physically arrives at an ORR-sponsored placement setting (ORR 2024b).

There are two types of placement decisions ORR makes when unaccompanied children arrive in the United States: the initial placement of children and any transfer of children from ORR placement settings to a sponsor. If the unaccompanied child has existing complex health, mental health, or legal needs, a more restrictive setting may be considered, such as a secure or staff secure setting, residential treatment facility, or long-term foster care setting. Throughout the placement process, ORR's placement process is guided by existing laws and regulations (e.g., the Flores Settlement Agreement), as well as child welfare best practices to ensure unaccompanied children are placed in the least restrictive setting possible (ORR 2024b).

Research shows that some placement settings, such as long-term foster care, have distinguishing characteristics that guide how unaccompanied children are supported and cared for. For example, one study found that child welfare outcomes for unaccompanied children fell under three broad areas: safety, permanency, and well-being (Crea et al. 2022). Based on data collected from long-term foster care social workers, the research revealed that many child welfare outcomes for unaccompanied children align with those of US native-born children in the domestic child welfare system. For example, physical and emotional safety were identified as vital for unaccompanied children. However, there are important differences for unaccompanied children. For unaccompanied children, ensuring safety, permanency, and well-being must also account for cultural adjustment, including navigating language barriers. In addition, unaccompanied children are in immigration court proceedings to seek adjustment of their status and receive relief from deportation, which is a distinct difference from domestic child welfare.

Transfers within ORR

While in ORR care, unaccompanied children begin the process of adjusting to the United States; however, they are not yet in a permanent and stable setting. At this point in their migration journey, unaccompanied children are not yet placed with their sponsor or family member. This stage in the placement process may be accompanied by feelings of anxiety and unfamiliarity for children, as they are unsure of the timeline for their placement with a sponsor. For some children, they anticipated arriving in the United States and living with their parent, aunt, uncle, or other family member. Some unaccompanied children may experience changes in their health or mental health that require transfers within ORR's network of care providers.

Any changes to a child's placement while they are in ORR custody are carefully considered and evaluated. ORR staff use ongoing evaluation to assess the child's current placement. When considering transfers to another placement, ORR staff use an array of information to make informed decisions. For example, ORR staff considers information from the referral source, clinical assessment tools, the location of the child's anticipated sponsor, as well as information from the child's attorney. If new information is gathered from these sources, and ORR determines a placement change is needed, ORR must make the recommendation within three days of knowing the new information.

Transfers within ORR should prioritize the least restrictive setting possible, as these are the settings that promote adjustment while keeping children safe as they await placement with their sponsor. If an unaccompanied child is placed in a restrictive setting, such as a secure, staff-secure, or residential treatment center, then the child's case must be reviewed at least once every thirty days. Because restrictive settings constrain a child's ability to engage with others and their community, thirty-day case reviews are a standardized process for ORR to consider new and existing information to determine possible placements in a lower restrictive setting. The thirty-day case review is based on a consultation between the care provider, meaning the staff member at the restrictive setting, and the ORR case coordinator. Any decision to continue placement in a restrictive setting must be documented with a "notice of placement in a restrictive setting" form. The documentation is subsequently shared with the child and their attorney, as well as the child's parents when appropriate, and the child advocate, if they request a copy. Continuous placement in a restrictive setting beyond ninety days results in ongoing evaluation of the placement every thirty days to determine possible transfer options. Children can remain in residential treatment centers only if a licensed psychologist determines the child is a danger to themselves or others (ORR 2024b).

The process to transfer unaccompanied children within ORR's network relies on a combination of careful documentation review and consultation with professionals and service providers in the child's life. It is a recognition that circumstances in a child's life can change, leading to special services and settings needed to meet unique and emergent needs in the child's life. More broadly, the specific process of a child transferring within ORR's network is further recognition that the migration journey that unaccompanied children experience is complex and not simply arriving in the United States to be placed with their sponsor or family member.

Transferring an unaccompanied child to a more or less restrictive setting is referred to as "stepping up" or "stepping down" the placement. More specifically, "stepping up" refers to a child transferring to a more restrictive placement, and "stepping down" refers to a child transferring to a less restrictive setting. Similar to other decisions to transfer a child within ORR's care network, stepping up a child's placement is based on careful consideration of available evidence, including the child's own reports. Case consultation occurs between the care provider, case coordinator, and ORR staff to evaluate evidence and determine if stepping up the placement is necessary. Stepping up placements is needed if the child is a threat to themselves or others or poses an imminent risk of running away from a placement (ORR 2024b). In some circumstances, unaccompanied children are stepped up in placement due to evidence or self-reports indicating the child was involved in criminal activity. In these circumstances, ORR care coordinators may consult with additional professionals, including local, state, and federal law enforcement officials, to determine if the reports or evidence of criminal activity merit stepping up the placement.

If stepping up the placement is determined to be the most appropriate course of action, ORR must clearly document the plan using a notice of placement in a restrictive setting form, and this must be shared with the child in language they can understand. The form and associated documentation must also be shared with any legal representatives supporting the child, as well as the child's parents if the circumstances allow. Communication with legal representatives and the child's parents must occur within forty-eight hours of the transfer to a more restrictive setting (ORR 2024b).

Stepping down a placement to a less restrictive setting occurs when available evidence no longer indicates a restrictive setting is the most appropriate placement for the unaccompanied child. Stepping down a placement is an objective for unaccompanied children to flourish in placements that are optimally aligned with child development needs. When considering a step down in placement, ORR staff, as well as the care provider and case coordinator, evaluate and consult on the available evidence. At times, ORR may also consider recommendations from immigration court if a judge has made determinations during a bond hearing (ORR 2024b). In each circumstance, stepping down placements cannot occur unless ORR is able to determine that services are available to keep the child and the community safe. Unfortunately, research shows that service availability differs throughout the United States, which may impede a child's ability to receive needed services in less restrictive environments (Roth and Grace 2015).

Long-Term Care

When unaccompanied children are in ORR care for longer than four months, they are considered to be in long-term care. Long-term care is necessary for unaccompanied children if an appropriate sponsor is not identified. This could include a sponsor not identified or a sponsor identified but deemed not appropriate by ORR for placement. Along with no sponsor identified, unaccompanied children are placed in long-term care if a legal services provider determines they may be eligible for immigration relief or the child is unable to return to their country of origin due to extenuating circumstances, such as a state of emergency in the country of origin. If a child is placed in long-term care, ORR attempts to minimize placement changes so the child can develop stable and secure relationships with caring adults in the placement. One type of long-term placement that can benefit unaccompanied children who do not have an identified sponsor is long-term foster care.

While special care is taken to ensure unaccompanied children are placed with family or other related sponsors, there are times when sponsors are not available or not identified. Unaccompanied children who cannot be placed with a sponsor, and who also do not meet criteria for staff secure or secure placements, may be placed in long-term foster care. Long-term foster care is broadly defined and can include "community-based foster care or a community-based group home" (ORR 2024b). Long-term foster care placements must be licensed at the state level and able to meet a child's cultural and linguistic needs. Unaccompanied children may be placed in long-term foster care if (1) a sponsor is not identified and one is not anticipated for four months or longer, and (2) if the child is under age seventeen years and six months at their time of apprehension (ORR 2024b).

ORR completes a comprehensive assessment to determine if long-term foster care is an appropriate placement for an unaccompanied child. This includes the child's age, any health or mental health needs, the child's capacity to live in a family setting, as well as placement availability. A child's legal status is also assessed, meaning a child's legal counsel may recommend placement in long-term foster care based on the child's eligibility for immigration legal relief in a certain state.

Legal counsel prepares a report for ORR to consider prior to making placement decisions, and this report must account for the potential for legal relief and the status of the child's legal proceedings in immigration court (ORR 2024b).

Placement decisions also account for unaccompanied children's desires. If the child is at least fourteen years old and is not diagnosed with a mental health disorder, they must consent to any recommendations for long-term foster care placements made by legal service providers or other service providers caring for the minor. Transferring to long-term foster care prioritizes the child's health and well-being. However, unlike domestic foster care, a complicating factor in determining the placement of a minor is the potential for a child's immigration relief.

Release from ORR Care

After a challenging migration journey to the United States, apprehension by US Border Patrol, and initial placement by the ORR, unaccompanied children who have an identified and appropriate sponsor are released by the ORR. Since this process involves transitioning the legal custody of unaccompanied children from the federal government to an individual, there are several policies and procedures to ensure unaccompanied children are protected as they move to a more permanent placement. Four different professionals are integral to ensuring an unaccompanied child's safe and timely release from ORR custody: ORR Federal Field Specialists (ORR/FFS), Case Managers, Care Coordinators, and Child Advocates.

The ORR/FFS is a government employee who works for the ORR to oversee the safe and timely release of unaccompanied children from ORR custody. ORR/FFS are located in different regions throughout the United States. As representatives of ORR, ORR/FFS has final authority on decisions regarding the release of unaccompanied children from ORR custody. ORR/FFS oversees the release process by acting as a liaison between the federal government (i.e., ORR) and service providers in the community. Along with approving release decisions for unaccompanied children, ORR/FFS are also responsible for determining if a home study needs to be completed before a child's release, or if post-release services are needed after a child is placed in the community.

Case managers are the primary direct service providers who help unaccompanied children who are released to sponsors in the community. Among the case manager's responsibilities are assessing the unaccompanied child and sponsors to identify their strengths and limitations in the context of release from ORR custody. In addition, case managers design individual service plans that outline the services an unaccompanied child will need for a safe and timely release to their sponsor. Case managers also routinely consult with ORR/FFS on a weekly basis to monitor an unaccompanied child's status to determine the appropriateness of their release to a sponsor. Along with the ORR/FFS, case managers also consult with legal service providers who are part of an unaccompanied child's care team to ensure they have the appropriate information related to release from ORR custody.

Case coordinators are professionals who work for nongovernmental organizations and who review unaccompanied children's case files and associated documents to make recommendations to ORR regarding a child's release to a sponsor. Case coordinators gather information and relevant data from all providers to create a release plan for the unaccompanied child. Similar to case managers, case coordinators meet with ORR on a weekly basis to evaluate unaccompanied children's status and their progress toward release from ORR custody. Case coordinators and case managers must agree on decisions regarding the release of unaccompanied children from ORR custody. If there is any disagreement, then the ORR/FFS provides additional support.

Child advocates are independent third-party professionals who are appointed by ORR to represent an unaccompanied child's best interests. ORR appoints child advocates for unaccompanied children who are victims of trafficking or are otherwise vulnerable due to complex health or mental health issues. In representing the best interests of the child, child advocates complete a document called the Best Interest Determination, which outlines the recommendations of the child advocate regarding a child's release from ORR custody. ORR and immigration courts consider the child advocate's Best Interest Determination form; however, there are no mechanisms that require ORR to follow the recommendations.

The safe and timely release of unaccompanied children from ORR custody is also known as "family reunification." This term applies to this process, even if the sponsor is not a biological family member of the child. Family reunification ensures children are placed in safe and stable settings in the community and are also protected from human trafficking and smuggling. The family reunification process includes several steps to meet the needs of the unaccompanied children and ensure their safety and well-being. These steps include identifying a sponsor, evaluating the sponsor's application, interviewing the sponsor, verifying the sponsor's relationship to the child, conducting background checks on the sponsor, conducting home studies in certain circumstances, and creating a plan for post-release services (PRS) (ORR 2024d).

Sponsor Application

Unaccompanied children who migrate to the United States often have a family member or other relative in their mind as an appropriate sponsor. The first step in the release process is identifying this sponsor. ORR identifies sponsors by collecting an array of information, including by interviewing unaccompanied children, their parents, legal guardians, or other family members in the child's life. If federal authorities, such as US Border Patrol, believe a child who is apprehended will be legally identified as an unaccompanied child, then ORR may receive this information before the child is transferred to ORR custody, allowing for the start of the sponsor identification process. These circumstances minimize the child being in a shelter setting or other unstable setting after arrival in the United States (ORR 2024d).

ORR prioritizes potential sponsor placements by the nature of the relationship between the child and the adult. There are five different categories of sponsor placements to help guide the sponsor placement process. Category 1 sponsors include the child's parent or legal guardian. In most circumstances, ORR prioritizes parents or legal guardians as the sponsor for an unaccompanied child. Category 2A sponsors include close family members, such as an unaccompanied child's brother, sister, grandparent, or other immediate biological relatives, such as aunts, uncles, or cousins who have been the child's primary caregiver in the past. In addition to these close biologically related sponsors, ORR also considers relatives through legal marriage. Category 2B sponsors include close family relatives, such as siblings, aunts, or uncles, who have not been the child's primary caregiver in the past. Category 3 sponsors are referred to as "other sponsors," including unrelated adults such as family friends or distant relatives. Category 4 indicates that no sponsor was identified. Unaccompanied children who have no sponsor identified will either transition to long-term care, such as long-term foster care, or ORR will continue trying to identify an appropriate sponsor for the child. While ORR strives to place unaccompanied children with their parents, ORR will decide against placements with parents if a court has terminated parental rights, or if there is clear evidence that the child's safety would be at risk if they were placed with their parent (ORR 2024d).

ORR is responsible for contacting and assessing potential sponsors. Within the sponsor application process, there are a variety of guidelines to help ORR evaluate the appropriateness of a sponsor placement. These guidelines include using interpreters to navigate language barriers, obtaining proof of a sponsor's relationship with the child, and screening for risk of exploitation, abuse, or human trafficking.

Once a potential sponsor is identified, the sponsor receives an application for reunification within twenty-four hours. The application is also referred to as the "Family Reunification Packet," and it contains multiple documents to help facilitate the placement process. These documents include authorizations for the release of information so ORR can communicate with care providers in the child's life, a formal family reunification application, a sponsor care agreement, and handouts with contact information for legal services and a sexual abuse hotline. ORR can assist the sponsor with completing the application; however, ORR may require the sponsor to complete the application on their own if there are safety concerns.

Human trafficking and economic exploitation are among the chief concerns for unaccompanied children when placed with sponsors in the United States. Many unaccompanied children migrate to the United States with a coyote, or smuggler. Families in countries of origin often need to spend thousands of dollars to ensure their child has safe passage to the United States. Unaccompanied children sometimes seek work to pay back coyotes or to help their families. Investigative reporting based in the United States reveals that unaccompanied children are at risk of working in unsafe conditions, including seafood processing plants, slaughterhouses, and construction jobs such as roofing. The sponsor identification and family reunification processes are designed to place unaccompanied children with individuals who can provide safe and stable home environments while also protecting children from exploitation and abuse (ORR 2024d).

Home Studies

Home studies are in-depth assessments completed by case managers who evaluate an individual's capacity to be a sponsor for an unaccompanied child and ensure the child's safety, health, and well-being. Home studies are multifaceted and are based on various types of data, including background checks of adults in the home, home visits to assess physical dwellings, and interviews of potential sponsors. Home studies result in a home study report that documents the adult's capacity to be a sponsor, provides potential sponsors with information to prepare them for the unaccompanied child's release from ORR custody, and confirms information that is collected during earlier parts of the reunification process, such as the sponsor assessment. ORR policy and federal law mandate home studies if certain criteria are met.

Home studies are mandated by ORR in the case of three different scenarios. First, home studies are mandated by ORR for any unaccompanied child under twelve years old. Home studies are also mandated if the potential sponsor is trying to care for two or more unaccompanied children, and at least one of the children in the home is unrelated to the sponsor. Home studies are also mandated by ORR if a sponsor cared for two or more unaccompanied children in the past and is now seeking to care for more children.

Home studies can also be mandated by federal law, specifically the TVPRA. Under TVPRA guidelines, home studies are mandated if there is clear evidence that the unaccompanied child has been the victim of human trafficking, abuse, or neglect, or there is evidence that indicates the child is at future risk of human trafficking, abuse, or neglect. Home studies are also mandated by TVPRA guidelines if the unaccompanied child has a special need that is defined by the Americans with Disabilities Act. Importantly, the home study guidelines outlined in TVPRA indicate that although unaccompanied children do not have permanent legal status in the United States, US federal law still seeks to protect their interests and preserve their well-being.

Home studies are typically completed by case managers at nonprofits that contract with ORR. Once ORR makes a referral for a home study, a case manager must be assigned within three calendar days. Following the referral, the case manager must then contact the child's sponsor within forty-eight hours to schedule the home study visit. Home visits occur in person, unless special exemptions are made by ORR for a virtual visit. Home studies follow a constricted timeline, with a written report submitted to ORR within ten days of the referral (ORR 2024d). Most unaccompanied children who migrate to the United States do not receive a home study before they are placed with a sponsor. For example, in 2022, 128,904 unaccompanied children were referred by the DHS to ORR. Of these 128,904 children, only 8,619 received a home study prior to placement with their sponsor (ORR 2024a). Home studies are brief and only one part of ensuring unaccompanied children are cared for after their placement with a sponsor. Additional services designed to help newly arrived unaccompanied children, and services provided for a much larger number of unaccompanied children, are PRS.

Post-Release Services

After an unaccompanied child is released from ORR care, they are placed with a sponsor in the community. Living in the community results in an assortment of challenges and opportunities as the child adjusts to life in the United States. Potential challenges and opportunities include making and keeping friendships, identifying available resources in the neighborhood, and enrolling in a school and learning how to navigate transportation systems. Across all of these experiences, unaccompanied children must navigate language barriers, which may limit their ability to engage with different parts of the community. The foundation of an unaccompanied child's support is their sponsor, who is often a family member and is familiar with the child's needs. To help unaccompanied children and their sponsors adjust to new communities, ORR offers PRS as a formal support offered to the unaccompanied child after their release from ORR custody.

PRS are case management services that are designed to help unaccompanied children adjust to new communities after their release from ORR custody. PRS is not provided directly by ORR. Instead, ORR provides contracts to nonprofit organizations throughout the United States that directly provide PRS for unaccompanied children. PRS are offered at three different levels, which differ in the intensity and the length of time services are provided. Level 1 PRS is the lowest level of PRS and includes three virtual check-ins between a case manager and the unaccompanied child across thirty days. Level 2 PRS are more structured case management services that help unaccompanied children connect with community-based supports, including legal services, enrolling in school, and accessing health and mental health services. Level 2 PRS lasts for up to six months. Finally, Level 3 PRS are intensive in-home services for unaccompanied children who have complex health or mental health needs that may be risk factors for the child's safety in the home. Level 3 PRS is designed to be intensive and short term; however, the services can be extended beyond thirty days after review by ORR (ORR 2024e).

Although PRS can be provided for any child released from ORR, there are some children who are legally mandated to receive PRS. For example, unaccompanied children who receive a home study as stipulated by TVPRA are legally required to receive a referral for PRS. Otherwise, PRS eligibility is prioritized based on the unique needs of unaccompanied children. For example, tender-age children (i.e., children between zero and twelve years old) who are legally required to receive PRS, children turning eighteen years old within two months of release from ORR care who are legally required to receive PRS, and children between thirteen and seventeen years old who are required to receive PRS are all prioritized by ORR. The remaining prioritization includes other tender-age children, children turning eighteen within two months of release from ORR care, and unaccompanied children between thirteen and seventeen years old. The method of prioritizing PRS for unaccompanied children is informed by existing law, such as TVPRA, as well as child welfare best practices for vulnerable children (ORR 2024e).

Depending on the area of the United States, PRS may not be readily available for an unaccompanied child, and there may be a wait-list. ORR will not delay a child's release from care due to a wait-list for PRS unless there is clear evidence that suggests a child is at risk of adverse health or mental health outcomes or they are at risk of harming themselves or someone else. Wait lists can be several weeks long, meaning many unaccompanied children may be placed in a community, with their sponsor, with limited formal support for navigating community-based supports.

A key component of PRS is assessment—gathering data from an array of sources to enhance understanding of an unaccompanied child's strengths, needs, and what supports will be most helpful for them to flourish in the United States. The role of assessment differs depending on the level of PRS. For Level 1 PRS, assessment is focused mainly on ensuring the sponsor is able to meet the child's immediate needs and can keep the child safe. Level 2 and Level 3 PRS assessments go deeper, and evaluate a range of domains in the child's life, including: "sponsor family functioning, legal services, education, medical care, behavioral healthcare (including substance abuse, mental health, and overall well-being), support appropriate for a child's personal belief system, healthy relationships, food and material goods security (e.g., adequate clothing for each season), transportation, housing, and any special circumstance" (ORR 2024e).

Three services in particular deserve closer attention—legal services, education services, and health and mental health services. Research shows these supports are critical to helping unaccompanied children adjust to life in the United States (Berger Cardoso et al. 2021). PRS case managers play a critical role in ensuring sponsors are able to bring the unaccompanied child to all legal proceedings that are part of their immigration court case. PRS case managers also connect sponsors and children with legal service providers to provide counsel and representation during immigration court proceedings. In cases where the sponsor is not the legal guardian, PRS case managers will also make referrals to legal service providers who can help sponsors adjust the custody status between the sponsor and the unaccompanied child.

Unaccompanied children, like all children without legal status in the United States, have a legal right to public education in the United States. PRS case managers play a critical role in helping unaccompanied children and their sponsors identify the correct public school in their neighborhood and also assist with enrolling the child in the school. Research shows school districts differ in the types of documents needed for immigrant children to enroll in school (Evans et al. 2020), and PRS case managers help sponsors access the correct types of documents needed for the child to attend school.

Research shows unaccompanied children experience a variety of stressors before, during, and after their migration to the United States that influences their migration journey. These stressors include family separation, gang violence, and widespread poverty (UNHCR 2014; UNICEF 2018). Furthermore, unaccompanied children are at risk of suffering from symptoms of trauma as a result of migration-related stressors (Berger Cardoso et al. 2021). PRS case managers help unaccompanied children access community-based health and mental health services. This includes helping children access health insurance, and making referrals to pediatricians, dentists, mental health clinicians, and other health care providers as needed (ORR 2024e).

The unaccompanied children program provides critical services and support for vulnerable children under age eighteen who arrive at a US border without a parent or legal guardian and who do not have legal status to remain in the United States. A completely different population of unaccompanied children in the United States is served by the URM program, which is a program distinctly separate from the Unaccompanied Children Program.

Unaccompanied Refugee Minors Program

The URM program is managed by ORR and "serves some of the most vulnerable minors in the world—those who fled persecution, violence, or abuse, and entered the United States without a parent or custodian" (ORR 2024f). Children in the URM program are eligible to receive the same services available to children in domestic foster care programs. Furthermore, the URM program strives to combine child welfare best practices with practices to identify and meet the complex needs of children who experience forced migration. At the inception of the URM program, eligibility was restricted to children under age eighteen who were living outside the United States and had refugee status. However, congressional changes to the URM program over time have expanded the program to a range of eligible populations, including refugees, asylees, and children from Cuba or Haiti, known as "Cuban and Haitian entrants." In addition, the URM program accepts children with a range of different immigration statuses, including Special Immigrant Juvenile Status (SIJS) and U status recipients and survivors of human trafficking. The URM program also adapts to changing global contexts and accepts Afghan unaccompanied children and Ukrainian unaccompanied children who have immigration parole in the United States (ORR 2024f). This section provides a general overview of the URM program, with special attention to features that distinguish it from other programs and services that support unaccompanied children.

The URM program is operated and funded at the federal level, by the ORR. The delivery of services is managed at the state level, by State Refugee Coordinators (SRC), who manage individual URM programs at the local level. Two national nonprofits, Global Refuge (formerly Lutheran Immigration and Refugee Service) and the United States Conference of Catholic Bishops, allocate funds and provide technical support to small provider agencies that deliver services in the URM program. Research shows that in 2020, there were twenty-two URM programs throughout the United States, in fifteen different states. URM programs at the local level are typically part of nonprofit organizations that provide other social services for vulnerable children, including domestic foster care and child welfare services (Foley et al. 2021).

Unlike the unaccompanied children program, a component unique to the URM program is a distinct relationship with state child welfare systems. URM programs are organized as either public or private. State child welfare agencies have legal custody of unaccompanied children in the URM program. For states with private URM programs, individual nonprofit organizations that deliver URM services have custody of unaccompanied children in the URM program and are overseen and licensed by state or county child welfare agencies. As of 2021, there were twenty-two URM programs that delivered services for unaccompanied children in the URM program, with eight in states with public custody arrangements and fourteen in states with private custody arrangements (Foley et al. 2021).

URM program services were first provided in the late 1970s in response to unaccompanied children displaced from the Vietnam War. Since then, the demographics of children served by the URM program have changed. These changes often reflect geopolitical events or natural disasters around the world that directly or indirectly involve the United States. For example, a 2010 earthquake devastated Haiti, killing thousands and resulting in a dramatic increase in the number of unaccompanied children who lost parents or caregivers. In Afghanistan, war throughout the beginning of the twenty-first century resulted in an increase in Afghan unaccompanied children arriving in the United States.

The demographic data of children served by the URM program demonstrates extraordinary diversity from around the world. According to research published by the Administration for Children and Families and the US Department of Health and Human Services, between 2014 and 2018, children in the URM program arrived from more than fifty countries around the world, and more than a hundred ethnicities were represented and eighty languages spoken (Foley et al. 2021). Between 2014 and 2018, most unaccompanied children entered the URM program as refugees, followed by children with SIJS, and finally trafficking victims. Most unaccompanied children in the URM program migrated from the "Americas" (44.5 percent), which includes North, Central, and South America. Nearly one in five children in the URM program during this time arrived from East Africa (19.2 percent), followed by children from Central Africa (14.4 percent), children from Central/South Asia (9.9 percent), the Middle East (8.2 percent), West Africa (3.3 percent), and East Asia (0.6 percent) (Foley et al. 2021). These numbers align with demographics in the unaccompanied children program, which shows that during 2014–18, most unaccompanied children migrated from El Salvador, Guatemala, or Honduras.

Between 2014 and 2018, nearly half of unaccompanied children in the URM program identified as Hispanic or Latino (40.4 percent), and nearly half spoke Spanish as their primary language (40.2 percent). Of all children in the URM program, most identified as male (68.3 percent), and this trend was consistent for each category of entry (e.g., asylees, trafficking victims, refugees, and special immigrant juvenile visas). Finally, most children in the URM program were seventeen years or older (62 percent), which indicates the importance of independent living services provided by the URM program (Foley et al. 2021).

The research by Foley et al. (2021) illuminates both the strengths and needs of children in the URM program using a variety of data, including interview, focus group, and survey data collected from program staff, foster parents, and children in the URM program. Foley et al. (2021) explain that program staff consistently describe children in the URM program as "resilient, goal-oriented, and hardworking." Most children identified work as a long-term goal; however, many children described education as a goal and explained how this aligns with their goal of being a doctor, lawyer, chef, writer, or other profession. Family support is a vital strength of children in the URM program, and technologies such as WhatsApp and other video conferencing technologies allow children to remain in contact with family in home countries.

Research also shows that unaccompanied children have specific needs that cluster in several categories: mental health, education and English-language skills, physical health, and legal service needs. Importantly, these areas of need align with the needs of children in the unaccompanied children program. Children in the URM program have demonstrated mental health needs. Many children enter the URM program after experiencing the devastating effects of climate change and natural disasters, political instability and government oppression, and widespread community violence. Entering the URM program, by definition, indicates a child has experienced some degree of forced separation from a parent or caregiver, which can exacerbate this trauma. Common mental health issues in the URM program include symptoms of posttraumatic stress disorder, depression, and adjustment disorder (Foley et al. 2021).

Many unaccompanied children in the URM program, along with trauma, have experienced major disruptions in formal education, along with limited English-language skills. A key priority of the URM program is ensuring children have access to public education supports, and this aligns with a demonstrated need reported by children and providers in the URM program. In addition, research shows the importance of English-language skills for newly arrived immigrants in the United States. Along with education needs, research shows a major area of need for children in the URM program is access to primary health services and dental services. Many youth who participated in Foley et al.'s study, for example, explained limited experience with primary health care in their country of origin. Furthermore, staff members and service providers noted instances of complex health needs that can tax an organization's ability to provide support for vulnerable children in the URM program. Finally, given the varied pathways into the URM program, and the range of legal statuses that children have when entering the program, access to legal services was identified as a primary need for children in the URM program. Staff members who participated in the study explained that children in the URM program may not have some of the legal protections that other refugees have when entering the United States (e.g., work authorization). This can result in stress related to "living in limbo" (Foley et al. 2021) that can limit a child's integration in the United States, as well as tax existing mental health issues, such as stress and anxiety.

Along with an overview of the URM program, including demographics, strengths, and needs of children in the URM program, the application and placement process explains how demographics, strengths, and needs of children are assessed so they are placed in appropriate settings.

URM Program Application and Placement Process

There are three primary pathways into the URM program. The first pathway is through the US Refugee Admissions Program. Historically, this was the only pathway into the URM program and is reserved for unaccompanied children who reside outside the United States and have refugee status. This pathway includes children who receive refugee status after experiencing war or political persecution and subsequently lose their parents or caregivers. For these children, they not only do not have a stable country to reside in, but they are also without stable family units.

The second pathway is the result of congressional changes to the URM program and includes children who arrive in the United States and are in ORR custody as part of the Unaccompanied Children Program. Certain children in the Unaccompanied Children Program may qualify for admission to the URM program, including asylees, Cuban and Haitian entrants, survivors of human trafficking, children with SIJS, or Afghan or Ukrainian unaccompanied children. This is an important pathway for these children, as it can increase access to resources that are part of the URM program. The third pathway into the URM program is through a community referral. Sometimes, unaccompanied children in the community may encounter family turmoil, or there may be health or mental health needs that emerge and require intensive services. Community referrals come from providers in the community, such as health care providers or educators (ORR 2024g).

The application and placement process for the URM program includes multiple components of review that ORR conducts to assess eligibility. At the beginning part of the process, an ORR official will review basic background information from the application and evaluate the needs of the child. This assessment includes identifying the child's age, gender, country of origin, and the circumstances that led to their arrival in the United States or their referral to the URM program if they are outside the United States. Using this information, ORR must determine if the child is eligible for the URM program according to existing laws and regulations. Since the URM program is for children under age eighteen, there must be enough time before the child turns eighteen years old to process the application material and identify an appropriate and available placement setting. ORR will also assess if the child has parents or other adults in the United States who can provide care and serve as a sponsor. If ORR decides that evidence indicates the child cannot be placed with a parent or guardian, parental consent may be needed to place the child in a URM placement. Finally, ORR will engage in case consultation with members of state refugee offices to gather and evaluate data related to a child who experienced a placement disruption (ORR 2024g).

URM Program Services

Children who are placed in the URM program have a variety of diverse and complex strengths and needs that influence the way they navigate resettlement settings and experience integration in the United States. To meet their complex needs and amplify their strengths, the URM program offers an array of services to support children and their caregivers.

The first set of services is designed to help with immediate and pressing needs in the first stages of arrival and resettlement in the United States. This begins with providing indirect financial support for housing, food, and other basic human needs such as hygiene products. Ensuring the child has access to health and mental health services is also vital, as children in the URM program often experience trauma before their arrival in the United States. To ensure children in the URM program have access to medical care, SRCs coordinate with state officials to determine if children qualify for Medicaid or the Children's Health Insurance Program. If a child does not qualify for Medicaid, then states are responsible for finding alternative funding to support children in the URM program. Existing ORR policy is that ORR funding cannot be used to meet a state's share of Medicaid.

The URM program also provides intensive case management services, which help children gain English-language support, enroll in school, and identify important parts of the community. Cultural orientation programs help unaccompanied children in the URM program navigate social norms in the United States, including how to access public transportation, how to access money in a bank, and how to purchase goods in stores. In addition, the URM program can help unaccompanied children access religious organizations and houses of worship that align with their faith beliefs.

Sometimes, unaccompanied children enroll in the URM program when they are near eighteen years old. These unaccompanied children are especially vulnerable, as they require unique support to help achieve independence. To accomplish this, the URM program can help unaccompanied children learn housing skills, such as how to read a rental lease agreement. In addition, URM case managers may help unaccompanied children gain job preparation skills such as how to build a resume, how to apply for a job, and how to prepare for an interview.

Conclusion

The United States has a long history of unaccompanied children arriving at its borders, and various laws and policies have emerged across US history that relate to unaccompanied children. Since 2014, the number of unaccompanied children in the United States has increased as a result of adversities in under-resourced countries with histories of political instability, widespread poverty, and pervasive violence that pose threats to the health and well-being of children. Upon arriving in the United States, unaccompanied children navigate a complex immigration system that begins with their apprehension at a US border and continues through initial processing and later placement with a sponsor or in another setting. Various services and programs are in place to assist unaccompanied children through this process as well as after their release. Chapter 2 explores in more depth some of the reasons unaccompanied children migrate, as well as the challenges they face during migration and after arrival at the US border. Problems, controversies, and solutions related to US immigration policy and programs are also discussed.

Further Reading

Administration for Children and Families. 2024. "Fact Sheet: Unaccompanied Children (UC) Program." https://www.hhs.gov/sites/default/files/uac-program-fact-sheet.pdf

Becker Herbst, Rachel, Raha Forooz Sabet, Amelia Swanson, Lauren G. Suarez, Denise S. Marques, Edward J. Ameen, and Etiony Aldarondo. 2018. "'They Were Going to Kill Me': Resilience in Unaccompanied Immigrant Minors." *The Counseling Psychologist* 46, no. 2: 241–68.

Berger Cardoso, Jodi, Kalina Brabeck, Dennis Stinchcomb, Lauren Heidbrink, Olga Acosta Price, Óscar F. Gil-García, Thomas M. Crea, and Luis H. Zayas. 2021. "Integration of Unaccompanied Migrant Youth in the United States: A Call for Research." In *Undocumented and Unaccompanied*, edited by Cecilia Menjívar and Krista Perreira, 77–96. Routledge.

Conde, Yvonne. 1999. *Operation Pedro Pan: The Untold Exodus of 14,048 Cuban Children*. Routledge.

Congressional Research Service. 2021. "Child Migrants at the Border: The Flores Settlement Agreement and Other Legal Developments." https://crsreports.congress.gov/product/pdf/IF/IF11799

Crea, Thomas M., Anayeli Lopez, Robert G. Hasson, Kerri Evans, Caroline Palleschi, and Dawnya Underwood. 2018. "Unaccompanied Immigrant Children in Long Term Foster Care: Identifying Needs and Best Practices from a Child Welfare Perspective." *Children and Youth Services Review* 92: 56–64.

Crea, Thomas M., Kerri Evans, Anayeli Lopez, Robert G. Hasson III, Caroline Palleschi, and Libby Sittley. "Unaccompanied Immigrant Children in Long-Term Foster Care: Identifying and Operationalizing Child Welfare Outcomes." *Child & Family Social Work* 27, no. 3 (2022): 500–12.

Evans, Kerri, Jaime Perez-Aponte, and Ruth McRoy. 2020. "Without a Paddle: Barriers to School Enrollment Procedures for Immigrant Students and Families." *Education and Urban Society* 52, no. 9: 1283–304.

Foley, Kimberly, Liza Rodler, Sam Elkin, and Sarah Catherine Williams. 2021. *Final Report of the Descriptive Study of the Unaccompanied Refugee Minors Program: Service Provision, Trends, and Evaluation Recommendations*. Vol. 81. OPRE Report.

Hasson, Robert G., III Clara A. Oliva, Bianca LaBella, and Dahiana Rodriguez. 2024. "'Little by Little, I Go': Multiple Dimensions of Distress and Support for Unaccompanied Children in the United States." *Children and Youth Services Review* 160: 107541.

H.R.3361, 108th Congress. 2003. Unaccompanied Alien Child Protection Act of 2003. https://www.congress.gov/bill/108th-congress/house-bill/3361

H.R.5005, 107th Congress. 2002. An Act to establish the Department of Homeland Security, and for other purposes. https://www.dhs.gov/sites/default/files/2023-11/03_0116_hr_5005_enr.pdf

H.R.7311, 110th Congress. 2008. An Act to authorize appropriations for fiscal years 2008 through 2011 for the Trafficking Victims Protection Act of 2000, to enhance measures to combat trafficking in persons, and for other purposes. https://www.congress.gov/bill/110th-congress/house-bill/7311/text

Lazarus, Emma. n.d. *The New Colossus*. Accessed December 8, 2022. https://poets.org/poem/new-colossus

Masten, Ann S. 2014. *Ordinary Magic: Resilience in Development.* Guilford Publications.

Migration Policy Institute tabulations of US Department of Homeland Security, Office of Immigration Statistics, Yearbook of Immigration Statistics. Various years. Available at www.dhs.gov/files/statistics/publications/yearbook.shtm

Office of Refugee Resettlement (ORR). 2012. "The Refugee Act." https://www.acf.hhs.gov/orr/policy-guidance/refugee-act

Office of Refugee Resettlement (ORR). 2024a. "Fact Sheets and Data." https://www.acf.hhs.gov/orr/about/ucs/facts-and-data

Office of Refugee Resettlement (ORR). 2024b. "ORR Unaccompanied Children Program Policy Guide: Section 1." https://www.acf.hhs.gov/orr/policy-guidance/unaccompanied-children-program-policy-guide-section-1

Office of Refugee Resettlement (ORR). 2024c. "ORR Unaccompanied Alien Children Bureau Policy Guide: Guide to Terms." https://acf.gov/orr/policy-guidance/unaccompanied-children-program-policy-guide-guide-terms#careprovider

Office of Refugee Resettlement (ORR). 2024d. "ORR Unaccompanied Children Program Policy Guide: Section 2." https://www.acf.hhs.gov/orr/policy-guidance/unaccompanied-children-program-policy-guide-section-2#2.1

Office of Refugee Resettlement (ORR). 2024e. "ORR Unaccompanied Children Program Policy Guide: Section 6." https://www.acf.hhs.gov/orr/policy-guidance/unaccompanied-children-program-policy-guide-section-6#6.1

Office of Refugee Resettlement (ORR). 2024f. "Unaccompanied Refugee Minors Program." https://www.acf.hhs.gov/orr/programs/refugees/urm

Office of Refugee Resettlement (ORR). 2024g. "ORR Guide to Eligibility, Placement, and Services for Unaccompanied Refugee Minors (URM): Section 1." https://www.acf.hhs.gov/orr/policy-guidance/orr-guide-eligibility-placement-and-services-unaccompanied-refugee-minors-urm#footiii

Padilla-Rodríguez, Ivón. 2020. "Child Migrants in 20th-Century America." In *Oxford Research Encyclopedia of American History.* https://doi.org/10.1093/acrefore/9780199329175.013.855

Roth, Benjamin J., and Breanne L. Grace. 2015. "Falling through the Cracks: The Paradox of Post-release Services for Unaccompanied Child Migrants." *Children and Youth Services Review* 58: 244–52.

Steinbock, Daniel J. 1989. "The Admission of Unaccompanied Children into the United States." *Yale Law & Policy Review* 7, no. 1: 137–200.

UNHCR (United Nations High Commissioner for Refugees). 2014. "Children on the Run: Unaccompanied Children Leaving Central America and Mexico and the Need for International Protection." http://www.unhcr.org/56fc266f4.html

UNICEF. 2018. "Uprooted in Central America and Mexico: Migrant and Refugee Children Face a Vicious Cycle of Hardship and Danger." https://www.unicef.org/media/47701/file/UNICEF_Child_Alert_2018_Central_America_and_Mexico-ENG.pdf

US Census. 2011. "Table 359. U.S.–Canada and U.S.–Mexico Border Lengths." https://www2.census.gov/library/publications/2010/compendia/statab/130ed/tables/11s0359.pdf

US Customs and Border Protection. 2023. "Locate a Port of Entry." https://www.cbp.gov/about/contact/ports

US Department of Homeland Security. 2023. "Creation of the Department of Homeland Security." https://www.dhs.gov/creation-department-homeland-security

US Department of Homeland Security Office of Inspector General. 2010. "CBP's Handling of Unaccompanied Alien Children." https://tracreports.org/tracker/dynadata/2010_10/OIG_10-117_Sep10.pdf

Vadasy, Richard. 2021. "The Trump Administration's War on the Flores Settlement Agreement Renewed amid COVID-19 Pandemic." *Children's Legal Rights Journal* 41, no. 1: 84–8.

Villegas, Rodrigo Dominguez. 2014. "Central American Migrants and 'La Bestia': The Route, Dangers, and Government Responses." Migration Policy Institute. https://www.migrationpolicy.org/article/central-american-migrants-la-bestia

2

Problems, Controversies, and Solutions

Unaccompanied children in the United States encounter a precarious experience of migration from their home country. Their reasons for migrating vary, and understanding those reasons adds important context to a journey that takes children away from their family and introduces them to a variety of stressors before and after arriving in the United States. These reasons often include widespread poverty and gang violence in their home country. Some of the main countries from which unaccompanied children migrate to the United States—El Salvador, Guatemala, and Honduras—have had among the highest rates of violence in the world along with high poverty rates, creating conditions that influence a child's migration. Other reasons for migrating are specific to the United States. For example, unaccompanied children seek family reunification, especially when a parent has already migrated to the United States. In addition, education opportunities are limited in parts of Central America, and unaccompanied children migrate to the United States seeking a quality education.

In addition to unpacking some of the reasons unaccompanied children migrate, this chapter offers analysis of the problems and controversies surrounding border crossings, human trafficking, and family separation. Each of these issues presents distinct challenges that impact the health and well-being of unaccompanied children. For example, border crossings at the US-Mexico border include initial apprehension by US Border Patrol agents and subsequent processing in border patrol facilities, which can be confusing and stressful for children without adult accompaniment. The US Border Patrol's sometimes conflicting goals of securing the border while also meeting the needs of unaccompanied children create a

---

Young migrants ride atop a freight train while en route to the US-Mexico border, 2023. Many unaccompanied children make the dangerous ride north through Mexico on a network of freight trains known as La Bestia (the Beast). (John Moore/Getty Images)

tension in policy that can be detrimental for children attempting to immigrate to the United States. Research shows that unaccompanied children are at risk of human trafficking, which can include sexual and economic exploitation. Like all children, unaccompanied children thrive in the context of a loving and supportive relationship with a parent or caregiver, which points to the central challenge that the problem of family separation presents for unaccompanied children as they migrate to the United States.

A growing body of research has shed light on issues related to unaccompanied children's mental health and education. After arriving in the United States and resettling in communities with family or sponsors, unaccompanied children are at risk of experiencing mental health symptoms related to trauma, depression, and anxiety. Although schools can provide an assortment of supports for unaccompanied children, research shows varying challenges that unaccompanied children encounter when trying to enroll and attend school. Exploring these issues, this chapter also examines the controversies and complexities surrounding family reunification, as children reconnect with family after their migration to the United States. For many children, living with a parent or family member they have not lived with in several years presents unique challenges to family systems.

The chapter concludes by exploring possible solutions to helping unaccompanied children, including legislation introduced to help reform immigration policies that focus on unaccompanied children in the United States. These policy proposals and associated debates mirror broader political divides on the issue of immigration in the United States. The chapter unpacks the different political perspectives that inform policy development and identifies the challenges with passing legislation that meets the needs of this vulnerable population of immigrants.

Reasons for Migration

Before migrating, unaccompanied children and their families answer a compelling question at the root of every child's decision to travel to the United States: Why? The answers to this question can be complicated, with various reasons influencing a child's migration journey. Many of these reasons overlap and inform one another. While each individual child carries with them a unique story, research shows broad patterns of common reasons for migrating to the

United States. Commonly referred to as "push-and-pull factors," these reasons include gang violence, poverty, and lack of education in the country of origin; the desire to reunify with family in the United States; and the desire to pursue education and work opportunities in the United States. Given that between 2012 and 2024, more than half of all unaccompanied children migrated to the United States from the Central American countries El Salvador, Guatemala, and Honduras, this section focuses mainly on these countries.

Children living in El Salvador, Guatemala, or Honduras—commonly referred to as the "Northern Triangle"—faced some of the highest murder rates in the world between 2012 and 2022. In fact, the Migration Policy Institute explained in 2016 that "Violence perpetrated by criminal gangs continues to plague the Northern Triangle—which represent three of the five countries with the highest murder rates in the world." Organized criminal gangs target younger adolescents, typically between twelve and fifteen years old. Limited economic and education opportunities in some Central American countries, such as El Salvador, can facilitate recruitment to gangs, providing a sense of opportunity and future. Other times, conscription to gangs is forced by the threat of violence.

Two of the most prominent gangs in El Salvador that drive community violence are MS-13 and the 18th Street Gang. MS-13 (formally called "Mara Salvatrucha 13") was first formed in the 1980s in Los Angeles among Salvadoran migrants who migrated to escape the civil war in El Salvador. After deportations, MS-13 strengthened in El Salvador throughout the 1990s, where there was limited government capacity and police presence to respond to the gang. According to the US Department of Justice, MS-13 is engaged in a variety of illegal activities, including weapons dealing, automobile theft, and human smuggling. Research consistently shows fleeing violence related to gangs like MS-13 is a primary reason for migration identified by unaccompanied children who migrate to the United States.

Along with violence, a second reason for migrating to the United States is widespread poverty and limited education opportunities. In addition to being some of the most dangerous countries in the world with three of the highest homicide rates, El Salvador, Guatemala, and Honduras also had three of the lowest-performing economies between 2012 and 2024. According to the International Monetary Fund, the economies of El Salvador, Guatemala, and Honduras had among the lowest gross domestic products (GDPs) in the world, lower than the GDPs of other Central American countries. Low GDP translates to limited job opportunities as well as prospects for high wages. For children in families that earn low wages and are in communities prone to higher unemployment, migrating to the United States unaccompanied has been viewed as a pathway to prosperity and a chance to earn money to support a family.

Along with low GDP, research shows that all three of these Central American countries have high poverty rates. In 2022, 26.6 percent of El Salvador's population and 48 percent of Honduras's population lived below the poverty line (Central Intelligence Agency 2024). Guatemala has an extensive history of having one of the highest poverty rates in Central America, and in 2014, more than half the population (59.3 percent) lived below the poverty line (Central Intelligence Agency 2024). Poverty also intersects with climate-related stresses that influence migration to the United States. Given that agriculture is an important component of the economies of many Central American countries—including El Salvador, Guatemala, and Honduras—natural disasters such as droughts and hurricanes can impact crop yield and exacerbate the effects of poverty already experienced by families. One of the common effects of poverty is food insecurity, which leads to unaccompanied children migrating to the United States to pursue work opportunities for their families. In fact, research shows remittances from migrants to family members account for approximately 20 percent of GDP in El Salvador, Honduras, and Guatemala (Central Intelligence Agency 2024).

Given the extensive histories of civil war, gang violence, and natural disasters in these countries, migration has long been an integral experience facing families in El Salvador, Guatemala, and Honduras. This migration has led to the separation of families, with mothers, fathers, aunts, uncles, and cousins making journeys to the United States to pursue work opportunities. Over time, children migrate to the United States to rejoin their family. In fact, family reunification is cited as among the most common factors influencing a child's decision to migrate to the United States. While individual contexts of family separation and reunification may differ, what is common is the dynamic of attachment and the importance of family relationships for children.

Extensive research from the United Nations High Commissioner for Refugees in 2014 focused on interviews with more than 400 unaccompanied children. This research found that family reunification overlapped with the desire to pursue economic or educational opportunities and was cited as a reason for migration among 84 percent of children from Guatemala and 80 percent of children from Honduras. Children from El Salvador were more likely to report gang violence as a primary driver. This finding aligns with other research for the American Immigration Council from Elizabeth Kennedy (2014), who interviewed 322 unaccompanied children from El Salvador and found that only one-third of children cited family reunification as their primary reason for migrating. Similar to children from Guatemala and Honduras, children from El Salvador experience family separation. However, research suggests that gang violence has been so widespread that it exceeds family reunification as a primary driver of a child's migration to the United States.

All children arriving in the United States come with experiences that tell the story of their migration. Some stories are explained by individual experiences, such as the separation of a child from their parent. Other stories are explained by systemic and structural dynamics that influence migration, such as natural disasters and the subsequent impact on a country's broader economy. As discussed, the primary reasons influencing unaccompanied children arriving in the United States have historically included different combinations of widespread gang violence, poverty and the pursuit of economic and educational opportunities, and the desire to reunify with family members in the United States. After deciding to migrate to the United States, unaccompanied children begin a journey that is thousands of miles long and can last months. Along the way, unaccompanied children encounter threats to their health and well-being while they pursue a path to safety and stability.

Hazards of the Migration Journey

Whether migrating due to poverty, gang violence, the desire to reunite with family, or a complex combination of these reasons, at some point unaccompanied children embark on a journey where they confront a variety of challenges and threats to their health and well-being. Some hardships are inherent in the environmental conditions of the journey, including fatigue, hunger, and exposure to elements such as excessive heat and cold. The travel methods and routes unaccompanied children take from Central America to the United States can also be unpredictable and dangerous. Other such threats include exposure to physical and sexual violence, economic exploitation, and human trafficking.

The timeline of migration journeys varies widely and can be impacted by detention while crossing borders on the way to the United States. For example, in response to increasing numbers of unaccompanied children arriving in the United States in 2014, the US government coordinated with the Mexican government to restrict border crossing between Guatemala and Mexico. According to

UNICEF (2018), this plan resulted in 18,300 children being apprehended and detained at the Mexico and Guatemala border. Unaccompanied children have reported migration journeys taking several weeks due to environmental challenges as well as detention from immigration authorities in Mexico.

One of the common methods of travel, especially for children whose families cannot afford the services of a coyote (smuggler), is riding on trains through Mexico to the border. Multiple rail lines traverse Mexico from the southern border with Central America to the northern border with the United States. Train routes arrive to towns and cities at or near the US border, including Nogales, Ciudad Juarez, and Reynosa. Traveling by train through Mexico has long been a popular method of transportation for immigrants migrating from Central America to the United States. In fact, research by the Migration Policy Institute suggests that more than 500,000 immigrants traveling through Mexico in 2014 traveled by train. This includes a substantial number of unaccompanied children. Although most unaccompanied children travel by other means, including buses or cars with the guidance of a coyote, unaccompanied children with limited financial resources may travel by train.

While travel by train is more affordable than other means, unaccompanied children must pay bribes to secure a spot on the train. Known as "La Bestia," or the Beast, trains through Mexico present a quicker and more affordable method of transportation; however, trains also pose significant dangers for unaccompanied children during their journey. Research demonstrates that riding on trains is accompanied by extraordinarily high risk for injury or death, leading most unaccompanied children to migrate by walking or buses. However, these other modes of transportation expose unaccompanied children to risks of robbery and kidnapping.

The trains in Mexico are exclusively freight trains, meaning the cars rattle along for miles across desert and around winding turns. Because the trains throughout Mexico are cargo trains with no passenger rail, migrants, including unaccompanied children, must ride on the top of freight railcars. They often do this after having to board a moving train. This poses enormous safety challenges. As trains shift with unexpected turns or speed changes, unaccompanied children are at risk of falling off the railcar, which could result in various injuries, including losing limbs. Children traveling by train often need to transfer multiple times along the way to the United States.

Along with dangers inherent in boarding and riding along the top of a speeding freight train, unaccompanied children are also at risk of violence from gang members, extortion, and kidnapping. Along the train routes, gangs control different stations and checkpoints, requiring payment for protection. Analysis by the Migration Policy Institute shows that criminal gang networks control various aspects of the rail network that migrants, including unaccompanied children, access. Briberies, extortion of train engineers and conductors, and threatening violence are all part of the gang's method of controlling who gets to travel by train. For unaccompanied children who are without supporting adults, navigating this network of extortion poses enormous challenges and threats to safety.

Journalists and academics have documented travel by train in Mexico at different times between 2010 and 2020, which included some years with record numbers of unaccompanied children arriving in the United States. Reporting for National Public Radio (NPR), Jason Beaubien (2011) describes how migrants experience the start of a journey on La Bestia:

> Finally, after three days, the freight train arrives in Tenosique. People run out of the shelter toward the tracks. Young men clutching small backpacks and large soda bottles filled with water emerge from the bushes. They scurry up the ladders of the moving freight cars and cling to the narrow platforms between the wagons. The train jerks violently as it picks up speed. There are about dozen people on top of the train. The vegetation sometimes hangs directly over the tracks, and so everyone has to lay almost flat to keep from getting swept off. At other times, the surface of the train gets so hot from baking in the intense midday tropical heat that you can't even touch it with your bare hand. As the train rolls on, more migrants appear along the tracks. They run and grab onto the moving beast as people on top yell out "Correle!"—"Run!"—as encouragement.

This reporting sheds important light on the lived experiences of young migrants, including unaccompanied children, who travel by train to the United States. Addressing the increased numbers of migrants traveling by train has proven difficult for government officials and train companies in Mexico. The Migration Policy Institute explains that government responses included different steps at different points in the migration journey. First, Mexican border officials increased border security with Guatemala, to address increasing numbers of migrants arriving from different parts of Central America. Along with enhanced border security, Mexican authorities also increased security at train stops throughout Mexico in an attempt to disrupt unauthorized migration. In addition to government responses, train companies also started initiatives to prevent unauthorized train travel after massive increases in migrant arrivals in the United States in 2014. For example, train companies in Mexico began building large cement columns along different parts of train tracks to prevent migrants from running alongside trains to board them. In addition, train companies began operating trains at higher speeds to discourage migrants from trying to board moving trains.

Many unaccompanied children are brought to the United States by a smuggler, or *coyote*, who is an adult who accompanies the child during the migration journey. Coyote services often cost thousands of dollars, usually paid for by a combination of family savings and debt for the child to pay upon resettlement in the United States. While coyotes provide an adult presence to help young children navigate difficult scenarios, too often coyotes exploit children or financially coerce them, by leaning on their inherent vulnerability as children in need of safety. Other children migrate with older siblings as a support; however, this unearths challenging dynamics as children worry about the health and well-being of their family members.

Social work researcher and anthropologist John Doering-White (2018) examined the dynamics of risk and protection for unaccompanied children using ethnographic research on a network of Mexican migrant shelters that assist migrants on their journey through the country. This pathbreaking research helped shed light on the conditions and types of assistance unaccompanied children encounter during their migration journey. For example, unaccompanied children often arrive at shelters in Mexico in the presence of an adult (coyote) or after losing contact with an adult caregiver during their journey. For children who arrive with an adult, humanitarian efforts at the shelters intersect with human smuggling. Doering-White elaborates on this intersection by explaining that smugglers are not formally allowed entry to migrant shelters; however, they are informally allowed entry and transit through migrant shelters with limited confrontation or inquiry from shelter workers. Part of the strategy behind this decision to turn a blind eye is to mitigate possible retribution by smugglers, and as Doering-White describes: "This approach maintains the possibility that continuing with a smuggler as opposed to seeking formal humanitarian recognition may be in the best interests of the young person."

The US government views coyotes as human smugglers who place vulnerable children at risk during dangerous journeys to the United States. In 2022, US Customs and Border Protection (CBP) launched an advertising campaign to encourage families to avoid coyotes. A CBP official explained: "Smugglers use lies to lure the vulnerable into a dangerous journey that often ends in removal or death. This digital ad campaign is an important component of U.S. government efforts to prevent tragedies and curtail irregular migration" (US Customs and Border Patrol 2022). A variety of advertisements share a common phrase: "Say no to the coyote." Despite the concerted effort by the US government to emphasize the dangers associated with coyotes, families in Central America face seemingly impossible decisions, and relying on a coyote is often seen as a necessary method to ensure their child travels with an adult to the US border. Reporting by outlets including NPR reveals a complicated reality within the world of coyotes. As NPR reporter John Burnett explained in 2014: "Federal border authorities demonize coyotes as ruthless criminals who kidnap, rape and abandon their clients. But it's more complicated than that. There are, to be sure, bad coyotes who do abuse their clients. But, as in any business, not everyone is the same."

US immigration policy is a topic that is heavily debated and contested, and unaccompanied children are not immune from political debates. Political dynamics in the United States can influence the ways in which unaccompanied children's migration journeys are portrayed. For example, viewing immigration policy through a conservative lens, through which the migration of unaccompanied children is discouraged for their own safety, coyotes are framed as human smugglers who unnecessarily place unaccompanied children in dangerous settings, especially at border crossings, kidnapping unaccompanied children and extorting their families for money. During President Biden's administration, conservative scholars believed that liberal Democratic policies encouraged the trafficking of unaccompanied children to the United States, declaring that Homeland Security Secretary Alejandro Mayorkas "basically advertised this opportunity for the Mexican drug cartels to smuggle children into the U.S. by repeatedly stating he would not turn unaccompanied children back from the border. The results have been gut-wrenching, as seen in videos and photos of children left at a river's edge, dropped over the border wall, abandoned" (Ries 2023). This statement was reinforced by incidents reported by US Border Patrol of young children, sometimes as young as one year old, who are brought to the US border by an adult and are simply left there for Border Patrol agents to find and take into custody. Although this type of incident highlights the extraordinarily perilous conditions unaccompanied children encounter during their migration to the United States, it is not clear that this is the experience of most unaccompanied children.

While conservative viewpoints tend to focus on preventing immigration as a way to discourage the dangerous smuggling and migration of unaccompanied children, liberal political views of immigration policy emphasize the complex conditions and subsequent trauma unaccompanied children experience during their journey to the United States. This manifests as a stronger focus on identifying and meeting the needs of unaccompanied children after they arrive in the United States and less focus on building policy to prevent their migration. Research from the Migration Policy Institute describes a tension between the goal of enforcing the border (preventing unaccompanied children from arriving in the United States) and the imperative to protect unaccompanied children who are fleeing gang violence or widespread poverty related to natural disasters or climate change-related disasters such as drought. Liberal views of immigration policy also recognize that a "one size fits all" approach is unlikely to work, given the varied experiences and circumstances that unaccompanied children bring with them on their migration journey. As the Migration Policy Institute explains, "ultimately, the tension between protection and enforcement can only be resolved on a case-by-case basis" (Rosenblum 2015). However, this strategy is difficult to implement, given the high numbers of unaccompanied children who migrate to the United States and the extent to which resources at the border and in the court system are overwhelmed.

After traveling thousands of miles using a combination of cars, buses, trains, and walking, unaccompanied children encounter their final step before entry to the United States. Approaching the United States in the desert of California, Arizona, New Mexico, or Texas brings children into the shadow of an unmistakable structure that divides the United States from Mexico for thousands of miles, from San Diego, California, to Brownsville, Texas. The physical border wall, although not present at each mile of the US-Mexico border, symbolizes the US government's attempts to maintain an orderly immigration system. For children who migrate to the United States without a parent or caregiver, the border wall presents another obstacle to overcome.

Border Detention and Screening Issues

Most unaccompanied children who migrate to the United States are apprehended at the US southern border, where they are processed by the US CBP, as discussed in Chapter 1. Children may arrive at the US border with limited personal resources, including food and water, which is an especially dangerous circumstance in the hotter summer months. Initial apprehension at the US border can be a confusing experience for unaccompanied children, who may not be familiar with the processes in place to appropriately identify and process them as unaccompanied migrants. Existing immigration policy that is court mandated, such as the Flores Settlement Agreement, and existing laws, such as the Trafficking Victims Protection Reauthorization Act (TVPRA), have clear guidelines to ensure that unaccompanied children are cared for and their human rights respected (see Chapter 1).

Unaccompanied children are held in detention on a "short-term basis," which is typically defined as twenty-four hours or less. However, the US Office of the Inspector General reports that CBP officials strive to transport unaccompanied children out of detention within twelve hours. Most children are held in short-term detention for forty-eight hours or less. Although limiting detention time for children is generally desirable, there is concern that rushing the screening process or subsequent placement process may put unaccompanied children in jeopardy, as they are returned to unsafe conditions in their country of origin or placed in settings within the United States that make them susceptible to human trafficking and economic exploitation.

While in short-term detention, CBP officials are required to provide certain resources and services for unaccompanied children to ensure their basic human needs are met. The Flores Settlement Agreement requires that CBP officials provide unaccompanied children: "(1) food and drinking water, (2) medical assistance in the event of emergencies, (3) toilets and sinks, (4) adequate temperature control and ventilation, (5) adequate supervision to protect minors from others, and (6) separation from unrelated adults whenever possible." However, one of the central problems that unaccompanied children face when in detention is threats to their health and well-being. According to research by physician and medical researcher Young and colleagues in 2024, one health risk factor for unaccompanied children is a lack of formal medical evaluation upon apprehension by CBP officials. Once apprehended at the border and transferred to a CBP location, unaccompanied children receive an initial medical screening by emergency medical technicians, who, according to Young and colleagues, may not have advanced training in pediatric health care. A formal assessment by a nurse or physician's assistant occurs within twenty-four hours of arrival at a CBP location. A potential problem with this framework is lapsed time before a child receives a formal medical evaluation, which could leave serious medical needs unmet.

Along with the problem of limited medical evaluation, a controversy related to the care of unaccompanied children has been lengthy stays in detention in overcrowded facilities. In a report published in 2024, titled "Kids in Care: Unaccompanied Children in Federal Government Custody," researchers Lauren Heidbrink and Sarah J. Diaz analyzed survey data collected from 135 individuals who have varying experiences working with unaccompanied children in detention facilities, including case managers, supervisors, and program directors. Along with survey data, the researchers also gathered qualitative data using in-depth interviews with fifty-five participants who work in detention facilities that serve unaccompanied children.

Among the findings, Heidbrink and Diaz found that most unaccompanied children (approximately 85 percent) are placed in congregate care settings that are substantially overcrowded. For example, most detention facilities identified in the study were designed to care for 50 to 200 children; however, some facilities had up to 1,400 unaccompanied children. The overcrowded conditions in detention facilities impacted the way unaccompanied children were cared for, including limiting their access to medical care and education services. The challenges identified in the report are even more pressing for vulnerable populations, including children with disabilities, pregnant or parenting children, LGBTQ+ children, and adolescents who are transitioning to adulthood. Each of these groups of unaccompanied children requires specialized services that are not consistently provided due to overcrowded conditions (Heidbrink and Diaz 2024).

There are several possible solutions to problems and controversies like limited medical care and overcrowded detention facilities. Heidbrink and Diaz (2024) recommend that congregate care be used only as a last resort, that care and services be child-centered, and that government oversight be increased to improve the monitoring and evaluation of detention facilities. Physician Paul Wise and researcher Lauren Stoffel (2024) explained in a peer-reviewed comment published in *Pediatric Research* that care for unaccompanied children must account for the intense political dimensions that influence the formation of controversies and perceived problems:

> In many ways, advocacy for migrant children must confront the collision of an idealized American vision of the innocent child in need of protection with the image of the southern migrant, an image that ignobly summons an enduring yet often veiled fear of the intruder, the outsider, the other. Pediatric advocacy for unaccompanied migrant children, therefore, must navigate this intensely contentious public discourse and ensure with both pragmatism and compassion the well-being of migrant children who come into the care of the people of the United States and come alone.

After unaccompanied children are processed by CBP officials and their identity and basic background information are verified, they follow two separate pathways to release: one pathway for unaccompanied children from contiguous countries (Mexico and Canada), which often results in voluntary return to their country of origin, and one pathway for unaccompanied children from other countries. Based on guidelines established in the TVPRA, unaccompanied children from Mexico are initially screened to determine if they are victims of trafficking, if they demonstrate fear of returning to Mexico due to persecution, or if they do not have the capacity to make an independent decision regarding their return to Mexico. This screening occurs while the child is held in detention and is conducted by CBP officials who do not have advanced training in trauma or child development. Furthermore, these initial screenings occur in a limited timeframe, which limits the assessment capabilities of CBP officials.

The voluntary return process for unaccompanied children is designed to facilitate repatriation for the US and Mexican governments; however, the process can overlook the best interests of children who may be returned to vulnerable and unsafe settings. Evidence suggests that, rather than promoting family reunification, the voluntary return process for unaccompanied children from Mexico can lead to children returning to at-risk settings, such as domestic violence, child maltreatment, or exploitation (Ataiants et al. 2018). If an unaccompanied child from Mexico demonstrates fear of persecution if they return to Mexico, or if evidence indicates they are a victim of human trafficking, then they are further processed by CBP and transferred to the Office of Refugee Resettlement (ORR), with the goal of placing the child with a sponsor in the United States.

Children who migrate from countries other than Mexico, also called "non-contiguous countries," are not subject to voluntary return. While in detention, after children from noncontiguous countries are processed by CBP, an Immigration and Customs Enforcement (ICE) Juvenile Coordinator is contacted, and the children are transferred to ICE custody. ICE transports unaccompanied children to ORR custody, and ORR is then responsible for placing the unaccompanied children with a sponsor or in long-term foster care if a sponsor is not identified or able to take custody of the child.

Many children file a claim for asylum, meaning they will need to present their case for remaining in the United States to a federal judge. However, given the large numbers of unaccompanied children who have arrived in the United States between 2014 and 2024, the average wait time to present an asylum case in court is more than four years long.

Human Trafficking and Economic Exploitation

According to the US Department of Homeland Security (2022), human trafficking is defined as "the use of force, fraud, or coercion to obtain some type of labor or commercial sex act." Immigrants and newcomers to the United States are vulnerable to human trafficking due to language barriers. Unaccompanied children are especially vulnerable, given the lack of adult support they have during their migration journey. In addition, female immigrants are especially at risk of sex trafficking.

Human trafficking is a violation of US federal law, based on the perpetrator's acts, means, and purpose. According to the US Department of State, the "acts" of a human trafficker refer to when a trafficker recruits, transports, or otherwise obtains a person for labor. The "means" of a human trafficker refers to the use of force, fraud, or coercion. For example, unaccompanied children, who do not have legal status to be in the United States, are vulnerable to a human trafficker exploiting their undocumented status. The "purpose" refers to the goal of the human trafficker and the reason why they engaged in trafficking to obtain labor. Unaccompanied children sometimes migrate with a coyote, an adult smuggler who is responsible for their safe arrival in the United States. Coyotes can cost families thousands of dollars, and unaccompanied children can be at risk of human trafficking if they are unable to pay back the coyote after their arrival in the United States.

Human trafficking impacts millions of people. According to the US Department of State, at any time in 2021 there were 27.6 million people who were victims of human trafficking around the world. Gathering reliable data remains difficult, given the fluid nature of human trafficking and challenges with identifying individuals who are harmed by human trafficking. The challenge is greater for unaccompanied children, who may experience human trafficking shortly after their processing at the US border and subsequent placement with a sponsor.

Investigative reporting in 2023 and 2024 revealed that unaccompanied children throughout the United States worked in settings that violated federal labor law, including dangerous construction and factory positions where minors are typically prohibited from working. Based on reporting from Alabama, Florida, Georgia, Michigan, Minnesota, South Dakota, and Virginia and interviews with more than 100 unaccompanied children, *The New York Times* reporter Hannah Dreier (2023) uncovered record numbers of children who migrated to the

United States from Central America to pursue education opportunities or escape violence, only to be coerced into dangerous work settings to support family or pay debts to smugglers. This economic exploitation occurs after a child arrives in the United States and after the federal government, including the Department of Health and Human Services, is aware the child is in the country. One challenge uncovered by this reporting is the limited follow-up for unaccompanied children after they are placed with a sponsor. Given the pressure to limit a child's time in detention after their arrival in the United States, a growing concern is that the placement process is too quick, and unaccompanied children are placed in settings that are prone to economic exploitation.

The New York Times investigative reporting conducted in 2023 aligns with findings from a study published in February 2024 by the US Department of Health and Human Services Office of Inspector General. To ensure the safety and well-being of unaccompanied children who arrived in the United States during an increase in referrals in early 2021, the Office of Inspector General "reviewed ORR's implementation of sponsor screening and post-release follow up calls" for a sample of 343 unaccompanied children (US Department of Health and Human Services 2024). A series of findings from the study uncovered substantial gaps in the sponsor screening process, which enhances the risk of human trafficking for unaccompanied children. First, the study found that 16 percent of case files in the sample lacked documentation of required sponsor safety checks. The study also found that almost one in five (19 percent) unaccompanied children were placed with sponsors when FBI or state child welfare agency background checks were still pending, and files were not updated with results. An additional documentation concern was poor legibility of sponsor IDs, found in 35 percent of unaccompanied children's files.

Within the sample, the study also found that two unaccompanied children did not receive mandatory home visits, and an additional four cases revealed concerns regarding the specificity of guidelines for home visits. In addition, there were gaps in the documentation of sponsor background. For 5 percent of cases, sponsor records were not updated with the latest information on their history or the results of child welfare background checks. Finally, more than one in five unaccompanied children (22 percent) did not receive timely safety checks from ORR officials to ensure their well-being in the community. These gaps in follow up and documentation, as described by the Office of Inspector General, reveal a tension between assessing child welfare concerns and ensuring the safe and timely release of unaccompanied children from ORR care. The report suggests that in many cases, the safe and timely release of unaccompanied children to sponsors in the community lacked necessary follow-up, which increased the risk for human trafficking and exploitation.

A final case that demonstrates the risk of exploitation unaccompanied children can experience in resettlement locations was documented by investigative reporting in New Bedford, Massachusetts, in 2023 (Sebai et al. 2023). This reporting followed the experiences of two minors who arrived in the United States as unaccompanied children and found work in a seafood processing facility. At fourteen and sixteen years old, the unaccompanied children were exposed to various occupational hazards that would otherwise prevent individuals their age from working in such a dangerous setting. Using fake IDs to gain work through an employment agency, the children earned $16.50 per hour and reported working twelve-hour shifts on a routine basis.

Many unaccompanied children describe working to pay debts to smugglers, to support family in their home country, or to support themselves in the United States. This reality, coupled with the children's desire to attend school and pursue education, reveals a harsh tension that exists for unaccompanied children. The complex migration journey takes a different form that can trap them in economic exploitation as they strive to accomplish goals and pursue dreams. This happens in every corner of the United States, in seafood processing plants on the coast, slaughterhouses in the heartland, and hotel rooms across the country.

Zero Tolerance and Family Separation

A unique pattern in migration began to emerge in 2020—increasing numbers of family units migrated to the United States. The reasons for families migrating to the United States were similar to the reasons driving children to migrate unaccompanied to the United States—violence in home countries, economic destitution, and the desire to reunify with family in the United States. Historically, family units that arrived at the US border and were apprehended by US CBP were processed through the immigration system as a family unit. In other words, all members of the family remained together while meeting with Border Patrol officials and awaiting release from immigration detention or expedited removal and deportation to their home country. However, an executive action in 2018 by President Donald Trump's administration made substantive changes to immigration policy at the US southern border. Among these changes was forcibly separating children from their parents after their apprehension at the border. Thousands of children were separated from their parents, and, as a result, children became unaccompanied as they were processed through the US immigration system.

The practice of forcibly separating children from their families was part of a larger policy called "Zero Tolerance." A press release from the US Department of Justice Office of Public Affairs on April 6, 2018, announced the arrival of President Trump's Zero Tolerance Policy, which aimed to deter unauthorized border crossings. US Attorney General Jeff Sessions explained that the Zero Tolerance Policy was "for offenses under 8 U.S.C. § 1325(a), which prohibits both attempted illegal entry and illegal entry into the United States by an alien" (US Department of Justice Office of Public Affairs 2018). Zero Tolerance changed the approach of the Department of Justice by pursuing criminal charges for any individual who crossed a US border without authorization. Under the framework of the policy, this included family units migrating to claim asylum. The press release explained that Zero Tolerance was in response to major increases in the number of individuals crossing the US border: "The implementation of the Attorney General's zero-tolerance policy comes as the Department of Homeland Security reported a 203 percent increase in illegal border crossings from March 2017 to March 2018, and a 37 percent increase from February 2018 to March 2018—the largest month-to-month increase since 2011" (US Department of Justice Office of Public Affairs 2018).

The decision to criminally prosecute all individuals who cross a US border without authorization, including members of family units, was planned for more than a year. Research from the US Department of Justice Office of Inspector General in 2021 "found that Department leadership and, in particular, the Office of the Attorney General (OAG), which had primary responsibility for the policy's development, failed to effectively prepare for, or manage, the implementation of the zero tolerance policy." The failure to adequately prepare for or manage the implementation of Zero Tolerance became clearer as children were forcibly separated from their parents, becoming unaccompanied children in the custody of the US government.

The practice of forcibly separating children from their parents officially lasted from April 2018 until June 20, 2018, when President Trump signed an executive order ending the Zero Tolerance Policy. After Attorney General Jeff Sessions announced the start of Zero Tolerance, nonprofits, nongovernmental associations, and prominent politicians in both the Democratic and Republican parties denounced the practice of forcibly separating children from their parents as a humanitarian disaster. On June 1, 2018, Human Rights Watch explained that the Zero Tolerance Policy "sends parents into detention and prosecutes them for the crime of entering the country illegally, while their children—including infants and toddlers—are taken into government custody separately and alone." Former First Lady Laura Bush, writing in an op-ed published in the *Washington Post*, argued that "people on all sides agree that our immigration system isn't working, but the injustice of zero tolerance is not the answer" (Bush 2018). A striking feature of the resistance to the Zero Tolerance Policy was the manner in which it transcended political ideology and sustained a focus on the vulnerable children, hundreds of whom were less than five years old, who were separated from a family member at the US border.

While the Zero Tolerance Policy officially ended on June 20, 2018, the practice of forcibly separating children from their families continued throughout President Trump's administration. A defining feature of the 2020 presidential election was immigration, and President Trump's Zero Tolerance Policy was cited often during debates about policy. President Biden's election in November 2020 signaled a change in approach to immigration policy, with a stronger emphasis on balancing the human rights of immigrants and the enforcement of immigration policy at the US border.

Changes to immigration policy manifested within days of President Biden taking office. On February 2, 2021, shortly after President Biden was inaugurated in January 2021, he signed Executive Order 14011 (E.O. 14011), "Establishment of Interagency Task Force on the Reunification of Families." This Executive Order called for the task force to identify children who were separated during the Zero Tolerance Policy and work to reconnect separated children with their families. In addition, the task force was called "to provide recommendations on providing additional services and support for the reunified families, including behavioral health services with a focus on trauma-informed care."

The task force was required to submit an initial report to the White House after the first 120 days. The 120-day initial report identified three different accomplishments. First, the task force identified "nearly all" children who were separated from their families as part of the Zero Tolerance Policy. The task force reported that between July 1, 2017, and January 20, 2021 (the date President Biden was inaugurated as president of the United States), 3,913 children were separated from their parents. Of these children, 1,786 were already reunified with family, leaving the task force to identify and reunify 2,127 children with their families.

The second accomplishment within the first 120 days was the establishment of a family reunification process. The task force organized a coordinated effort between multiple government agencies to harness the full power of the federal government to reunify children with their families and ensure they received the appropriate care and resources during the reunification process. This included involvement of the US Department of Homeland Security, Department of Justice, Department of State, and Department of Health and Human Services. The task force also recommended that the Department of Homeland Security allow adult family members parole of up to thirty-six months so they could return to the United States and reunify with their children.

The third accomplishment within the first 120 days of the task force was the beginning of reunifying separated children with their families. According to the task force in an Initial Progress Report on June 2, 2021, 1,779 children were reunified with their parents before the task force was formed. This reunification effort was largely facilitated by nongovernmental organizations (NGOs). After 120 days, the task force identified seven children who were reunified with their families, 37 individual cases that were processed by immigration authorities, and an additional 48 families that filed formal requests for reunification. As reported in a progress report on April 22, 2024, the task force made substantial progress across three years in the effort to reunify children with their families. For example, the task force reported that "As of March 20, 2024, the Task Force has facilitated the reunification of 795 children with their parents in the United States and made behavioral health services available to those families" (Interagency Task Force on the Reunification of Families 2025, 1). As of April 22, 2024, the task force identified 1,360 children who were not yet reunified with their families.

Outside of the US government, scholars have begun to examine the impact of family separation on the lives of children. In 2019, Dr. Ben Roth, a social work professor from the University of South Carolina College of Social Work, and a group of scholars published a study titled "Detached and Afraid: U.S. Immigration Policy and the Practice of Forcibly Separating Parents and Young Children at the Border." This study was based on analysis of twenty in-depth interviews with case managers and service providers working at transitional foster care settings that provided services for children recently separated from their parents. The analyses revealed three main themes: (1) the impact of separation on children, (2) challenges with building trust, and (3) the need for programs to adapt.

Roth and his colleagues uncovered clear descriptions of how forcibly separating children from their parents impacts children's mental health. Clinicians and service providers described how children in their placements were confused and disoriented because they assumed they would remain with their parents after arriving in the United States. Symptoms of trauma were more profound for tender-age children—children under five years old. Many tender-age children did not have the verbal communication skills to report their feelings to case managers. As a result, children often struggled with trauma symptoms, such as abrupt crying, with little warning. Case managers described having difficulty recognizing these symptoms because children were unable to consistently communicate their feelings.

A second main theme uncovered in the analysis was difficulty building trust with children who were separated from their parents. Children often remained in the foster care placements for limited periods of time, which created challenges for case managers to build trust with the children. Throughout the immigration process, children were transferred among multiple placements. These included apprehension by border patrol officials, short-term processing at a border patrol facility, placement at a short-term shelter, transition foster care, and then transfer to their family or sponsor in the United States. Roth and colleagues learned that these multiple placements were especially taxing on children who were separated from their families because they did not have time to build relationships with trusting and caring adults. The transfer between placements exacerbated the trauma from family separation by stressing attachments between children and the adults in their lives.

Along with difficulty building trust, the practice of family separation also required case managers and supervisors to make substantial changes to their programs. Case managers described unique challenges presented by tender-age children who were separated from their families. These children, especially children in toddlerhood, required physical support, such as being held, to help them soothe and manage their feelings. The arrival of tender-age children also required that programs have spaces designated for napping, as well as resources to promote developmental skills through play. Finally, given the limited information that tender-age children could communicate to case managers, the study also revealed how case managers required substantial amounts of time to track down information from other sources.

While Roth and colleagues examined the impact of the family separation policy on the lives of individual children and how it impacted service providers, the policy was also influenced by politics at a broader, societal level. Zero Tolerance, including the practice of forcibly separating children from their families, was a highly polarizing policy from its inception through long after the policy ended. The conservative political lens framed Zero Tolerance as a necessary effort to end unauthorized border crossings and secure the southern border. This framework was emphasized during President Trump's administration, including by the Attorney General, Jeff Sessions. As Caitlin Dickerson (2022), in her reporting for *The Atlantic Monthly*, explained:

> Jeff Sessions is exactly the sort of person one might expect to be responsible for a policy that would result in widespread family separations. Throughout his career, his approach to both criminal justice and immigration enforcement could be defined by the phrase *zero tolerance*, a law-enforcement term of art that is almost always used euphemistically, because snuffing out all crime is impossible. But for Sessions, the phrase is literal. He supported enforcing all laws—or at least the ones that he deemed important—to the fullest extent possible, with no room for nuance or humanitarian exception.

While the Zero Tolerance Policy aligned with a long-standing conservative view of restricting undocumented immigration, the practice of forcibly separating children from their parents violated humanitarian norms that guided how the United States framed and carried out immigration policy at the border. A liberal political lens framed family separation as a violation of human rights. For example, the American Civil Liberties Union (ACLU) described the family separation policy as "one of the darkest chapters of the Trump administration" and a "horrific practice" (American Civil Liberties Union 2023). In response to the Zero Tolerance Policy and the subsequent forced separation of children from their parents, the ACLU filed a lawsuit, and in December 2023, a federal court approved a settlement in favor of the children and families. The settlement requires the US government to support reunification of children and their families, allow pathways for asylum for affected families, and provide access to a range of benefits to support adjustment in the United States, including housing support and work authorization. Requiring that the federal government provide mental health services for the children separated from their families as part of the Zero Tolerance Policy was also a part of the settlement achieved by the ACLU lawsuit. For unaccompanied children more broadly, mental health issues are a prominent challenge.

Unaccompanied Children and Mental Health

Unaccompanied children encounter a variety of conditions before, during, and after their migration journey that are associated with adverse mental health outcomes. Being separated from parents in childhood threatens the bond formed between a child and parent and can stress attachment. Gang violence, poverty, child maltreatment, and economic and sexual exploitation are all risks that unaccompanied children can experience during different parts of a migration journey. The result can be a variety of psychiatric symptoms that emerge as different mental health issues. Social isolation, depressed mood, sleep and appetite disruptions, verbal or physical aggression, intrusive memories, suicidal ideation, and self-harm behavior are all symptoms that can indicate an unaccompanied child is suffering from trauma experienced during the migration journey. In this section, the importance of this topic is demonstrated by a review of research on unaccompanied children and mental health.

Research from the United Nations High Commissioner for Refugees shows that substantial numbers of children who migrated from Central America reported gang violence in their home country as a primary reason for their migration to the United States, especially for unaccompanied children who migrate from El Salvador and Honduras. The trauma associated with gang violence—including physical beatings, being robbed, and being threatened—can exacerbate trauma-related mental health symptoms such as intrusive memories, depressed mood, hypervigilance, and sleep disruptions. Gang violence can disrupt a child's sense of safety, which is further challenged by dangers inherent in the migration journey.

Along with risk factors before migration, unaccompanied children also encounter risks to mental health during their migration journey. Some of these risk factors include exposure to sexual violence, which is especially prevalent for female unaccompanied children. In addition, research from UNICEF shows that kidnappings and economic exploitation are high among unaccompanied children who migrate to the United States, which reflects their vulnerability as children. During the migration journey, many unaccompanied children ride on trains to travel to the United States. Trying to board moving trains presents an array of challenges, including the risk of serious injury or death. Unaccompanied children may experience stress and trauma during the migration journey due to the unpredictable nature of train travel.

After arriving in the United States, the apprehension process at the border, followed by subsequent detention before transfer to ORR custody, are also mental health risk factors. Research also shows that challenges to integration in the United States, such as language barriers, can be associated with symptoms of mental distress, such as depressed mood, for unaccompanied children who are resettled in the United States.

Research on mental health outcomes for unaccompanied children in the United States is a growing area among scholars. One of the first forays into this topic was from Jodi Berger Cardoso (2018), a social work scholar at the University of Houston Graduate School of Social Work. Dr. Berger Cardoso's article, titled "Running to Stand Still: Trauma Symptoms, Coping Strategies, and Substance Use Behaviors in Unaccompanied Migrant Youth," analyzed quantitative and qualitative data to answer three broad research questions. First, the study aimed to understand what trauma unaccompanied children experienced after their arrival in the United States. Second, the study aimed to understand the coping skills unaccompanied children use to manage symptoms of trauma. Finally, the study aimed to understand how trauma symptoms and coping strategies are associated with substance use behavior.

The study included a total of thirty unaccompanied children who resettled in the United States after migrating from Mexico, El Salvador, Guatemala, and Honduras, with an equal proportion of male (fifteen) and female (fifteen) participants. Among the main findings was that children in the study experienced an average of 8.27 traumatic events in their lifetime. Common traumatic events included being separated from a family member, which was reported by 73.3 percent of children in the study, and witnessing physical violence and being hurt in a natural disaster, both of which were reported by 66.7 percent of children in the study. Along with experiencing trauma, the study also found that more than 50 percent of children met criteria for posttraumatic stress disorder (PTSD), 30 percent met criteria for major depressive disorder, and 30 percent reported experiencing suicidal ideation in the last year. Dr. Berger Cardoso placed these findings in context by explaining that the experiences of threats to mental health were greater than in recently sampled adult immigrants from Central America.

Along with determining adverse mental health outcomes, Dr. Berger Cardoso also explored how unaccompanied children coped with trauma-related symptoms. Children in the study cited religion, family, and "healthy distraction," such as playing sports or listening to music, and social support from friends as important coping skills. Social support, including speaking with friends, counselors, teachers, or family members, was an especially important coping skill. Engaging with faith communities, such as churches, provided children in the study an outlet for using faith and spirituality as a coping skill to manage negative feelings related to traumatic experiences.

However, the study also unearthed maladaptive coping skills that children engaged in to manage stress and mental health symptoms. These coping skills included "social isolation and withdrawal, avoidance, self-harm behavior, and substance use" (Berger Cardoso 2018). Social isolation and withdrawal are especially problematic maladaptive coping skills because they complicate the stresses related to integration that immigrants navigate as they adjust to new communities. Finally, some children in the study described substance use as a way to "numb" the pain experienced prior to migrating to the United States. This study, one of the first to examine symptoms of trauma and coping strategies in a sample of unaccompanied children in the United States, offers important insights into the ways vulnerable immigrant children experience mental health issues while they adjust to their new country.

One challenge for meeting the needs of immigrant children, including unaccompanied children, is limited culturally informed mental health assessments. Many mental health instruments used in the United States were created by US citizens and tested on populations of people born in the United States. However, it can be unclear if these measures accurately capture mental health symptoms experienced by unaccompanied children. In other words, while unaccompanied children from Central America and children from parts of the United States may both experience gang violence, it is unclear if the resulting symptoms of trauma are experienced in the same way. To address this, a study by Robert G. Hasson III and colleagues (2021) explored the extent to which one trauma measure, the Child PTSD Symptom Scale (CPSS), accurately assesses symptoms of trauma.

The CPSS is a twenty-item questionnaire that measures different symptoms of trauma. The results of the CPSS, when scored, can indicate whether or not a child has PTSD. The CPSS measures four different "clusters" of PTSD symptoms, including intrusion symptoms, avoidance symptoms, changes in cognition or mood, and increased arousal and reactivity symptoms. In addition to the subscales, the CPSS also measures overall symptom severity.

In their study, Hasson III and colleagues analyzed CPSS data from a sample of 149 unaccompanied children who were resettled in the United States. The analysis revealed that, rather than four clusters of symptoms, unaccompanied children exhibited trauma symptoms that aligned with three different clusters. The first cluster included all four types of symptoms (e.g., intrusion symptoms, avoidance symptoms, changes in cognition or mood, and increased arousal and reactivity symptoms). This suggests that unaccompanied children experience a broad range of trauma-related symptoms. The second cluster identified in the analysis included symptoms from the intrusion, changes in cognition or mood, and reactivity clusters. However, the third cluster identified in the analysis included only reactivity symptoms. This suggests that unaccompanied children who experience trauma may experience unique challenges with reactivity symptoms, such as anger outbursts and having difficulty concentrating.

Hasson III and colleagues expanded on this research in 2022 in a study titled "Mental Health Services for Unaccompanied Children in the United States" (Hasson, Diaz-Valdez, and Underwood 2022). The study explored what factors are associated with unaccompanied children reporting mental health services as their primary need. After placement with a sponsor in the United States, some unaccompanied children begin case management services, called Post-Release Services (PRS). Case managers help unaccompanied children identify their primary need when starting PRS. Among the several needs that unaccompanied children report are mental health services.

In their study, Hasson III et al. found that, among a total sample of 851 unaccompanied children, 23.5 percent reported mental health services as their primary need. Older unaccompanied children and children from Honduras both reported higher odds of identifying mental health services as their primary need. Male unaccompanied children, compared to female unaccompanied children, reported lower odds of identifying mental health services as their primary need. This research sheds light on the important role of family relationships in supporting unaccompanied children who may struggle with mental health challenges (Hasson, Diaz-Valdez, and Underwood 2022). These results also highlighted important areas for future research, which Hasson III and colleagues explored in a separate study.

Building on Berger Cardoso's 2018 study, Hasson III and colleagues completed a qualitative study in 2024 that explored how unaccompanied children describe their mental health challenges, as well as the supports they find most helpful (Hasson, Oliva et al. 2024). This study was based on in-depth interviews with sixteen unaccompanied children who were resettled in Rhode Island and were receiving case management services. The study aimed to amplify the voices of unaccompanied children who experienced hardship before, during, or after their migration to the United States and provide them space to describe the supports they found most helpful.

The study identified three broad categories of challenges. First, unaccompanied children described language barriers that complicated socialization during the integration process in resettlement areas. This could manifest in different ways. For example, an unaccompanied child who recently arrived in Rhode Island may live near a park with other children playing soccer. However, with limited English-language skills, the child may have difficulty navigating how to join the game and make new friends in the neighborhood. Similarly, children who were newcomers to their neighborhood in Rhode Island explained feeling symptoms of anxiety when trying to access stores in their neighborhood if they did not know if the employee in the store spoke their language. Unaccompanied children often cite education as a primary reason for migrating to the United States, and the pressure to learn English can also complicate the stresses inherent with starting at a new school and not having any friendships.

Along with language barriers that complicate the integration process, Hasson III and colleagues also found that family separation is a unique stressor experienced by unaccompanied children, and this family separation results in a complex constellation of trauma symptoms. Not all unaccompanied children experience poverty and lack of basic human needs, or experience gang violence or natural disasters. However, a stressor that is experienced by all unaccompanied children is separation, at some point and for some duration, from their family. Hasson III and colleagues found that family separation was associated with a unique profile of trauma symptoms that may not align with existing diagnostic tools. Intrusive memories, depressed mood, and hyperactive responses may all emerge; however, the timeline for these symptoms, and the duration of their acuity, may expand beyond the boundaries of diagnostic frameworks.

Interestingly, Hasson III and colleagues found that, along with family separation, children also described family reunification as a stressor during the integration process. Families undergo a lot of change in the context of migration, and these changes can have an outsize effect on children. One example of family changes an unaccompanied child may experience is the loss of, and then reconnection with, a parental figure. For example, an unaccompanied child's father may migrate to the United States when the child is in early childhood. Then, after the father is in the United States for several years, the unaccompanied child may migrate to the United States to reunify. However, now the unaccompanied child is in adolescence, which is a developmental stage that requires parenting skills that are different from parenting skills used with a young child. In the United States, after resettlement, family turmoil may arise when parents try to set expectations in the home that the child is not used to. Along with various stressors, Hasson III and colleagues also uncovered three main types of support that unaccompanied children described.

The first support identified by unaccompanied children was family support. Despite the challenges with reunification, unaccompanied children consistently cited family support as a primary mechanism of resilience. This included direct family support in the United States, as well as family support a child received from family members in their home country. With the benefit of technology such as WhatsApp, Skype, and FaceTime, unaccompanied children reported being able to receive emotional support from family in home countries.

The second support identified by unaccompanied children in the sample was education. Children in the study described education as a gateway for socialization and a catalyst for integration. Most unaccompanied children in the study identified education as a reason for their migration to the United States. In describing the importance of education, children explained that school is where most socializing occurs with peers. In fact, some children explained to researchers that they did not have friends yet because they had not yet started school. In other words, even though some children had not yet been to school, the idea of school was one that conjured ideas of friendship and the accompanying social support that is critical for integration. Schools foster this type of social support in various formal and informal ways. Lunchtime in the cafeteria and visiting a locker in between classes both provide children unstructured moments for connecting with peers. Clubs, sports, and after-school activities provide more structured settings for children to socialize with others.

A final form of social support that is helpful for unaccompanied children is support from NGO staff. Hasson III and colleagues described the importance of NGO staff for identifying and meeting the needs of unaccompanied children after they arrive in the United States. Many unaccompanied children require basic human needs upon their arrival. For many children in the study, they resettled in the Northeast United States in the winter. Receiving a winter coat from an NGO staff member was identified as a critical type of material support. Likewise, receiving school supplies when enrolling at school was described as helpful support. However, Hasson III and colleagues unearthed an important nuance to the support the children received. Unaccompanied children reported that the relational support provided by NGO staff was as meaningful as the material needs, and in some instances more important. In other words, for some unaccompanied children, it was not *what* they received that was most helpful, but it was *who* provided it that made the most difference.

Unaccompanied Children and Education

Whether it's on the playground in elementary school, in the hallways between classes in middle school, or in the cafeteria at lunchtime in high school, schools provide ample opportunities for unaccompanied children at any grade level to have formal and informal learning experiences. This includes the important building blocks of English-language skill building, as well as the informal relationship building that children encounter in hallways and cafeterias. Taken together, these learning opportunities can facilitate socializing and catalyze integration for vulnerable immigrants in the United States, including unaccompanied children. Research shows the sheer positive impact that education can have on unaccompanied children in the United States. However, unaccompanied children and their families may struggle with enrolling in school, which is a major barrier to integration. Despite laws that protect access to public education for all immigrant children, research shows clear patterns of struggle with enrollment processes.

All immigrant children in the United States, including unaccompanied children, have a right to public education. This was decided as part of *Plyler v. Doe*, a 1982 Supreme Court case in which the court ruled that "A state cannot prevent children of undocumented immigrants from attending public school unless a substantial state interest is involved." This ruling extends to unaccompanied children, many of whom may be seeking asylum in the United States or are otherwise without permanent legal status to reside in the United States.

According to the US Department of Education, all K-12 schools must be open to all students, regardless of their immigration status or the immigration status of their family members. In addition, all K-12 schools must offer language support for students who have limited English-language skills so they can fully participate in their own education. Finally, all K-12 schools are required to have school information available in non-English languages to enhance accessibility. This includes information about how to enroll children in school, class information, and education programs. Despite these requirements, unaccompanied children and their families may encounter various challenges when trying to access public education. Children may have difficulty enrolling if schools request Social Security numbers or copies of a US birth certificate. According to the US Department of Education, valid documents for enrolling unaccompanied children in schools include a "Verification of Release Form" or a vaccination record from the ORR.

Unaccompanied children may encounter additional challenges once enrolled in a school. One challenge unaccompanied children may encounter is with assessment. Schools may administer proficiency tests at the beginning and end of a school year; however, unaccompanied children may not be included if they were enrolled partway through the school year. Unaccompanied children may also be deterred from enrolling in special academic programs (e.g., gifted and talented programs, Advanced Placement classes) because they are English-language learners or have a history of interrupted education due to migration. Many unaccompanied children live with sponsors who are family members and have limited English-language skills. Schools may not provide language assistance so family members can actively participate in decision-making about their child's education. This problem could emerge during a parent-teacher conference, or a special education meeting. If a school does not provide language services, sometimes students who are multilingual may be asked to act as a translator for an unaccompanied child and their family. This creates barriers for unaccompanied children, as well as for multilingual students. Finally, the US Department of Education describes scenarios where unaccompanied children and their families are informed they need to choose between language services or special education services, when they are, in fact, entitled to both.

The rights that unaccompanied children have to access education, as well as the barriers they encounter with enrolling as well as after enrolling in school, are part of a larger problem with unaccompanied children encountering discrimination. These threats are identified in an array of research on the experiences of unaccompanied children in education systems in the United States. One study examines the policies that create systemic barriers for immigrant children, including unaccompanied children, to access education. In a policy analysis titled "Without a Paddle: Barriers to School Enrollment

Procedures for Immigrant Students and Families," social work professor Kerri Evans and colleagues (2020) identified documentation and discrimination and bias as key challenges immigrant children may experience when trying to enroll in schools.

For documentation challenges, Evans explains that birth certificates, documents proving residency, and health records are all materials that unaccompanied children and their families may not have, due to the unpredictable nature of forced migration. After enrollment, Evans and colleagues explain that discrimination and bias can prevent unaccompanied children from accessing certain education services. For example, unaccompanied children who require English-language services may be placed in alternative education settings that are primarily focused on behavior challenges. Evans and colleagues also identify differences at the school district level—some school districts allocate resources to promote bilingual and bicultural learning, whereas other school districts face penalties such as lawsuits for not providing the required services for immigrant children, including unaccompanied children.

This research was expanded in additional scholarship that focuses on the perspectives of practitioners who work with unaccompanied children. In 2022, Evans and colleagues completed a study that included analysis of qualitative data collected from focus groups. The study included seventy-nine participants in twenty-two different focus groups, and each participant had experience working directly with unaccompanied children. Among the participants were teachers and school personnel. The results of the study unearthed several themes that describe the central challenges unaccompanied children face when trying to access education.

First, the study explained that, in many ways, the education system in the United States has a limited capacity to meet the complex needs of unaccompanied children. At the school level, participants in the study described challenges with deciding how to place unaccompanied children at certain grade levels, wondering whether age, academic level, or other criteria should inform grade placement decisions. Other challenges were related to the amount of resources available for schools to provide programming. For example, participants explained that with limited funding, schools were unable to support sports, clubs, or other after-school activities that are central for helping immigrant students with adjustment and integration.

A second challenge identified in the study was language barriers. Similar to other research (see Hasson, Oliva et al. 2024), Evans and colleagues learned from participants that some schools lacked translation services for English-language learners. When translation services are requested, delays of weeks can disrupt the flow of education for unaccompanied children in the classroom. Complicating matters further are the numbers of unaccompanied children who do not speak English or Spanish but rather migrate from Guatemala and speak an indigenous language.

A third challenge described by participants was a general lack of preparedness on the part of children that was observed in education settings. Evans and colleagues explain that many unaccompanied children drop out of school in their home country or experience extended gaps in learning as a result of migration to the United States. These learning gaps, the researchers explain: "create complications in terms of grade placement, emotional stability, and can hinder healthy social and academic adjustment to the school environment" (Evans et al. 2022, 202). A resulting challenge is placing an adolescent unaccompanied child in a lower grade level that meets their reading and writing level but may not meet their social needs by being placed with students who are significantly younger.

Evans and colleagues also found that a culture clash can impact an unaccompanied child's education. More specifically, caseworkers who participated in focus groups explained that unaccompanied children sometimes struggle to adjust to new norms and expectations in the classroom, leading to behavioral challenges and difficulty with maintaining positive study skills. In addition, this analysis also highlighted the tension between an unaccompanied child's desire to pursue education and the pressure they feel to work and support their family members. While the norm in the United States is to remain in school and attend school consistently, unaccompanied children miss classes due to the perceived need to work, which can subsequently result in learning loss, dropping out, and later pursuing a Generalized Educational Development (GED). Participants in the study explained that school districts struggle to manage the culture clash that magnifies different norms surrounding education. A result of this struggle is a lack of programming and policy to meet the unique needs of unaccompanied children.

A final challenge identified by Evans and colleagues was complex health and mental health challenges that can impact an unaccompanied child's ability to access education. This challenge emerged at both the micro and macro levels. At the micro level, participants explained that histories of trauma led to mental health symptoms that unaccompanied children experienced and struggled to manage in classroom settings. Histories of trauma also complicated other peer interactions in school settings, such as bullying, which led to physical altercations in the school. At the macro level, participants reported that schools lacked the resources—both funding and personnel—to support unaccompanied children who presented complex mental health symptoms related to trauma. Additional research has explored what factors are associated with an unaccompanied child requiring support with education.

Hasson III and colleagues completed a study in 2022 titled "Educational Services for Unaccompanied Immigrant Children in the United States" (Hasson, Corbett et al. 2022). When unaccompanied children first arrive in the United States, they receive an assessment from ORR to begin the placement process. As part of this evaluation, unaccompanied children are able to report their primary needs to help focus any case management supports, such as PRS. Hasson III and colleagues found that in a sample of 851 unaccompanied children who received PRS in 2019, a total of 219 reported that education services were their primary need. This meant that 25.7 percent of unaccompanied children in the sample described needing support with enrolling in school or accessing education services such as English-language classes.

The researchers also uncovered different patterns in the educational needs of unaccompanied children. For example, the researchers found that most unaccompanied children who reported education as their primary need identified as male (65.75 percent) and that most migrated from Guatemala (59.36 percent). Unaccompanied children who reported education services as their primary need received case management services for a significantly shorter period of time (7.2 months) compared to unaccompanied children who reported other types of needs, such as mental health services or family stabilization services (9.82 months). Along with these patterns, the researchers also found that each additional month that unaccompanied children received case management services was associated with 26 percent lower odds of reporting education services as their primary need. In addition, unaccompanied children who were placed with their mothers who were resettled in the United States, compared to unaccompanied children placed with other sponsor types, had 55 percent lower odds of reporting education services as their primary need.

The results of this study help explain the conditions where unaccompanied children may require assistance with navigating education systems. For example, the results suggest that when an unaccompanied child is placed with their mother, they are less likely to need support with education. The authors of the study suggest that this finding reinforces existing research that indicates mothers in Hispanic or Latino families communicate high expectations that emerge in children striving for educational attainment. Because of these high expectations, mothers may not need the supports in PRS that are aimed at navigating education systems.

A wide body of research suggests that integration is associated with educational attainment in the United States. More specifically, education levels tend to rise after first-generation immigrants arrive in the United States, with second and third generations attaining higher levels of education. For unaccompanied children, pursuing education, and specifically learning English, is a commonly identified reason for migrating to the United States. Furthermore, education provides a pathway for unaccompanied children to build relationships and achieve goals. However, research shows that unaccompanied children and their families navigate a host of challenges with accessing education, including documentation requirements and discrimination. These challenges exist despite the fact that US law clearly requires public schools to allow all children, regardless of immigration status, access to public school. A growing body of research shows that unaccompanied children can benefit from specific services, like PRS, when trying to access public education.

Challenges with Family Reunification

Unaccompanied children share a common stressor that threatens their health and well-being throughout their migration journey to the United States. By definition, each unaccompanied child experiences, for a certain period of time, separation from a family member. Migrating to the United States without a parent or caregiver stresses a child's ability to cope with the material stresses of migration, such as lack of food or fresh water, as well as the challenge of not having emotional support to manage traumatic exposure that arises from violence or threat of violence during a migration journey. Many unaccompanied children, after processing by US Border Patrol and assessment by ORR partner agencies, are reunified with their families in the United States. However, many factors, such as navigating new family dynamics and adhering to new cultural expectations, contribute to reunification being a stressful experience for some unaccompanied children.

Liza Barros-Lane and her colleagues are researchers who completed a study in 2022 that examined the experiences of unaccompanied children who reunified with their family in the United States. The study analyzed qualitative data collected during focus groups with thirty participants who were twelve to seventeen years old and had arrived in the United States within the previous three years. The study revealed four themes that explain the experiences of unaccompanied children who reunify with their families: perceiving parents as strangers, struggling with loss and loneliness, changing norms in a family system, and adjusting to a new family system.

Children in focus groups described encountering disagreements with their parents; however, since there was limited foundation between the child and parent, the relationship was stressed beyond what was developmentally appropriate for the age and stage of the child. The separation of children from their parents created an emotional distance that was difficult to navigate in resettlement settings. With limited trust in the relationship, children perceived parents as strangers, unable to meet their needs.

Along with perceiving their parents as strangers, children in the study described struggling with feelings of loss and loneliness. Many parents in the study reported working multiple jobs per week, which resulted in prolonged absence and periods of isolation for children who recently reunited with them. Results from the study revealed that loneliness emerged as a continued separation between parents and children due to work requirements to meet financial demands. Although a physical connection was established as part of the reunification process, participants described consistent feelings of loss due to emotional distances.

Barros-Lane and colleagues also found that family systems shifted after children reunified with their families, resulting in stress. An important dynamic between children and parents in Latinx families is respect, or "respeto." However, this study found that excessive separation between children and their parents resulted in children feeling ambivalent about respecting their parents. Prolonged separation can also complicate a child's perception of who has authority to discipline children in the family, which can lead to additional stress for children and the parents.

Finally, the study highlighted how children experienced stress when adjusting to new family systems. This was especially prevalent for children who reunified with a stepparent. Barros-Lane and colleagues describe the unique nature of this dynamic: "While some of these challenges were not unique (i.e., they are common among blended families), many of the participants were getting to know a stepparent at the same time they were reacquainting with the biological parent" (2022, 13).

Barros-Lane and colleagues provide empirical evidence that begins to explain the unique challenges unaccompanied children and parents experience after reunifying in the United States. While the attachment relationship with a parent is among the most important relationships in a child's life, research shows the reunification experience can complicate this foundational connection. Rather than healing the difficult emotional wounds that can result from family separation, family reunification introduces new stresses on a family system that are unique to unaccompanied children. Loneliness, ambivalence, loss, and confusion can all arise as unaccompanied children enter new family systems, adjust to new expectations, and negotiate how to meet the inner emotional needs in an unfamiliar environment. If these challenges are identified early on in the process of family reunification, unaccompanied children can receive family stabilization services as part of case management supports.

In 2024, Hasson III and colleagues completed a study that explored the factors associated with unaccompanied children reporting family stabilization services as their primary need (Hasson, LaBella et al. 2024). Family stabilization services are clinical services that help preserve family units and support families with the reunification process. In many ways, family stabilization services aim to address the challenges with reunification identified in existing research, such as challenges with navigating new family systems (Barros-Lane et al. 2022).

Hasson III and colleagues explored the experience of family stabilization services in a sample of 851 unaccompanied children who received PRS in 2019. Of the sample, nearly one in five unaccompanied children (19 percent) reported family stabilization services were their primary need. Analyses revealed interesting patterns for children requiring support with reunifying with their family. For example, unaccompanied children who reported family stabilization services as their primary need were significantly younger (14.27 years old) than unaccompanied children who reported some other type of need, such as education services or mental health services (16.05 years old). Furthermore, each additional year in an unaccompanied child's age at their time of discharge from PRS was associated with 45 percent lower odds of reporting family stabilization services as their primary need.

The study also revealed interesting relationships between sponsor type and country of origin and family stabilization services. For example, children who were placed with their fathers, compared to placement with other sponsor types, had more than two times greater odds of reporting family stabilization services. In addition, children from Honduras, compared to children from other countries, had more than two times the odds of reporting family stabilization services as their primary need.

These findings suggest that younger unaccompanied children may require specific support for navigating new family dynamics. Building on Barros-Lane and colleagues (2022), it may be that younger unaccompanied children struggle with loneliness and adjusting to new family systems due to limited emotion regulation skills. Moreover, children placed with their fathers have significantly greater odds of reporting family stabilization services as their primary need. This finding suggests that unaccompanied children placed with fathers may not receive high levels of affection, which is more common in maternal parenting practices in Latinx cultures. Finally, the finding that children from Honduras have greater odds of reporting family stabilization services as their primary need is explained by the fact that research also shows that 80 percent of unaccompanied children from Honduras report family reunification as their main reason for migrating to the United States (United Nations High Commissioner for Refugees 2014).

When unaccompanied children migrate to the United States, they each encounter the same challenge—migrating thousands of miles without their parents or caregivers to support them. After arriving in the United States, unaccompanied children who are placed with their families experience the process of family reunification, which brings with it a unique set of challenges. After extended periods of time—sometimes years—away from their parents, unaccompanied children struggle with navigating new family dynamics and adjusting to new family systems. With the right supports in place, unaccompanied children and their families are able to build new bonds in a family system that can serve as the foundation for integration in the United States.

Unaccompanied Children and Immigration Law

Unaccompanied children who migrate to the United States and are apprehended at the US border encounter a complex immigration system that includes laws and policies that can be adversarial in nature and at times conflict with the best interests of children. Rather than being the end of the migration journey, arriving at the border is the start of a new journey through a bureaucratic maze full of legal twists and policy turns that may not fully recognize and respond to the conditions that influenced a child to migrate to the United States. Furthermore, these laws and policies risk overlooking the hopes, aspirations, and dreams that unaccompanied children carry with them from their home countries to the US border. To understand the stress, uncertainty, and confusion unaccompanied children encounter in the US immigration system, one must understand the laws and policies that form the foundation of this broken system.

By definition, unaccompanied children do not have legal status to be in the United States. To address this, unaccompanied children seek immigration relief in different ways. Some unaccompanied children apply for asylum status, pursue Special Immigrant Juvenile Status (SIJS), or apply for a U visa. Each of these pathways provides for relief from the threat of deportation, and some include a pathway to permanent status to remain in the United States. Each has distinct differences.

According to US Citizenship and Immigration Services, asylum is a pathway through immigration court that is reserved for people who have a credible fear of returning to their home country because they have suffered, or there is a threat of persecution, due to race, religion, nationality, membership in a particular social group, or political opinion. Unaccompanied children are able to apply for asylum under certain conditions: if they are under age eighteen, have no legal status to remain in the United States, and there is no parent or legal guardian in the United States to provide care and physical custody.

The US Citizenship and Immigration Services outlines different procedures asylum officers should follow when interviewing an unaccompanied child. The guidelines offered by US Citizenship and Immigration Services align with the best interests of the child and are intended to inform the interview techniques used by asylum officers. However, while the best interests of the child guide interview techniques, they do not inform the decisions made regarding an unaccompanied child's claim for asylum.

The guidelines from US Citizen and Immigration Services include encouraging asylum officers to build rapport by using an opening statement, which is "a rapport-building activity intended to create a relaxing atmosphere, to make the child feel secure and confident, and to provide the child with general information about the asylum interview" (US Department of Justice Immigration and Naturalization Service 1998). Furthermore, the guidelines emphasize that "reassurance, empathic support, carefully-framed questions, encouragement, and topic-shifting are important techniques for children's cases." While the guidelines offered in this memo offer robust strategies that align with the best interests of the child, asylum officers and other border patrol officials do not have advanced mental health, child development, or psychological training or education.

Data on the numbers of unaccompanied children filing for asylum is difficult to gather. The Transactional Records Access Clearinghouse (TRAC) "is a data gathering, data research and data distribution organization at Syracuse University" that has historically gathered and analyzed data on unaccompanied children who are in immigration court (TRAC 2021). However, TRAC has stopped analyzing data since 2017, due to "serious, unresolved deficiencies" in the data shared by the US Department of Justice's Executive Office of Immigration Review (EOIR). According to TRAC data, between 2005 and 2014, a total of 101,850 immigration cases for unaccompanied children were filed in immigration court (TRAC 2014). Of this number, there were stark differences for unaccompanied children who were represented by legal counsel compared to those who were not.

For unaccompanied children who did not have legal counsel during their immigration case, 77 percent received an order of removal for deportation from the United States, 13 percent elected for voluntary departure, meaning they voluntarily chose to return to their country of origin, and only 10 percent were allowed to remain in the country. Unaccompanied children who did have legal counsel during their immigration court cases experienced significantly different outcomes: 28 percent received a removal order, 26 percent chose voluntary departure, and 47 percent were allowed to remain in the United States (TRAC 2014). This data suggests that unaccompanied children who had access to an attorney during their immigration were allowed to remain in the United States more than four times as often as unaccompanied children who did not have an attorney during their immigration case.

Along with asylum, SIJS is a different pathway for unaccompanied children to remain in the United States. SIJS is a visa that protects individuals under age twenty-one who are survivors of child maltreatment. Furthermore, SIJS can lead to lawful permanent residency in the United States in the form of a Green Card. According to the US Citizenship and Immigration Services (2025), for children to qualify for SIJS, "The juvenile court order must contain the required determinations made under relevant state law regarding dependency or custody, parental reunification, and best interests."

SIJS is designed for any noncitizen person under age twenty-one who is a survivor of maltreatment, including unaccompanied children. There are a series of eligibility requirements for a child to qualify for SIJS. At the time of filing an application for SIJS, the person must be under age twenty-one, unmarried, and in the United States at the time of filing the application. In addition, the individual must be the subject of an order from a juvenile court that makes determinations on custody, family reunification, and the best interests of the child.

More specifically, the juvenile court must determine that the child is "dependent on the court, or in the custody of a state agency or department or an individual or entity appointed by the court" (US Citizenship and Immigration Services 2025). In addition, the court must determine that the child is unable to reunify with one or both parents because of concerns of abuse, neglect, or maltreatment as defined by state law. The abuse, neglect, or maltreatment may have occurred in the child's home country, or in the United States. Finally, the juvenile court must determine that it is not in the child's best interest to return to their country of origin. There are a variety of professionals who can help unaccompanied children receive immigration relief from SIJS, including child welfare professionals and PRS case workers.

The pathway to receiving SIJS includes several steps. According to the Migration Policy Institute, the process starts with an unaccompanied child being apprehended at the US border and placed in foster care, the juvenile justice system, or with a guardian. With the support of legal counsel, the child then attempts to determine SIJS eligibility in a state court. Because state court is separate from immigration court, the child then must submit an SIJS application and evidence of a state court determination to the US Citizenship and Immigration Services. The US Citizenship and Immigration Services reviews the application and relevant state court determination documents and decides on the child's SIJS application. If approved, the child can remain in the United States and possibly later apply for permanent residency through a Green Card.

Thousands of children have applied for SIJS. According to the Migration Policy Institute, more than 70,000 applications have been filed between 2010 and 2017. Applications rose steadily beginning in 2014, which aligns with a dramatic increase in the number of unaccompanied children who migrated to the United States from El Salvador, Guatemala, and Honduras. In fact, more than 21,000 SIJS applications were filed in 2017.

Along with SIJS, unaccompanied children may qualify for a U visa if they are victims of a crime, or a T visa if they are survivors of human trafficking. According to the US Citizenship and Immigration Service (2024a), "the U nonimmigrant status (U visa) is set aside for victims of certain crimes who have suffered mental or physical abuse and are helpful to law enforcement or government officials in the investigation or prosecution of criminal activity." The U visa is designed to help law enforcement investigate and prosecute crimes by protecting individuals who are victims of crime and may not be US citizens. The U visa was initially included in the Victims of Trafficking and Violence Protection Act, which Congress first passed in October 2000.

The T visa is "a temporary immigration benefit. It enables certain victims of a severe form of trafficking in persons to remain in the United States for an initial period of up to 4 years if they complied with any reasonable request for assistance from law enforcement in the detection, investigation, or prosecution of human trafficking" (US Citizenship and Immigration Service 2024b). The US government defines "severe trafficking" as either sex trafficking or labor trafficking, which research shows unaccompanied children are vulnerable to experience during their migration journey to the United States, as well as after their resettlement in the United States.

Although there are pathways through the immigration system for unaccompanied children to adjust their status, including asylum, SIJS, and special visas like the U visa and T visa, the way some unaccompanied children have had to navigate the US immigration system has resulted in some controversy. For example, Senator Patrick Leahy, a Democratic senator representing Vermont, described circumstances where unaccompanied children presented to court with no legal counsel. During a hearing on unaccompanied children before the Senate Judiciary Committee on February 23, 2016, Senator Leahy explained:

> These children are particularly vulnerable and many of them can qualify under our laws for humanitarian protection in the United States. But our immigration system is extremely complex. We expect children and those with little education, who do not speak English and have suffered serious trauma, to navigate it without legal guidance. Some of them are as young as three years old, and often show up before an immigration judge unrepresented when they are summoned to present their case for relief. (US Senate Committee on the Judiciary 2016)

Conversely, Senator Charles Grassley, a Republican senator representing Iowa, remarked that policies from the Obama White House led to increased numbers of unaccompanied children migrating to the US border. Because of the dramatic increase in arrivals, many "shortcuts" in the processing of arrivals, such as accepting copies of birth certificates and not pursuing fingerprints for potential sponsors, led to some unaccompanied children suffering from human trafficking.

Ultimately, Senator Grassley's tone echoed a broader conservative sentiment of not responding to the human rights of unaccompanied children but rather seeking to secure the border and uphold existing immigration law, even when it overlooks the best interests of children. Furthermore, Senator Grassley explained:

> We need to be prepared to take care of these unaccompanied minors crossing the border, while at the same time ensuring their safety, and the safety of the community, when placing them with sponsors. This will require the administration to stop shirking its responsibility and monitor these individuals after placement. They need a plan, they need to learn from their mistakes, they need to ensure that the minors are quickly and safely returned to their home country, and they need to be held accountable. (US Senate Committee on the Judiciary 2016)

One solution may be the A Fair Day in Court for Kids Act (H.R. 4646), first introduced in the 114th Congress. One of the main components of the bill was an amendment of the Immigration and Nationality Act that would provide legal counsel at government expense to immigrants presenting their case in immigration court. The bill would provide undocumented immigrants with access to all documents pertinent to their case, as well as access to legal counsel while in immigration detention facilities. The bill was focused especially on the unique needs of unaccompanied children, providing legal counsel, at government expense, to unaccompanied children who were in removal proceedings. Furthermore, the bill called for the Department of Homeland Security to "establish a pilot program to increase the court appearance rates of unaccompanied alien children and particularly vulnerable individuals by contracting with nongovernmental, community-based organizations to provide such aliens with case management services." The case management services proposed by H.R. 4646 would support unaccompanied children with accessing legal counsel, complying with court-related deadlines and other legal obligations as a result of findings from the court, accessing housing and enrolling in school, and accessing health and mental health services in the community.

The A Fair Day in Court for Kids Act has been introduced into several sessions of Congress but so far has not passed into law. In 2023, the bill was introduced to the 118th Congress as "S.3065—Fair Day in Court for Kids Act of 2023" by Senator Mazie Hirono, a Democrat from Hawaii. It included twenty-eight cosponsors, all of whom are Democrats. This is an indication of the lack of bipartisan support for the bill. Furthermore, it is a signal of the complex political context that surrounds immigration policy broadly, even as it relates to the most vulnerable immigrants, including unaccompanied children (Congress.gov 2023).

S.3065 includes many of the provisions of earlier versions of the bill. For example, it focuses specifically on providing legal counsel, at government expense if necessary, for vulnerable immigrants, including unaccompanied children who may be in removal proceedings. However, it does not include case management services that were part of earlier versions of the bill. The bill does include a provision requiring routine reporting on access to counsel. Specifically, the bill requires the Secretary of Health and Human Services, in coordination with the Attorney General, to submit a report to the Senate and House of Representatives committees on justice. The report should include the number and percentage of unaccompanied children who were provided legal counsel in the previous year. The report also requires details of each child's case, including the stage of the legal process when each child received legal counsel description of whether each child was in government custody when they received access to legal counsel, and demographic data for each child, including nationality and age. The report should also include the number and percentage of children who received legal screenings and a description of the processes used for "identifying, recruiting, and training pro bono counsel to represent unaccompanied children" (Congress.gov 2023).

The Vera Institute for Justice is a nonprofit organization based in the United States that seeks "to end mass incarceration for people of color, immigrants, and people experiencing poverty" (Vera Institute of Justice n.d.). With a focus on immigrants, the Vera Institute for Justice published a report in 2021 that provided detailed analysis of the experiences of unaccompanied children who navigate immigration court in the United States. Importantly, immigrants in the United States who are trying to navigate court cases do not have a right to legal representation, as individuals in other court systems do. This is because immigration law is considered a civil matter, and the right to an attorney is only extended to individuals in criminal court. This can have extraordinarily detrimental impacts on unaccompanied children who are in immigration court. As the Vera Institute for Justice reported, between 2005 and 2017, only 64 percent of unaccompanied children received legal counsel at some point during their court case (Snider and DiBennardo 2021). Furthermore, unaccompanied children with legal counsel at some point during their case were more than seven times as likely to receive a court decision that would allow them to remain in the country.

This stark statistic is supported by data offered from the Congressional Research Service, which in 2024 published data that described the stark differences in legal outcomes for unaccompanied children when navigating immigration court (Kandel 2024). Between 2005 and 2017, for unaccompanied children with legal counsel, 8,942 received legal relief from deportation. However, during the same time period, only 308 unaccompanied children without legal counsel received immigration relief. This comprised less than 1 percent of unaccompanied children who did not have legal counsel. In fact, most children without legal counsel (84 percent) received a removal order, meaning they were subject to deportation from the United States. Furthermore, significant numbers of unaccompanied children never had legal counsel during their immigration court proceedings. Data indicates of all unaccompanied children in immigration court between 2005 and 2017, 36 percent did not have any legal counsel (Kandel 2024).

Further Reading

American Civil Liberties Union. 2023. "Court Approves Historic Settlement in ACLU's Family Separation Lawsuit." https://www.aclu.org/press-releases/court-approves-historic-settlement-in-aclus-family-separation-lawsuit

Ataiants, Janna, Chari Cohen, Amy Henderson Riley, Jamile Tellez Lieberman, Mary Clare Reidy, and Mariana Chilton. 2018. "Unaccompanied Children at the United States Border, a Human Rights Crisis That Can Be Addressed with Policy Change." *Journal of Immigrant and Minority Health* 20: 1000–10.

Barros-Lane, Liza, Kalina Brabeck, and Jodi Arden Berger Cardoso. 2022. "'Es Como Que no los Conociera': Reunification of Unaccompanied Migrant Youth with Their US Families." *Social Work Research* 46, no. 1: 5–16.

Beaubien, Jason. 2011. "Atop a Train, Migrants Begin Dangerous Trek to U.S." National Public Radio. https://www.npr.org/2011/07/06/137528534/atop-a-train-migrants-begin-dangerous-trek-to-u-s

Berger Cardoso, Jodi. 2018. "Running to Stand Still: Trauma Symptoms, Coping Strategies, and Substance Use Behaviors in Unaccompanied Migrant Youth." *Children and Youth Services Review* 92: 143–52.

Burnett, John. 2014. "Who Is Smuggling Immigrant Children across the Border?" NPR, July 15, 2014. https://www.npr.org/sections/parallels/2014/07/15/331477447/who-is-smuggling-immigrant-children-across-the-border

Bush, Laura. 2018. "Laura Bush: Separating Children from Their Parents at the Border 'Breaks My Heart.'" *Washington Post*, June 17, 2018. https://www.washingtonpost.com/opinions/laura-bush-separating-children-from-their-parents-at-the-border-breaks-my-heart/2018/06/17/f2df517a-7287-11e8-9780-b1dd6a09b549_story.html

Cavendish, Betsy, and Maru Cortazar. 2011. *Children at the Border: The Screening, Protection and Repatriation of Unaccompanied Mexican Minors*. Appleseed.

Central Intelligence Agency. 2024. "The World Factbook." https://www.cia.gov/the-world-factbook/

Congress.gov. 2023. "Cosponsors—S.3065—118th Congress (2023–2024): Fair Day in Court for Kids Act of 2023." October 17, 2023. https://www.congress.gov/bill/118th-congress/senate-bill/3065/cosponsors

Crea, Thomas M., Robert G. Hasson III, Kerri Evans, Jodi Berger Cardoso, and Dawnya Underwood. 2018. "Moving Forward: Educational Outcomes for Unaccompanied Refugee Minors (URM) Exiting Foster Care in the United States." *Journal of Refugee Studies* 31, no. 2: 240–56.

Dickerson, Caitlin. 2022. "The Secret History of the US Government's Family-Separation Policy." *The Atlantic* 2.

Doering-White, John. 2018. "Evidencing Violence and Care along the Central American Migrant Trail through Mexico." *Social Service Review* 92, no. 3: 432–69.

Dreier, Hannah. 2023. "Alone and Exploited, Migrant Children Work Brutal Jobs across the U.S." *New York Times*, February 28, 2023. https://www.nytimes.com/2023/02/25/us/unaccompanied-migrant-child-workers-exploitation.html

Evans, Kerri, Jaime Perez-Aponte, and Ruth McRoy. 2020. "Without a Paddle: Barriers to School Enrollment Procedures for Immigrant Students and Families." *Education and Urban Society* 52, no. 9: 1283–304.

Evans, Kerri, Gabrielle Oliveira, Robert G. Hasson III, Thomas M. Crea, Sarah Elizabeth Neville, and Virginia Fitchett. 2022. "Unaccompanied Children's Education in the United States: Service Provider's Perspective on Challenges and Support Strategies." *Cultura Educación y Sociedad* 13, no. 1: 193–218.

Frankel, Katherine K., Kalina M. Brabeck, and Sarah A. Rendón García. 2022. "Understanding Unaccompanied Immigrant Youth's Experiences in US Schools: An Interdisciplinary Perspective." *Journal of Education for Students Placed at Risk (JESPAR)* 27, no. 1: 27–58.

Geltman, Paul L., Wanda Grant-Knight, Supriya D. Mehta, Christine Lloyd-Travaglini, Stuart Lustig, Jeanne M. Landgraf, and Paul H. Wise. 2005. "The 'Lost Boys of Sudan': Functional and Behavioral Health of Unaccompanied Refugee Minors Resettled in the United States." *Archives of Pediatrics & Adolescent Medicine* 159, no. 6: 585–91.

Goebertus Estrada, Juanita. 2024. "El Salvador's Cycles of Violence through a Teenager's Eyes." Human Rights Watch. https://www.hrw.org/news/2024/04/09/el-salvadors-cycles-violence-through-teenagers-eyes

Hasson, Robert G., III, Antonia Diaz-Valdez, and Dawnya Underwood. 2022. "Mental Health Services for Unaccompanied Children in the United States." *Journal of Loss and Trauma* 28, no. 7: 599–615. doi:10.1080/15325024.2022.2141515

Hasson, Robert G., III, Bianca LaBella, Antonia Díaz-Valdés, and Dawnya Underwood. 2024. "Family Stabilization Services for Unaccompanied Children in the United States." *Families in Society* 105, no. 4: 507–19. doi:10.1177/10443894231186194

Hasson, Robert G., III, Caitlin Corbett, Antonia Diaz-Valdés, Kerri Evans, Thomas M. Crea, and Dawnya Underwood. 2022. "Educational Services for Unaccompanied Immigrant Children in the United States." *Journal of Social Service Research* 48, no. 5: 606–16. doi:10.1080/01488376.2022.2096746.

Hasson, Robert G., III, Clara A. Oliva, Bianca LaBella, and Dahiana Rodriguez. 2024. "'Little by Little, I Go': Multiple Dimensions of Distress and Support for Unaccompanied Children in the United States." *Children and Youth Services Review* 160: 107541.

Hasson, Robert G., Scott D. Easton, Antonia Díaz-Valdés Iriarte, Laura M. O'Dwyer, Dawnya Underwood, and Thomas M. Crea. 2021. "Examining the Psychometric Properties of the Child PTSD Symptom Scale within a Sample of Unaccompanied Immigrant Children in the United States." *Journal of Loss and Trauma* 26, no. 4: 323–35.

Heidbrink, Lauren, and Sarah J. Diaz. 2024. "Kids in Care: Unaccompanied Children in Federal Government Custody." Center for the Human Rights of Children at Loyola University Chicago School of Law. https://www.luc.edu/media/lucedu/law/centers/chrc/pdfs/Kids-In-Care.pdf

Human Rights Watch. 2018. "US Policy Forcibly Separating Children from Parents Is Inhumane." June 1, 2018. https://www.hrw.org/news/2018/06/01/us-policy-forcibly-separating-children-parents-inhumane

Immigration Policy Center. 2014. *Children in Danger: A Guide to the Humanitarian Challenge at the Border*. American Immigration Council.

Interagency Task Force on the Reunification of Families. 2025. "Family Reunification Task Force." https://www.dhs.gov/family-reunification-task-force

Kandel, William A. 2024. "Unaccompanied Alien Children: An Overview." Congressional Research Service. https://www.congress.gov/crs-product/R43599

Kennedy, Elizabeth. 2014. *No Childhood Here: Why Central American Children Are Fleeing Their Homes (Perspectives)*. American Immigration Council.

Lorenzen, Matthew. 2017. "The Mixed Motives of Unaccompanied Child Migrants from Central America's Northern Triangle." *Journal on Migration and Human Security* 5, no. 4: 744–67.

Massey, D. S. 2014. "Children of Central American Turmoil and the US Reform Impasse." In *SSN Forum on the Immigration Impasse*. https://scholars.org/children-central-american-turmoil-and-us-reform-impasse

Meyer, Peter J. 2024. "Central American Migration: Root Causes and US Policy." Congressional Research Service, 27.

Migration Policy Institute tabulations of US Department of Homeland Security, Office of Immigration Statistics, Yearbook of Immigration Statistics. Various years. Available at www.dhs.gov/files/statistics/publications/yearbook.shtm

Miller, Leila. 2018. "For Cities Where MS-13 Lives, a Fight to Keep Youth from Gang Life." February 15, 2018. https://www.pbs.org/wgbh/frontline/article/for-cities-where-ms-13-lives-a-fight-to-keep-youth-from-gang-life/

Murray, Eli, Hannah Dreire, and K. K. Rebecca Lai. 2024. "Where Migrant Children are Living, and Often Working, in the U.S." *New York Times*, December 28, 2024. https://www.nytimes.com/interactive/2023/12/28/us/migrants-children-data.html

Office of Refugee Resettlement (ORR). 2023. "Facts and Data." https://www.acf.hhs.gov/orr/about/ucs/facts-and-data

Patel, Zabin S., Elizabeth P. Casline, Cedrin Vera, Vanessa Ramirez, and Amanda Jensen-Doss. 2024. "Unaccompanied Migrant Children in the United States: Implementation and Effectiveness of Trauma-focused Cognitive Behavioral Therapy." *Psychological Trauma: Theory, Research, Practice, and Policy* 16, no. S2: S389.

Rafieifar, Maryam, Miriam Potocky, Hui Huang, Richard L. Beaulaurier, and Sloan Bruan Lorenzini. 2023. "Experiences of Undocumented Parents Reuniting with Children Who Entered the United States as Unaccompanied Minors." *International Journal of Environmental Research and Public Health* 20, no. 5: 4496.

Ries, Lora. 2023. "Congress Must End the Exploitation of Unaccompanied Alien Children." The Heritage Foundation, May 10, 2023. https://www.heritage.org/border-security/commentary/congress-must-end-the-exploitation-unaccompanied-alien-children

Rose, Austin. 2018. "For Vulnerable Immigrant Children, A Longstanding Path to Protection Narrows." Migration Policy Institute. https://www.migrationpolicy.org/article/vulnerable-immigrant-children-longstanding-path-protection-narrows

Rosenblum, Marc R. 2015. "Unaccompanied Child Migration to the United States: The Tension between Protection and Prevention." Migration Policy Institute. https://www.migrationpolicy.org/sites/default/files/publications/TCM-Protection-UAC.pdf

Roth, Benjamin J., and Caroline S. Hartnett. 2018. "Creating Reasons to Stay? Unaccompanied Youth Migration, Community-Based Programs, and the Power of 'Push' Factors in El Salvador." *Children and Youth Services Review* 92: 48–55.

Roth, Benjamin J., Thomas M. Crea, Jayshree Jani, Dawnya Underwood, Robert G. Hasson III, Kerri Evans, Michael Zuch, and Emily Hornung. 2019. "Detached and Afraid: U.S. Immigration Policy and the Practice of Forcibly Separating Parents and Young Children at the Border." *Child Welfare* 96, no. 5: 29–50.

Roy, Diana, and Amelia Cheatham. 2023. "Central America's Turbulent Northern Triangle." Council on Foreign Relations. https://www.cfr.org/backgrounder/central-americas-turbulent-northern-triangle

Salgado, Lucía, Susan Fratzke, Lawrence Huang, and Emma Dorst. 2024. *Managing International Protection Needs at Borders*. Washington, DC: Migration Policy Institute. https://www.migrationpolicy.org/sites/default/files/publications/mpi-bta_border-processes-2024-final.pdf

Sebai, Nadine, Nina Sparkling, and Bruce Gil. 2023. "Underage and Unprotected: Migrant Teens Worked in Risky Jobs in New Bedford Seafood Processing Plants." *The Public's Radio*, September 18, 2023. https://thepublicsradio.org/article/migrant-teens-worked-in-risky-jobs-in-new-bedford-seafood-processing-plants/

Snider, Alyssa, and Rebecca DiBennardo. 2021. "Representation Matters: No Child Should Appear in Immigration Proceedings Alone." Vera Institute of Justice. https://vera-institute.files.svdcdn.com/production/downloads/publications/representation-matters.pdf?dm=1641336655

The Transactional Records Access Clearinghouse (TRAC). 2014. "New Data on Unaccompanied Children in Immigration Court." https://tracreports.org/immigration/reports/359/

The Transactional Records Access Clearinghouse (TRAC). 2021. "About Us." https://trac.syr.edu/aboutTRACgeneral.html

UNICEF. 2016. "Broken Dreams: Central American Children's Dangerous Journey to the United States." https://www.justice.gov/eoir/file/888441/download

UNICEF. 2018. "Uprooted in Central America and Mexico: Migrant and Refugee Children Face a Vicious Cycle of Hardship and Danger." https://www.unicef.org/media/47701/file/UNICEF_Child_Alert_2018_Central_America_and_Mexico-ENG.pdf

United Nations High Commissioner for Refugees (UNHCR). 2014. *Children on the Run: Unaccompanied Children Leaving Central America and Mexico and the Need for International Protection*. http://www.unhcr.org/en-us/children-on-the-run.html

US Citizenship and Immigration Service. 2024a. "Victims of Criminal Activity: U Nonimmigrant Status." https://www.uscis.gov/humanitarian/victims-of-criminal-activity-u-nonimmigrant-status

US Citizenship and Immigration Service. 2024b. "Victims of Human Trafficking: T Nonimmigrant Status." https://www.uscis.gov/humanitarian/victims-of-human-trafficking-t-nonimmigrant-status

US Citizenship and Immigration Service. 2025. "Special Immigrant Juveniles." https://www.uscis.gov/working-in-US/eb4/SIJ

US Customs and Border Patrol. 2022. "CBP Launches Digital Ad Campaign 'Say No to the Coyote' to Warn Migrants about Smuggler Lies." https://www.cbp.gov/newsroom/national-media-release/cbp-launches-digital-ad-campaign-say-no-coyote-warn-migrants-about

US Department of Health and Human Services Office of Inspector General. 2024. "Gaps in Sponsor Screening and Follow-Up Raise Safety Concerns for Unaccompanied Children." February 2024. OEI-07-21-00250. https://oig.hhs.gov/oei/reports/OEI-07-21-00250.pdf

US Department of Homeland Security. 2022. "What Is Human Trafficking?" https://www.dhs.gov/blue-campaign/what-human-trafficking
US Department of Homeland Security. 2024. "Family Reunification Task Force." https://www.dhs.gov/family-reunification-task-force
US Department of Justice Immigration and Naturalization Service. 1998. "Guidelines for Children's Asylum Claims." https://www.uscis.gov/sites/default/files/document/memos/ChildrensGuidelines121098.pdf
US Department of Justice Office of Inspector General. 2021. "Review of the Department of Justice's Planning and Implementation of Its Zero Tolerance Policy and Its Coordination with the Departments of Homeland Security and Health and Human Services." January 2021. https://oig.justice.gov/sites/default/files/reports/21-028_0.pdf
US Department of Justice Office of Public Affairs. 2018. "Attorney General Announces Zero-Tolerance Policy for Criminal Illegal Entry." https://www.justice.gov/archives/opa/pr/attorney-general-announces-zero-tolerance-policy-criminal-illegal-entry
US Department of State. 2024. "About Human Trafficking." Accessed on August 12, 2024. https://www.state.gov/humantrafficking-about-human-trafficking/
US Senate Committee on the Judiciary. 2016. "The Unaccompanied Children Crisis: Does the Administration Have a Plan to Stop the Border Surge and Adequately Monitor the Children?" https://www.judiciary.senate.gov/committee-activity/hearings/the-unaccompanied-children-crisis-does-the-administration-have-a-plan-to-stop-the-border-surge-and-adequately-monitor-the-children
Vera Institute of Justice. n.d. "About Us." https://www.vera.org/what-we-do
Wise, Paul H., and Lauren Stoffel. 2024. "Remember These Are Children: Unaccompanied Migrant Children in Detention." *Pediatric Research* 96, no. 3: 571–3.
Young, Janine, Warren Binford, Michael Garcia Bochenek, and Jordan Greenbaum. 2024. "Health Risks of Unaccompanied Immigrant Children in Federal Custody and in US Communities." *American Journal of Public Health* 114, no. 3: 340–6.

ORIGINAL TASTE
12

3

Perspectives

In this chapter, four contributing essay writers explore some of the challenges unaccompanied children and their families face as they enter the United States, as well as the challenges faced by service providers attempting to assist these children. Kerri Evans, who has case management and social work experience with unaccompanied immigrant children and whose research focuses on improving service delivery, takes a look at problems and solutions in relation to access and participation in education for unaccompanied children. Zayna Lyon, a PhD student whose research focuses on immigration, discusses labor exploitation faced by unaccompanied children who find themselves needing to work upon their arrival in the United States. Maryam Rafieifar, whose research focuses on the effects of immigration policies on immigrant children and families, reflects on the challenges of reuniting families who become separated. Finally, Silvia Melgar shares her experiences as a youth services coordinator at a nonprofit organization in support of unaccompanied children and their sponsors, shedding light on the challenges service workers face.

Challenges and Solutions to Navigating the US Education System for Unaccompanied Children

Kerri Evans

Introduction

As of the writing of this essay at the beginning of 2025, unaccompanied children can and, in many cases, are mandated to attend public school when they are in the United States (US Civil Rights Act of 1964; *Plyler v. Doe*, 1982).

A ten-year-old Honduran immigrant helps shop at Walmart a day after arriving to live with her extended family on April 24, 2021, near Clarksville, Indiana. The unaccompanied minor was released from US Health and Human Services custody after spending nearly eight weeks in shelters. (John Moore/Getty Images)

However, the Trump administration has made a claim that may change this policy and restrict access to public education for unaccompanied children (American Civil Liberties Union 2024). Nonetheless, there are currently many challenges that unaccompanied children face in accessing and participating in school. In this essay, Iwill walk through a handful of the common challenges faced, followed by solutions and examples of programs working to minimize these challenges.

Positionality

I have worked with unaccompanied children as a social worker in a few different capacities. My first role with this group of children was providing post-release services (PRS). At the time, this role included providing in-home visits about once a month to help the child integrate into the local community and also to help them integrate into the family unit. On visits, I would check in to see how they were doing overall, as well as specifically ask them about school, mental health, and friendships; ensure they had food and other basic needs; and take time to educate them on US culture in relevant ways. For example, I often talked to families about mandated attendance, ensuring they knew what was expected and how truancy officers could get involved if the child did not report to school regularly.

My second role with unaccompanied children was working at a national nonprofit that provides a host of services through local community organizations. Here my role was to facilitate a safe release of the unaccompanied child to their family members. Specifically, this entailed assessing what we knew about the family and asking follow-up questions so that the PRS worker would have the knowledge they needed to implement effective services starting at the first visit. Second, I would work with local nonprofits in the community that were trained to work with unaccompanied children to determine which had the best resources to help each individual child, and I would match the child with the appropriate post-release caseworker. I would hold a phone call with the worker before the child was released from the Office of Refugee Resettlement's (ORR) care to explain what I knew about the case and share my recommended service plan. It should be noted that this is no longer the process of assigning a post-release worker. As the numbers of unaccompanied children drastically increased in 2014, ORR had to change its policies and reduce the amount of coordination and screening that could be done prior to release.

My third role with unaccompanied children was oversight of foster care programs for both unaccompanied children in long-term foster care and Unaccompanied Refugee Minors (URM). This role could largely be considered quality assurance of the foster care program. I held monthly phone calls with each individual agency to check in on the well-being of children, and to troubleshoot issues, and I also held monthly network calls where multiple foster care agencies attended the phone call and were able to share best practices and troubles and gain insight from one another. I hosted ongoing webinar trainings for staff in the foster care programs and visited each site (long-term foster care programs were once a year and URM were every two to three years) to check on operations firsthand.

Since becoming a social work professor, I have maintained communication with nonprofits serving unaccompanied children and have maintained an active research agenda on the topic through these partnerships. I now work to answer questions that the agencies have and to help provide data to support their efforts in program development/modification and in seeking grants. My work with unaccompanied children has gone from direct service to macro-level service, to research, bringing well-rounded experience to the topic today.

Common Challenges (and Solutions) Unaccompanied Children Experience in US Schools

Enrollment Issues

Enrolling in school should be a simple logistical step, but for many unaccompanied children living in the community, this is not true (Booi et al. 2016; Evans et al. 2020). They often face barriers due to the fact that school districts mandate specific paperwork for enrollment, paperwork that many unaccompanied children do not have available. For example, students enrolling in public schools are generally asked to provide an original birth certificate. However, when people flee their homes without much notice, they do not always bring this along; children born in rural areas may never have received one; and for those who do have one, it may be in another language, and the school district may not accept this.

Next, prospective students are generally asked to provide proof of residence as proof that they are zoned for the local school. Many low-income and undocumented families live in shared homes (Westbrook 2024), and therefore generally only one person's name is on the lease. School districts generally expect to see the parent/caregiver's name on the lease, and this may not be available, especially for undocumented families who want to stay under the radar. (Throughout this essay, I intentionally use the term caregiver because many unaccompanied children are living in the United States with another relative, such as an aunt, older sibling, or grandparent, and some are even living with nonrelatives, while their parents still live in their country of birth.)

Next, families are asked to provide proof of immunizations to enroll. The immunizations given vary from country to country around the globe, and as stated previously, if someone is fleeing for their life, they may not think to bring this documentation to the United States. Lastly, the enrollment process is not always immigrant friendly. School staff members may not have multilingual skills or may not have forms readily available in other languages. But even worse, there is some evidence that some schools have proactively discriminated against immigrant students trying to enroll due to the fact that they are less likely to graduate on time, and in many districts there is more funding available to schools with better graduation rates (American Civil Liberties Union of Pennsylvania 2016).

Solutions and Promising Practices for Enrollment

As with any challenge, there are some solutions that can be implemented to mitigate its impact or effectiveness. When an unaccompanied child does not have a birth certificate, we need to remember that the real reason for this request is to prove the child's age to assign the correct grade level. Families or social workers can go to the consulate of their country and try to get a copy. However, this process may be lengthy and costly. At times an affidavit that establishes age can be used, such as from a pediatrician, a dentist, or a bone density scan. When formal proof of residence is unavailable, families can enroll children in school under the McKinney Vento Act of 2008, which was designated to assist homeless children in minimizing delays in school entry. Unaccompanied children are generally given immunizations while in ORR shelter care, and caregivers should have been given this paperwork when the child arrived home. Alternatively, some medical testing can be done to show antibodies for vaccines received, or a waiver of immunization can be completed with the school. Overcoming the barriers to racism and xenophobia present in the enrollment process is much more complicated. Research shows that bystander trainings and advocacy work can be effective in helping to both educate enrollment staff about unaccompanied children (Evans et al. 2020) and to change attitudes and beliefs (Kuntz and Searle 2023).

Gaps in Schooling

Many unaccompanied children arrive in the United States having not attended school the previous year or a few years prior (Szlyk et al. 2020). In some cases, this is because the school in their hometown was not affordable, not available to females, or not safe, or because the child needed to work for the family to survive (financially or to help maintain the farm, etc.). In other cases, this is because the child's journey to the United States took a significant amount of time. Upon arrival in the United States, unaccompanied children attend school in shelters. These classes are often in Spanish and are focused on very basic academics because most youth are in shelter for only a few weeks or months (Diebold et al. 2019; Office of Refugee Resettlement 2024). While it is good to start educational programming as soon as possible, there are challenges with this model. Many unaccompanied children do not speak Spanish, and the curriculum does not always meet the students at an educationally appropriate level. However, in recent years, I have heard social workers tell me how amazing it is when Afghan or Ukrainian children learn Spanish in the shelter and how it can really advance their trajectory in the United States.

This gap in schooling often means that the child has a harder time adjusting to the academic space and engaging in learning (Szlyk et al. 2020). This can be due to trouble sitting for long periods of time, being overwhelmed with academic curriculum, or even being worried that they need to work and contribute to the family/pay off debt from a coyote. The gap in schooling can make it hard for school districts to know if the child should enter the grade where they belong based on (1) age, (2) knowledge, or (3) somewhere in between. An age gap in students could make them more susceptible to bullying or dropping out, but being placed in a grade too high academically leads to lower grades, increased stress for students, and a longer time to graduation.

Solutions and Promising Practices for Gaps in Schooling

For students who are struggling academically, tutors can be very beneficial. For students struggling with the school routine and ability to sit, the school social worker may be able to get involved and assist with fidgets, breaks from class, or other remedies. For students needing to work in the evening, it is important that we ensure they are getting their basic needs met (e.g., sleep) and that they understand the implications associated with working instead of studying or even missing classes for work. School staff may be able to help them locate scholarships that would reduce the need to work, or could help them find jobs that may allow more flexibility around times when there are exams, etc. The school social worker can also engage with the student and family to ensure that the unaccompanied child is not being forced or trafficked into employment and to help find alternative solutions to financial struggles.

Alternative classroom settings are another very common way to overcome these educational challenges. For example, one solution to this struggle of gaps in educational schooling and grade placement is newcomer schools. Many cities have a charter school that caters to new immigrants, and others have smaller centers in multiple schools (e.g., Denver Public Schools). These are most common for children of high school age who need to learn English skills, and who need to learn classroom content before they can transition to mainstream schools in their neighborhood. These schools are excellent at addressing the gap in schooling and at helping new immigrant students make friends and find a social circle among their immigrant peers. However, sometimes these schools do not have sports teams, art/music classes, and other extracurricular programs due to a lack of funding or numbers of students to sustain these programs.

Another solution is summer programs. School districts, county parks and recreation programs, and nonprofit organizations in many communities have chosen to create programs similar to summer school, especially for immigrant students. These offer new immigrant students the chance to get familiar with a US classroom environment, to learn English, to make friends, and to get up to speed in content they will need to succeed in their classes for the following year (e.g., Summer Rising in New York). The major downside to these programs is that they are not available to students who arrive at other times during the year, and funding for them varies widely.

School Districts Unprepared: Space, Resources, and Mental Health

Over the past few decades, there have been times when the number of unaccompanied children arriving one year far exceeded the year before. For example, in 2013 we saw 24,688, but the next year that more than doubled to 57,496

(Office of Refugee Resettlement 2024). More recently, in 2019 there were 69,488 arrivals, compared to 49,100 in 2018. There was a stark reduction in the number of arrivals in 2020 due to the Covid-19 pandemic, when there were only 15,381 arrivals. The number of arrivals increased to 122,731 in 2021 (Office of Refugee Resettlement 2024). In these cases, school districts in high-destination areas have felt overwhelmed and often been unprepared to meet the needs of the number of new students coming to the school. Schools use their enrollment rates from one year to predict classroom sizes, seek state and federal funding, and employ teachers who are adequate for the predicted number of students the following year. Summer is often a high time for migration, and therefore schools can struggle to meet the demand when the number of students significantly outpaces their predictions. This can lead to overcrowded classrooms. In these cases, there may be a lack of bilingual support for children and their caregivers or limited resources (i.e., tutoring) that these families need to succeed (Evans et al. 2022).

At times, the trauma histories that unaccompanied children bring with them may make it more difficult to engage in traditional classrooms and could impede their ability to learn or participate in the classroom (Hasson et al. 2021; Szlyk et al. 2020). Most school systems do not have enough mental health providers to adequately meet the needs of the student population (Whitaker et al. 2019), nor are these staff always knowledgeable about unaccompanied children in particular. Similarly, many unaccompanied children struggle to adjust to the social and cultural norms in the United States and to build friendships (Evans et al. 2022; Szlyk et al. 2020), which can directly impact their attendance and willingness to engage in the classroom.

Solutions and Promising Practices for Unprepared School Districts

Under prior presidential administrations, there have been funding streams available to schools seeing an increase in immigrant students; for example, the EL/Title III funding has been something that schools with 5 percent or 100 person growth could apply to. However, those funds may not always be available. In terms of mental health, we should continually advocate for more mental health providers in schools and, likewise, continually advocate for more training on diverse populations, including immigrants and unaccompanied children.

Baltimore City School District has established the Newcomer Support Team, which was developed when the city saw a large increase in the number of unaccompanied children entering their schools. The team implements a social-emotional learning program specifically focused on Refugee and Immigrant Student Empowerment. The multilingual team now consists of social workers and social work interns who see only new immigrant students (though no longer only unaccompanied children) who need assistance adjusting to the United States and to US schools. They can help families with basic needs, understand graduation requirements, provide individual and group counseling, and more. This program is one example of an innovative approach that allows staff to specialize in working with culturally diverse youth.

When unaccompanied children enroll in public school, there are some steps we can take to help them adjust. Offering a holistic orientation in the student's native language for both the child and caregivers can be beneficial to ensure that the child feels welcome and safe to enter the school and knows where things like lockers, bathrooms, classrooms, the school social worker's office, etc. are located. This helps to instill confidence on day one of school. Peer mentoring programs or exchange programs are used in many schools to help new immigrant students make friends, increase confidence (Messiou and Azaola 2018), and navigate the school system, but cross-cultural mentoring can have benefits for both groups (Oberoi 2016).

Graduation Requirements and College

US public schools vary in what courses students need to take to graduate, and navigating this process can be complicated for many. This process is even more complicated when adding in the possibility that the student has taken some courses in their home country and that they may or may not have a degree record explicitly saying that. This process can be very stressful for unaccompanied children and families and can sometimes lead to a longer time to graduation. There is a common misconception that undocumented immigrants cannot attend college in the United States, or if they can, that there is no financial aid available to do so. These policies vary by state, but in many places, they can do both.

Solutions and Promising Practices for Those Graduating from High School

School districts should work to explain the graduation requirements to families and to provide resources in languages other than English. One promising practice is the Arizona State University initiative, WeGrad, which provides information to parents on the education system targeted for elementary, middle, and high school. The program is available in English and Spanish, online and free, and helps parents orient themselves to US public education expectations and resources and graduation requirements.

For unaccompanied children who enter the United States at ages close to eighteen, there are General Educational Development (GED) programs which may simplify the process of getting some educational record before moving on to work. However, there are also some programs that work with adults to obtain a high school diploma (often preferred to the GED). In Baltimore, the Excel Center is one such program that has worked specifically to recruit immigrants to attend their programming and get a high school diploma. These programs often focus on one or two classes at a time rather than a standard school day so that students can work, and so they can complete each class in a shorter period of time before moving on to the next class. They also often have weekend and evening classes for those who need them.

While undocumented students (all unaccompanied children entering the United States are undocumented, and many are never able to obtain legal status) are not eligible to complete the Free Application for Federal Student Aid for federal financial aid at this time, there are other avenues available to assist them in going to college. Many community colleges offer low-cost tuition and have counselors that can help them transfer to a four-year university and may even know of scholarships available specifically for immigrant students. Many private scholarships allow immigrants to apply, and some specifically target immigrant students wishing to contribute to certain careers. Lastly, some states offer state-based financial aid to undocumented students, such as in Maryland through Maryland High Education Commission §§15–106.8. Importantly, more advocacy in this area is needed to change the narrative and ensure that people know they can pursue higher education opportunities.

Conclusion

While unaccompanied children may face more struggles than their US-born counterparts, or even than other immigrant students in school, there is much we can do to ease the burdens. Being intentional and taking the time to find resources and opportunities in your local area can greatly increase these students' sense of welcome and belonging.

Resources

- Women's Refugee Commission Technical Assistance Packet. https://www.womensrefugeecommission.org/research-resources/schools-stability-and-community-prosperity-new-students-seeking-asylum/
- US Department of Education's Newcomer Tool Kit. https:// www2.ed.gov/about/ offices/ list/oela/newcomers- toolkit/index.html
- Demystifying the College Financial Aid Process for Immigrants and Refugees Webinar. https://www.youtube.com/watch?v=t-Vy2lwIfSg
- Arizona State University's WeGrad Virtual Training Program. https://eoss.asu.edu/wegrad
- Baltimore City Schools Newcomer Support Team. https://sites.google.com/bcps.k12.md.us/nst/home
- Denver Public Schools. https://mle.dpsk12.org/page/newcomer-centers
- Excel Center Baltimore. https://goodwillches.org/the-excel-center-2/
- Summer Rising in New York. https://www.schools.nyc.gov/learning/multilingual-learners/summer-for-multilingual-learners

Further Reading

American Civil Liberties Union. 2024. "Trump on Immigration." https://www.aclu.org/publications/trump-on-immigration

American Civil Liberties Union of Pennsylvania. 2016. "ACLU and Education Law Center Sue School District of Lancaster for Illegally Denying Immigrant Youth an Education." https://www.aclupa.org/news/2016/07/19/aclu-and-education-lawcenter-sue-school-district-lancaster

Booi, Zenande, Caitlin Callahan, Genevieve Fugere, Mikaela Harris, Alexandra Hughes, Alexander Kramarczuk, Caroline Kurtz, Raimy Reyes, and Sruti Swaminathan. 2016. "Ensuring Every Undocumented Student Succeeds." Georgetown Law Human Rights Institute Fact-Finding Project.

Diebold, Kylie, Kerri Evans, and Emily Hornung. 2019. "Educating Unaccompanied Children in US Shelters." *Forced Migration Review* 60: 53–5.

Evans, Kerri, Jaime Perez-Aponte, and Ruth McRoy. 2020. "Without a Paddle: Barriers to School Enrollment Procedures for Immigrant Students and Families." *Education and Urban Society* 52, no. 9: 1283–304.

Evans, Kerri, Gabrielle Oliveira, Robert G. Hason III, Thomas M. Crea, Sarah E. Neville, and Virgginia Fitchett. 2022. "Unaccompanied Children's Education in the United States: Service Provider's Perspective on Challenges and Support Strategies." *Cultura Educación Sociedad* 13, no. 1: 193–218.

Hasson, Robert G., III, Scott D. Easton, Antonia Díaz-Valdés Iriarte, Laura M. O'Dwyer, Dawnya Underwood, and Thomas M. Crea. 2021. "Examining the Psychometric Properties of the Child PTSD Symptom Scale within a Sample of Unaccompanied Immigrant Children in the United States." *Journal of Loss and Trauma* 26, no. 4: 323–35.

Kuntz, Joana C., and Freya Searle. 2023. "Does Bystander Intervention Training Work? When Employee Intentions and Organisational Barriers Collide." *Journal of Interpersonal Violence* 38, no. 3–4: 2934–56.

Messiou, Kyriaki, and Marta Cristina Azaola. 2018. "A Peer-Mentoring Scheme for Immigrant Students in English Secondary Schools: A Support Mechanism for Promoting Inclusion?" *International Journal of Inclusive Education* 22, no. 2: 142–57.

Oberoi, Ashmeet K. 2016. *Mentoring for First-Generation Immigrant and Refugee Youth.* National Mentoring Resource Center.

Office of Refugee Resettlement. 2024. "Facts and Data." https://www.acf.hhs.gov/orr/about/ucs/facts-and-data

Szlyk, Hannah Selene, Jodi Berger Cardoso, Liza Barros Lane, and Kerri Evans. 2020. "'Me perdía en la escuela': Latino Newcomer Youths in the US School System." *Social Work* 65, no. 2: 131–9.

Westbrook, Marisa. 2024. "'I Don't Have a Pile of Money to Take Care of Things': Financial Stress and Housing Insecurity among Low-Income Hispanic/Latinx Immigrant Families during COVID-19." *Journal of Family and Economic Issues* 45, no. 2: 315–26.

Whitaker, Amir, Sylvia Torres-Guillén, Michelle Morton, Harold Jordan, Stefanie Coyle, Angela Mann, and Wei-Ling Sun. 2019. *Cops Not Counselors: How the Lack of School Mental Health Professionals Is Harming Children.* American Civil Liberties Union.

Kerri Evans, PhD, is an associate professor of social work at the University of Maryland Baltimore County School of Social Work. Her research focuses on service providers' questions to improve service delivery and make policy recommendations that will improve the lives of immigrants and refugees in the United States. She has both case management and macro social work experience with refugees and unaccompanied immigrant children in the United States.

Unaccompanied Children and Labor Exploitation in the United States

Zayna Lyon

Introduction

When children migrate to the United States without a parent or legal guardian, they often arrive with limited resources and no access to public assistance. Most of them face the immediate pressure of meeting basic needs by working. Many of these children are unaware of their rights both as minors and as workers, which leaves them vulnerable to exploitation in unsafe or informal jobs. This essay examines how immigration, social welfare, and labor policies interact to create structural conditions that contribute to the labor exploitation of unaccompanied children. It concludes with policy recommendations to address the issue.

Immigration Policy

In the last decade, tens of thousands of children migrated to the United States alone each year. The primary driver for their migration is extreme poverty (Lorenzen 2017), which limits access to education, destabilizes communities, and increases vulnerability to violence and environmental disaster. For most, migrating alone is seen as the only viable option for survival or improvement, and they face pressure to work to not only care for themselves but also provide for the families they left behind (Canizales 2024).

But why do children migrate alone, as opposed to whole families migrating together to seek asylum? In some cases, children lack an adult caregiver to accompany them, while in other instances, families alter their plans to migrate in response to US immigration policy changes (Escamilla García 2024). Between 2018 and 2024, US immigration policies restricted family-based migration while allowing unaccompanied children to enter to apply for asylum. (See Migrant Protection Protocols, Title 42, and Proclamation 10773.) Such policies discouraged families from migrating to seek asylum together in the hope of increasing their children's chances of entry (Escamilla García 2024). While these policies enabled children to enter to seek asylum, the physical separation from their families left them with limited support, making it harder to meet basic economic needs and exposing them to greater risks of exploitation (Glind

2010). In short, restrictive US immigration policies that limited family-based migration encouraged families to send children alone, inadvertently exposing them to socioeconomic precarity.

Immigration policies that restricted family-based migration were an early factor in creating conditions that pushed unaccompanied children into the labor force, where their uncertain legal status, lack of physical parental support, and limited knowledge of their rights made them especially vulnerable to exploitation (Polaris 2017). After they entered the United States, many were at some point apprehended into federal custody. These children receive short-term support that is meant to mirror child welfare best practices from the ORR until they are released to a sponsor in the United States (ORR 2025). Once released, ORR transfers the responsibility of caring for the unaccompanied child to the designated adult sponsor in the United States while the child awaits his or her immigration court hearing. However, sponsors often lack the social and economic resources needed to care for an unaccompanied child, and ORR does not offer any direct services to help sponsors meet children's needs (Greenberg et al. 2021). Once released from ORR care, most children cannot access essential services such as medical and mental health care and legal services due to high costs or limited availability (Heidbrink 2024; Roth and Grace 2015). The lack of adequate resettlement services leaves children with little choice but to work to provide for their own basic needs.

Social Welfare Policy

Unaccompanied children face a contradictory social welfare policy landscape. They are recognized as minors requiring protection but treated under federal immigration law as unauthorized individuals who are generally ineligible for public benefits (O'Connell Davidson 2011). US law restricts access to programs like Medicaid, Supplemental Nutrition Assistance Program (SNAP), and housing assistance to citizens and lawfully present individuals.[1] Furthermore, state immigration policies differ significantly, with some adopting more restrictive measures that exclude immigrants from accessing essential services and others offering more protection and inclusion to immigrants, affecting the safety and well-being of unaccompanied children differentially across states (Samari et al. 2021). Denied access to many essential public benefits, unaccompanied children are often left with no choice but to work in order to meet their basic needs.

Labor Policy

While immigration and social welfare policies create the conditions that compel unaccompanied children to enter the workforce, gaps and weaknesses in US labor policy enable and perpetuate their exploitation once they begin working. US labor laws, such as the Fair Labor Standards Act, were designed to protect children from working in hazardous industries and regulate the hours and conditions of youth employment. However, these laws are often undermined by unscrupulous employers due to a lack of funding and resources for enforcement agencies, making it difficult to address violations effectively. Instead, enforcement agencies rely heavily on worker complaints to identify violations (Gleeson 2010; Weil and Pyles 2005). However, due to the power imbalance between young workers and employers, their immigration status, and the lack of knowledge of their rights as workers, unaccompanied children are among the least likely to report labor law violations (Gleeson 2010; Polaris 2017; Rejman 2024).

Since 2021, during the same time as the influx of unaccompanied children to the United States, several states have introduced or passed laws weakening child labor regulations, expanding work hours, reducing safety standards, and shielding employers from liability in cases of injury or death (Sherer and Mast 2023). Many of these states had already passed "Right to Work" laws that have significantly reduced the private sector union rate (Ellwood and Fine 1987), eliminating a key source of worker protection and labor law enforcement within the workplace (Freeman 1987). A recent study examining the impact of these relaxed laws found a correlation between an increase in unaccompanied children entering a state and a rise in child labor violations, highlighting the growing risk of exploitation for unaccompanied children in states with weaker child labor protections (Bao and Kabra 2024). While immigration policies shape the conditions that push unaccompanied children into the labor force, weak and poorly enforced labor laws create an environment where their labor is exploited.

Recommendations

To mitigate the labor exploitation of unaccompanied children, several systemic changes are necessary. First, immigration policies should prioritize family unity and provide clear pathways for families to migrate together rather than encouraging children to migrate alone to ensure children maintain the support provided by the physical closeness of a parent. Strengthening pathways to asylum for families, offering enough work permits to meet labor needs in the United States, and allowing for cyclical migration can reduce the need for children to migrate alone. Moreover, the resettlement services for unaccompanied children should be reformed to ensure that unaccompanied children are given the resources and support they need after they are released from ORR custody. ORR should provide comprehensive support services to children, including mental health assistance, legal aid, and access to social services.

Second, federal social welfare policies should expand eligibility for social services to cover all children, including unaccompanied children. States should not be able to exclude children from federally funded social welfare services. Expanding eligibility for programs like Medicaid, SNAP, and Temporary Assistance for Needy Families will provide the support many unaccompanied children need to prevent them from being pushed into exploitative work.

Finally, policymakers should pursue labor law reform that makes it easier for workers to unionize, expands eligibility to form unions to occupations excluded from coverage, and increases resources and funding for enforcement agencies to investigate labor law violations (see Weil 2023 for labor policy recommendations to address child labor violations). Unions help balance the power between workers and employers, equipping child workers with the knowledge and confidence to detect and report labor violations. Enforcement agencies should also collaborate with community-based organizations such as PRS providers, worker centers, and legal advocacy groups, which are often better connected to immigrant communities (Fine 2017). These organizations can act as trusted intermediaries, helping bridge the gap between unaccompanied children and authorities.

Conclusion

The labor exploitation of unaccompanied children is a complex issue fueled by intersecting failures in immigration, social welfare, and labor policies. US immigration laws encourage children to migrate alone, while social welfare programs exclude them from vital services, leaving them vulnerable to exploitation. The weakening of labor unions and inadequate enforcement of labor protections further exacerbate the problem, particularly in states where child labor laws have been weakened.

These policies fall short of safeguarding children and instead push unaccompanied children into situations where they must work to survive, often in exploitative conditions. Addressing these issues requires comprehensive reform that prioritizes family unity in immigration policies, ensures adequate resettlement services, expands social services eligibility, and reforms labor law to help balance the power between workers and employers.

Note

1. According to federal law, unaccompanied children are excluded from access to food stamps, healthcare, and social security insurance. See eligibility requirements for: Supplemental Nutrition Assistance Program, US Department of Agriculture, "Supplemental Nutrition Assistance Program (SNAP)," https://www.fns.usda.gov/snap/recipient/eligibility; Medicaid Centers for Medicare & Medicaid Services, "Medicaid," https://www.medicaid.gov/medicaid/eligibility-policy/index.html; and SSI (Supplemental Security Income) Social Security Administration, "Supplemental Security Income (SSI)," https://www.ssa.gov/ssi/spotlights/spot-non-citizens.htm.

Further Reading

Bao, Fred Jiacong, and Ashish Kabra. 2024. "State Mandated Employment Certificate for Minors Reduces Child Labor Violations in the US." Ashish, State Mandated Employment Certificate for Minors Reduces Child Labor Violations in the US (June 7, 2024).

Canizales, Stephanie L. 2024. *Sin Padres, Ni Papeles: Unaccompanied Migrant Youth Coming of Age in the United States*. University of California Press.

Escamilla García, Ángel A. 2024. "The Externalization of Legal Categories: How U.S. Immigration Law Shapes Central American Youth Migrants' Journeys through Mexico." *Ethnic and Racial Studies* 48, no. 4: 906–26. https://doi.org/10.1080/01419870.2024.2404490

Ellwood, David T., and Glenn Fine. 1987. "The Impact of Right-to-Work Laws on Union Organizing." *Journal of Political Economy* 95, no. 2: 250–73.

Fine, Janice. 2017. "Enforcing Labor Standards in Partnership with Civil Society: Can Co-Enforcement Succeed Where the State Alone Has Failed?" *Politics & Society* 45, no. 3: 359–88. https://doi.org/10.1177/0032329217702603

Freeman, Richard B. 1987. "Unionism and Protective Labor Legislation." Industrial Relations Research Association Series, Proceedings, 260–7.

Gleeson, Shannon. 2010. "Labor Rights for All? The Role of Undocumented Immigrant Status for Worker Claims Making." *Law & Social Inquiry* 35, no. 3: 561–602. https://doi.org/10.1111/j.1747-4469.2010.01196.x

Glind, Hans van de. 2010. *Migration and Child Labour: Exploring Child Migrant Vulnerabilities and Those of Children Left-Behind.* International Labour Organization.

Grace, B. L., and B. J. Roth. 2021. "Bureaucratic Neglect: The Paradoxical Mistreatment of Unaccompanied Migrant Children in the U.S. Immigration System." *Journal of Ethnic and Migration Studies* 47, no. 15: 3455–72. https://doi.org/10.1080/1369183X.2020.1788378

Greenberg, Mark, Kylie Grow, Stephanie Heredia Kira Monin, and Essey Workie. 2021. "Strengthening Services for Unaccompanied Children in US Communities." Migration Policy Institute. https://www.migrationpolicy.org/sites/default/files/publications/mpi-unaccompanied-children-services_final.pdf

Heidbrink, Lauren. 2024. "From Congregate to Community-Based Care: Strengthening Reunification and Support of Unaccompanied Children." Women's Refugee Commission. https://www.womensrefugeecommission.org/wp-content/uploads/2024/10/From-Congregate-to-Community-Based-Care-Strengthening-Reunification-Support-Unaccompanied-Children-Report.pdf

Lorenzen, Matthew. 2017. "The Mixed Motives of Unaccompanied Child Migrants from Central America's Northern Triangle." *Journal on Migration and Human Security* 5, no. 4: 744–67. https://doi.org/10.1177/233150241700500402

O'Connell Davidson, Julia. 2011. "Moving Children? Child Trafficking, Child Migration, and Child Rights." *Critical Social Policy* 31, no. 3: 454–77. https://doi.org/10.1177/0261018311405014

Office of Refugee Resettlement. 2025. "About the Unaccompanied Alien Children Bureau." https://acf.gov/orr/programs/uac/about

Polaris. 2017. "A Dangerour Journey North." https://polarisproject.org/blog/2017/03/a-dangerous-journey-north/

Rejman, Ewa. 2024. "Child Migrant Workers: The Invisible Children?" *Denver Journal of International Law and Policy* 52, no. 2: 255–82.

Roth, Benjamin J., and Breanne L. Grace. 2015. "Falling through the Cracks: The Paradox of Post-release Services for Unaccompanied Child Migrants." *Children and Youth Services Review* 58: 244–52.

Samari, Goleen, Amanda Nagle, and Kate Coleman-Minahan. 2021. "Measuring Structural Xenophobia: US State Immigration Policy Climates over Ten Years." *SSM-Population Health* 16: 100938.

Sherer, Jennifer, and Nina Mast. 2023. "Child Labor Laws Are under Attack in States across the Country: Amid Increasing Child Labor Violations, Lawmakers Must Act to Strengthen Standards." Economic Policy Institute. https://www.epi.org/publication/child-labor-laws-under-attack/

Weil, David. 2023. "'This Ancient Atrocity': The Return of Child Labor in the United States: Why Now? What Should Be Done?" Harvard Kennedy School. https://ash.harvard.edu/resources/this-ancient-atrocity-the-return-of-child-labor-in-the-united-states-why-now-what-should-be-done/

Weil, David, and Amanda Pyles. 2005. "Why Complain-Complaints, Compliance, and the Problem of Enforcement in the U.S. Workplace United States." *Comparative Labor Law & Policy Journal* 27, no. 1: 59–92.

Zayna Lyon is a PhD student at the Schar School of Policy and Government at George Mason University. Her research focuses on issues in immigration and labor policy, and child and family welfare. Zayna brings ten years of experience from her prior roles as a service coordinator supporting youth with behavioral challenges, a program evaluator and organizer for immigrant workers, and an associate director of quality assurance for programs serving unaccompanied children and refugees through resettlement services. Prior to PhD studies, Zayna earned a BA in history/political science and an MSW from Rutgers University.

Navigating the Immigration System to Reunite Families with Their Separated Children

Maryam Rafieifar

In 2021, the United States saw a surge in unaccompanied minors crossing the southern border after the peak of Covid-19. At the time, I volunteered as a grant writer for a small community organization in Florida that helped undocumented families locate their children in the immigration system. Many of these parents, terrified of contacting authorities for fear of deportation, turned to the organization for help. They were desperate, overwhelmed, and had no idea where their children had been taken after being processed at the border.

Although my primary role was in grant writing, during this critical time, the organization was short-staffed, and I offered additional support where I could. My role was not to directly update families—many of whom spoke only Spanish or Indigenous languages—but rather to contact shelters, check databases, and communicate with lawyers handling the cases. In situations where the parents spoke some English and I could use my limited Spanish, we managed to communicate.

Parents Searching for Their Children

One of the hardest realities for these families was not knowing where their children were. Many knew their children had made it across the border and were likely in a shelter, but beyond that, information was scarce. The parents who came to the organization were undocumented and feared any contact with authorities might lead to their deportation. The organization became their lifeline, assisting them and navigating the complex system on their behalf. In the following examples, the names have been changed to protect people's privacy.

Ana's case was particularly difficult. She was living in Nebraska and had her three children—a nineteen-year-old daughter and eight-year-old twins—travel to the US border in hopes of reuniting with them after years. Her eldest daughter, acting as the twins' guardian, was deported upon arrival because she was legally considered an adult, while the twins were taken into custody and placed in a shelter in Texas. Ana struggled to prove her relationship to her children due to limited documentation. The process was confusing, and she had difficulty communicating with her caseworker. My role was to help track down her children by calling shelters and working with a *pro bono* lawyer who was handling the legal hurdles. It took weeks of phone calls and relentless follow-ups, but after nearly two months, Ana was finally reunited with her children. She later shared a picture of their tearful reunion at the airport—a moment of relief after so much uncertainty.

Another heartbreaking case involved Elena, a mother in Florida whose husband and seven-year-old daughter, Itzel, tried to cross the border together. The father was deported, while the daughter was taken into custody and placed in a shelter in Michigan. She spoke only an Indigenous Guatemalan language—neither English nor Spanish—which created a major communication barrier in the shelter. Because she could not communicate with the staff, they did not understand why she was crying for days. It was only after she was finally reunited with her mother that we learned she had been suffering from an untreated toothache the entire time. This case was a painful reminder of how vulnerable these children were—not only because of separation from their families but also because their needs were often overlooked in a system not equipped to accommodate language diversity.

Why Children Are Classified as Unaccompanied Minors

For many, the idea of parents sending their children on a dangerous journey to the United States alone may seem unthinkable. It is easy to assume that these parents are abandoning their children or making reckless decisions. However, the reality is far more complex. Most families making these journeys come from countries marked by extreme poverty, violence, and the constant threat of gang activity. At the same time, migration is expensive, and families rarely have the financial means to travel together. In many cases, one or two family members—usually a parent—migrate first, hoping to find work and establish some stability. Once they have saved enough money, they arrange for their children or other relatives to join them. These parents are not abandoning their children; they are making impossible choices in an effort to reunite their families after months or even years of separation.

Another critical factor is that, despite being classified as "unaccompanied," most children do not actually travel alone. They are often accompanied by a trusted adult—an older sibling, a family friend, or a distant relative—who is tasked with bringing them safely to the US-Mexico border. However, once they arrive, immigration protocols frequently result in their separation. Because the accompanying adult is not their legal guardian or parent, the child is categorized as an "unaccompanied minor" and placed in the custody of US authorities.

For example, Ana's eldest daughter was deported after accompanying her younger twin siblings to the border. Although she had been responsible for their safety throughout the journey, immigration officials did not recognize her as their legal guardian, and she was sent back to their home country. The twins, meanwhile, were taken into US custody and placed in a shelter alone. This pattern played out in many of the cases I worked on.

The Role of Small Organizations in a Big System

Unlike large nonprofits or government agencies, the organization I volunteered with was small and community driven. It relied on volunteers to handle everything from grant writing to case tracking. Parents didn't have a direct line to government shelters, so we had to make calls, cross-check information, and work with legal teams to push cases forward. The system itself was overwhelming.

Shelters were overburdened, and getting through to the right person often took multiple attempts. Many times, I would call different places, sometimes in various states, following vague leads in hopes of confirming a child's location. When I finally reached someone who could confirm a child was safe, it felt like a small but significant victory.

The devastation of family separation was something I witnessed up close. Parents carried heavy feelings of guilt and helplessness, wondering if they had made the right decision in sending their children to the border. They often cried on the phone, expressing how much they missed their children and how powerless they felt in the face of an unfamiliar system. For the children, separation was equally traumatic. Many had already endured hardship—violence, poverty, or instability in their home countries. In addition to the very dangerous journey they had just undertaken, being separated from their families in an unfamiliar country only added to their fear.

Reflections on This Experience

Although my role in the organization was originally focused on grant writing, stepping in to assist during the influx of unaccompanied minors left a lasting impact on me. I saw firsthand the resilience of parents and children, as well as the importance of small organizations in helping families navigate an overwhelming system. One of the biggest lessons I learned was how vital it is for parents to have someone they can trust. For these families, reaching out to an unknown organization for help was a leap of faith. They were entrusting their children's fate to people they had never met, hoping that someone would advocate on their behalf. The case of the seven-year-old Itzel in Michigan continues to stay with me. She suffered in silence simply because no one understood her language. Her story represents so many others—children whose pain and struggles go unnoticed because the system isn't designed for them.

While immigration policies will continue to shift, what remains constant is the human reality behind these cases. Families will continue to make impossible choices in hopes of a better future, and small, community-based organizations will remain essential in helping them navigate a system that is often unprepared to meet their needs. My experience showed me that even in a vast, bureaucratic process, persistence, empathy, and community support can make a meaningful difference.

Maryam Rafieifar, PhD, is an assistant professor in the School of Social Work at the University of Texas at Arlington. Her research focuses on how immigration policies affect the well-being of children in immigrant and refugee families, especially when it comes to the risks of family separation. She has also been a longtime volunteer with community-based organizations that support immigrant children and families, which inspired the chapter she contributed to this book.

Serving Children in a System That No Longer Serves Them

Silvia Melgar

When I began working as a Youth Services Coordinator at an immigrant-serving nonprofit organization, I joined a team that grew to seven. We were a dedicated group brought together by a shared purpose: to support unaccompanied children and their sponsors through some of the most vulnerable and uncertain periods of their lives. In doing so, we became witnesses to the deep fears and struggles they faced—fears of leaving their homes, of family members departing and not returning, and of wanting to pursue a better future but being met with constant barriers. The desire to further their education was often hindered by these obstacles, and sometimes we were their only advocates, stepping in to ensure they felt a sense of belonging. We found ourselves in schools, fighting for their right to be heard educating staff on the importance of providing documents in languages they could understand. Beyond the classroom, we delivered food and household supplies to families too fearful to leave their homes, and we saw a decline in after-school and summer programs, as parents and sponsors feared that their children might be taken if they participated. These experiences were a constant reminder of the profound impact fear and uncertainty had on every facet of their lives.

Today, that team has been reduced to just two of us. It is hard to describe what it feels like to go from a room full of colleagues sharing ideas, dividing up referrals, and celebrating family reunifications to a near-empty office, where the silence is heavy. The weight is physical, emotional, and deeply personal. And while the losses we've experienced internally have been challenging, the real devastation lies with the children and families we can no longer reach or properly serve.

Since January 2025, when the Trump administration returned to office, everything has changed. New policies impacting refugee resettlement, home study, and PRS programs have created even more barriers for these children. The abrupt elimination of grants that once helped unaccompanied minors afford legal representation for their court hearings has left children as young as one year old to defend themselves in court, with no proper guidance or support. These inhumane policies have only further pushed the narrative that these children do not have the right to be here, despite their efforts to go through the system the "right way." It is a stark reminder of how the system continues to fail those who are already the most vulnerable, subjecting them to an ongoing cycle of fear and uncertainty. Case managers began reporting that sponsors who once welcomed home visits were becoming hesitant, guarded, or completely disengaged. Some stopped answering their phones altogether. Children who had once begun to settle in—starting school, building routines—were now expressing fear, withdrawing emotionally, or exhibiting signs of distress again. I don't work directly with the children or sponsors. But as the person supporting and overseeing the case management team, I hear their stories daily. I hear the worry in my case managers' voices after each difficult visit—or worse, when there's no visit at all because the family is suddenly unreachable. I hear the exhaustion when they talk about how hard it is to build trust when the broader system feels hostile. And I feel their heartbreak when they recount the fear in a child's eyes or the quiet resignation in a sponsor's voice.

The sudden loss of legal support services was one of the most destabilizing developments this year. Being one of the agencies that provided in-house legal representation to our clients, the loss of legal support left us trying to find any way to provide legal services for our children. We went from establishing legal representation within weeks to the process taking months, leaving some children to age out without having had legal representation. The lack of resources and funding left us scrambling and needing longer time periods to obtain legal aid. Our biggest fear was that any of our children would have to face a judge on their own. Furthermore, language barriers could present barriers for them understanding what would be happening to them and their families. Without legal representation, children fear that even when they do show up for court, they may face detention. When the administration abruptly ended contracts that provided legal aid for unaccompanied minors, case managers were left scrambling to find resources. We've had families with pending court dates and struggling to find representation children midway through their immigration cases who now had no one to guide them. I watched my team struggle with the implications of this shift.

They weren't just losing a referral source—they were losing a safety net. I witnessed team members share the guilt of having to tell a family that a referred attorney could no longer represent them, unfortunately due to funding being stripped away.

The changes to our team happened almost overnight, suddenly, and without warning. Within a matter of weeks, what had been a fully staffed program began unraveling. Team members were let go, some walked away, and the impact was immediate and deeply felt. It wasn't just about losing staff—it was about losing the trust they had built with clients, the cultural understanding they brought to the work, and the emotional support they provided to one another. For months, the team fluctuated in uncertainty until eventually, we were down to just two. While the overall caseload did decrease due to shifts under the new administration, the complexity and urgency of the remaining cases remained just as high—and the loss of staff meant that even reduced numbers still felt overwhelming.

While I don't work directly with children and sponsors, the stories I hear from my case managers are deeply affecting. They speak of sponsors growing terrified—about kids showing increased anxiety, asking heartbreaking questions like, "Will they take my family too?" The sponsors, who are often the child's only sense of stability here, live in constant fear that they could be next. These aren't abstract concerns. They're the lived reality for many of the families we've tried so hard to support. Some days, the emotional toll is palpable. As a coordinator, I try to support however I can—offering structure, resources, and encouragement—but I also know what they're carrying. The trauma they absorb from their clients. The moral injury of wanting to do more but being limited by time, funding, and policy. We've had to adapt constantly, leaning on community organizations, informal networks, and whatever limited resources we can pull together. We're in a perpetual state of triage, often putting out fires instead of building sustainable solutions. What once was a proactive, holistic support system has turned into reactive crisis management. But my team shows up. They keep showing up, even when the system feels stacked against them. I believe in this work, and in the people doing it. I believe in my team, even as it has shrunk to two of us. I stay because every time one of our case managers helps a family navigate a difficult circumstance, or finds a resource that eases a sponsor's burden, or simply reminds a child that they are not alone—we are doing something powerful. The strength I see in my team, and in the children and sponsors they serve, is what fuels me. Even when our capacity is limited, our commitment is not. The stories I hear are painful—but they're also reminders of what's possible when care, compassion, and resilience meet in the same space.

This experience has shown me how the system can be rebuilt to better serve unaccompanied children. We need stable funding. Stable funding will allow for consistent case management presence in the community and in the lives of unaccompanied children. We need immigration policies that prioritize child welfare and family unity. We need legal resources, access to trauma-informed care, and a system that treats unaccompanied children not as a problem to be managed, but as people to be supported. Legal resources could include *pro bono* attorneys who specialize in immigration law and are equipped to handle the unique challenges of unaccompanied minors. These attorneys would not only provide representation in court but also advocate for the child's best interests throughout the entire immigration process, ensuring their voices are heard and their rights protected. Trauma-informed care would involve services such as counseling or support groups specifically designed for survivors of migration-related trauma, where children can safely process their experiences and begin to heal. These services would recognize the complex emotional and psychological impacts of their journeys and offer a space for recovery, dignity, and empowerment. We need to restore trust between communities and the services designed to help them. And that starts by recognizing the harm that's been done—and choosing to repair it. Since January 2025, we've watched the system meant to protect unaccompanied children unravel. Programs have been gutted, trust has been eroded, and families have been left more isolated than ever. Although nonprofits are experiencing funding cuts, the commitment to serving unaccompanied children remains. We may be just two now, but we're still here. And that matters. Because these children still matter. And we refuse to forget that.

Silvia Melgar is a nonprofit professional who has experience with program management, grant development, and case coordination. She is based in Rhode Island.

KIND
KIDS IN NEED OF DEFENSE
CELEBRATING 10 YEARS
BOOM EVENTS
BOLON

4

Profiles

This first section of this chapter presents brief profiles of organizations involved with unaccompanied children. Some are government organizations that are mandated by law to provide services and support for unaccompanied children. Others are nongovernmental organizations that receive funding from government agencies to provide direct services for unaccompanied children in the United States. These services may include case management for unaccompanied children who are resettled in the United States, as well as legal services for unaccompanied children who are navigating immigration court. The chapter concludes with a section of profiles of individuals who have extensive expertise in advocating for unaccompanied children in a variety of leadership roles.

Organizations

Bethany Christian Services

Bethany Christian Services is a US-based nonprofit organization that provides social services for vulnerable children and families. Based in Michigan, Bethany Christian Services provides services in twenty-eight states. The organization was established as Bethany Christian Home in 1944 after two friends named Marguerite Bonnema and Mary DeBoer welcomed an infant girl who unexpectedly needed shelter. The friends later took in and cared for additional

---

Wendy Young, President of Kids in Need of Defense (KIND). KIND provides legal services for vulnerable immigrants, including unaccompanied children, and advocates for policy reform to promote a system that recognizes children's rights and advances their health and well-being. (Hutchinsphoto/Dreamstime.com)

infants, and their organization continued providing services for children in need of shelter over the coming years, becoming a licensed adoption agency in 1951 (Bethany Christian Services 2025a).

Bethany Christian Services is a Christian organization that believes families are the best setting for raising children. The organization's mission statement explains that "Bethany demonstrates the love and compassion of Jesus Christ by protecting children, empowering youth, and strengthening families through quality social services" (Bethany Christian Services 2025b). Furthermore, "Bethany envisions a world where all children, youth, and families are safe, loved, and connected" (Bethany Christian Services 2025b). Bethany Christian Services is guided by five values: faith, support, justice, excellence, and long haul (i.e., a commitment to sustained support for vulnerable individuals). The organization served a total of 53,766 children and families in 2024, including 21,334 immigrant children and families.

Bethany Christian Services is organized into four main areas: foster care, adoption, family strengthening, and refugees and immigrants. The organization provides local foster care as well as adoption from foster care. Within the adoption program, Bethany Christian Services offers an array of services across all stages of the adoption process, including adoption from foster care, infant adoption, home studies, pregnancy support, post-adoption support, and support for adult adoptees. For family-strengthening services, Bethany Christian Services offers individual and family therapy and intensive therapeutic services for families experiencing maltreatment, conflict, domestic violence, substance use, and mental health challenges. In addition, the organization provides parent coaching to help parents strengthen their capacity to care for their children.

The organization's final program area focuses on immigrant children. Bethany Christian Services provides an array of services for unaccompanied children, including home studies and post-release services for unaccompanied children who are placed with a sponsor, as well as long-term foster care for unaccompanied children who do not have an identified sponsor in the United States. The organization provides these services as part of a partnership with the Office of Refugee Resettlement, which allocates funding for nonprofit organizations to support unaccompanied children. The immigrant children program helps unaccompanied children cope with mental health challenges that may result from migration-related trauma and also helps unaccompanied children flourish in their resettlement community as they integrate in the United States (Bethany Christian Service 2025c).

Center for Immigration and Child Welfare

The Center for Immigration and Child Welfare (CICW) is an organization based at the University of California, Berkeley, that engages in advocacy and research to support children of immigrants and families who navigate the immigration system in the United States. The organization "pursues and supports research that advances our mission to improve policy and practice with immigrant children and families at risk of involvement with the child welfare system" (Center for Immigration and Child Welfare n.d.).

Research from the organization focuses on pre-migration contexts, the migration journey, and experiences in resettlement. The organization seeks to use research to inform policies that will enhance the health and well-being of immigrant children and families, as well as address risks for trauma that may be experienced within the child welfare system. Examples of research studies include "The Strengthening Border Families Research Project" and a study that explores child welfare systems that support immigrant children who are transitioning to adulthood. Along with research, CICW also provides training for child welfare professionals and service providers who work with immigrant children and families to strengthen capacity and inform service delivery. Trainings have helped child welfare organizations improve their services, coordinate community-based supports, and support family reunification following a deportation.

Church World Service

Church World Service (CWS) is a nonprofit organization that provides social services for individuals living on the margins of society. The mission statement of CWS states: "Church World Service is a faith-based organization transforming communities around the globe through just and sustainable responses to hunger, poverty, displacement and disaster" (Church World Service n.d.a). CWS is guided by values including justice, hope, belonging, excellence, collaboration, and integrity. CWS envisions a world "where all have food, voice and a safe place to call home" (Church World Service n.d.a).

Like other nonprofit organizations who serve immigrants, CWS was established after the Second World War, when record numbers of people were displaced due to war and violence. Seventeen separate Christian organizations joined together to provide direct support to individuals in need, including providing more than 11 million pounds of food and resettling more than 100,000 refugees in the first ten years. CWS has responded to humanitarian crises around the world, including famine in Ethiopia and natural disaster in Haiti. Beginning in the 1960s, CWS began focusing on development work, including food and water security, sanitation, and health programs. Since the 1980 US Refugee Act, CWS has resettled more than 865,000 refugees in the United States (Church World Service n.d.c).

Among the many services CWS provides in the United States are services specifically for unaccompanied children. Two specific services CWS provides for unaccompanied children are home studies and post-release services. These services are provided at sixteen different offices in three locations. CWS collaborates with the Office of Refugee Resettlement to support unaccompanied children who migrate to the United States. First, case managers conduct home visits. They "interview each member of the household and ensure this is a safe placement for the child while supporting the sponsor to prepare for the responsibility of promoting the arriving child's safety, rights and needs" (Church World Service n.d.b). Next, CWS also provides ongoing post-release services for unaccompanied children in need of additional support. Case managers work with unaccompanied children and their sponsors to create a treatment plan that will ensure unaccompanied children have access to school, legal services, and health and mental health services. According to CWS, 9,749 children received services from CWS between January 2023 and December 2023. In 2022, CWS completed ninety-five home studies and provided post-release services to 3,287 unaccompanied children in thirty-six states. In 2022, CWS also created a "Unaccompanied Children Action Alert" to engage in advocacy for policies that support unaccompanied children (Church World Service n.d.b).

Dorcas International Institute of Rhode Island

An example of a small nonprofit that provides case management services for unaccompanied children is Dorcas International Institute of Rhode Island (DIIRI). DIIRI is a small nonprofit in Rhode Island that is based at two different locations in the state's capital city, Providence. DIIRI was established in 2013 when two separate organizations joined together: the International Institute of Rhode Island and the Dorcas Place Adult and Family Literacy Center. Dorcas Place was first established in 1981 and focused on providing social services, including literacy classes, for low-income adults. The International Institute of

Rhode Island was first established in 1921 as an affiliate of the YMCA. Starting in 2013, DIIRI provided a range of social services for immigrants and newcomers who arrived in Rhode Island.

DIIRI's mission statement describes a pursuit of building community for the betterment of individuals. Specifically, the organization explains that: "We cultivate an inclusive community for immigrants and those seeking refuge by providing integrated services, fostering cross-cultural understanding, and nurturing strong partnerships" (Dorcas International Institute of Rhode Island [DIIRI] 2025a). Moreover, DIIRI describes a vision that promotes welcoming communities that help individuals flourish: "We envision a future where everyone is welcome and has the opportunity to thrive and prosper" (DIIRI 2025a). The organization pursues this work guided by a set of core values, including respect, integrity, agility, and inclusivity.

DIIRI provides a range of services for immigrants and refugees in Rhode Island. The organization helps individuals navigate the immigration system and supports immigrants with a variety of immigration statuses, including citizenship and naturalization. It provides education and training programs to help immigrants learn new skills and gain employment. DIIRI provides translation and interpretation services to help individuals access services. It also operates a clothing collaborative, where individuals can access clothing for job interviews and different work settings, and provides services for specific immigrant groups, including refugees and unaccompanied children.

DIIRI provides community-based case management services for unaccompanied children as part of a contract with Heartland Human Care Services. The services DIIRI case managers provide for unaccompanied children begin even before a child arrives in Rhode Island. The process begins with the Office of Refugee Resettlement sending a referral to Heartland Human Care Services. Upon receiving a referral for case management services from Heartland Human Care Services, DIIRI starts with conducting a background check and intensive home study with the sponsor who will serve as the legal guardian of the unaccompanied child. This home study ensures the child will be placed in a safe home environment, that the sponsor has access to basic human needs, including food and clothing, and that the sponsor has the capacity to provide ongoing support for the child upon their arrival to Rhode Island.

Upon the child's arrival in Rhode Island, DIIRI case managers provide ongoing visits with the child and their sponsor to ensure the child has access to health, mental health, education, and legal services. Case managers provide referrals for doctors and other health specialists, support the minor and their sponsor with enrolling in local public schools, and also connect children with *pro bono* legal services. DIIRI has also established a volunteer-based mentor program, where unaccompanied children are connected with mentors who help them navigate new communities. According to DIIRI's website, the organization provides services to approximately eighty to ninety families per year in the unaccompanied children program (DIIRI 2025b).

Endeavors

Endeavors is a faith-based nonprofit located in San Antonio, Texas, that "passionately serves vulnerable people in crisis" (Endeavors 2025a). In its vision statement, Endeavors explains that "We are committed to providing a helping hand to restore dignity and improve the quality of life for every client, every time, in every community we serve" (Endeavors 2025a). Endeavors' work is guided by a set of core values, including accountability and integrity, care and compassion, teamwork, commitment to making a difference, and community involvement. Among the services that Endeavors provides are mental health and wellness services, shelter services for vulnerable populations, rapid response for individuals experiencing crisis, and case management.

Endeavors was established in 1969 when five Presbyterian churches in San Antonio joined together and formed the San Antonio Urban Council. The history of Endeavors is marked by various evolutions that included collaborations and partnerships, as well as expanding services for vulnerable individuals. The Council focused on supporting individuals struggling with homelessness and poverty and also providing education and health services, as well as services for older adults. In 1971, the organization evolved into San Antonio Urban Ministries, growing to include thirty-five different churches. In 1976, the organization opened an emergency shelter for adolescent boys, called Roy Maas Youth Alternatives, and in 1977 it opened Fairweather Lodge, which supported individuals discharged from San Antonio State Hospital. Continued partnerships and collaborations emerged in the 1980s and 1990s, expanding Endeavor's capacity to support vulnerable individuals. In the 2000s, continued expansion of services included job training and employment support. In 2010, Endeavors received federal funding to focus on ending veteran homelessness. Endeavors added disaster relief services in 2015 and expanded Supportive Services to Veteran Families in a variety of states, including Alabama, Florida, and North Carolina (Endeavors 2025c).

Among the several programs and services operated by Endeavor are Migrant Children's Services. Endeavors operates two shelters that provide services for unaccompanied children who are apprehended by the US Customs and Border Protection. These shelters serve youth aged 13–17 years old who are awaiting reunification with a sponsor in the United States. The shelters include a wide range of services to support unaccompanied children, including case management, health and mental health services, food and shelter, education and recreational programming, and know-your-rights orientations (Endeavors 2025b).

Global Refuge

Global Refuge, formerly called Lutheran Immigration and Refugee Service (LIRS), is a national nonprofit organization based in the United States that provides social services for immigrants and people experiencing forced migration. Beginning in 1918 as the National Lutheran Council (NLC) in New York City, Global Refuge helped resettle 522 refugees in the first year of operation by coordinating with the city's Welfare Department. Becoming Global Refuge in 1939, the organization grew in response to people displaced due to the Second World War.

Originally focused on refugees from Germany and Eastern Europe, Global Refuge has since helped refugees and immigrants from around the world find "new beginnings" in the United States. The organization has provided an array of social services, including economic empowerment, mental health services, and family reunification services, for people from various countries, including Uganda, Vietnam, the Balkans, Afghanistan, and Iraq. Responding to the needs of vulnerable people fleeing conflict and chaos, Global Refuge seeks to uplift those who have experienced the trauma of forced migration and look to new beginnings to pursue ambitions and dreams. Global Refuge has adapted to meet the needs of different groups of people experiencing forced migration throughout history.

Global Refuge resettled 30,263 refugees in the immediate years following the Second World War. In October 1956, more than 50,000 Hungarians escaped government oppression, and Global Refuge responded by helping to resettle 1,500 refugees in the United States. Similarly, in 1959, Cuba experienced a revolution, resulting in more than 100,000 Cubans migrating to the United States to seek safety and freedom. Global Refuge supported their resettlement by providing social services. Global Refuge responded in a similar manner to people fleeing government persecution in Uganda in 1972, helping to resettle 600 of the 75,000 who were expelled by the government. This trend continued in the 1970s, with Global Refuge helping resettle Vietnamese refugees, as well as refugees escaping conflict in the Balkans in the 1990s. In the 2000s, Global Refuge continued the trend of welcoming refugees escaping war-related conflict by providing resettlement support to individuals and families from Afghanistan. Throughout each of the responses to these conflicts, Global Refuge adapted to provide support and resources that matched the context of specific groups of people.

The mission of Global Refuge is "fostering a world of just and welcoming communities" (Global Refuge 2025b). Along with responding to the needs of individuals, an important part of Global Refuge is the organization's efforts to shape a culture of communities in the United States that promote a sense of welcoming and respond to injustices related to forced migration. These efforts are rooted in core values, including welcome, prophetic wisdom, integrity, innovation, and interdependence. Among the different services Global Refuge provides are refugee resettlement support, mental health services, inclusion and empowerment programs that promote economic self-sufficiency, and immigration legal services. In addition, Global Refuge provides services specific to unaccompanied children.

Global Refuge helps provide the basic human needs for unaccompanied children who arrive in the United States and do not have family in the country, as well as children who arrive without family. For children who migrate to the United States and do not have family available to meet their needs, Global Refuge helps place children in foster care settings that provide shelter and adult support. For unaccompanied children who already have family in the United States, Global Refuge provides family reunification services that help children adjust to their new family setting, including accessing important parts of their community. Because many children who migrate to the United States have experienced trauma before, during, and even after their arrival, Global Refuge also provides an array of mental health services to address mental health issues such as anxiety, depression, and posttraumatic stress disorder that can impede a child's ability to flourish in their community. Among the specific services that Global Refuge provides are individual counseling, case management, and group therapy for children.

Across the twentieth, and into the twenty-first century, Global Refuge has shown how organizations can respond directly to the needs of people on the move, fleeing political persecution, government oppression, and the chaos caused by war and violence. Global Refuge seeks to offer a range of services that welcome, support, and uplift refugees, immigrants, and children who arrive in the United States for safety and opportunity. For unaccompanied children, specifically, these supports include foster care, family reunification, and mental health services to address complex symptoms resulting from the stresses of migration. Through advocacy, as well as direct services, Global Refuge is an organization that is "redefining what it means to come home" (Global Refuge 2025b).

Heartland Human Care Services

Heartland Human Care Services is a national nonprofit organization based in Chicago, Illinois, that provides an array of social services for vulnerable and marginalized individuals, including unaccompanied children. In its mission statement, Heartland Human Care Services explains that it is "dedicated to partnering with individuals facing poverty, displacement, and injustice, to support them in achieving ongoing safety, stability, and long-term success" (Heartland Human Care Services 2024b).

As an organization, Heartland Human Care Services has experienced multiple evolutions across different time periods in US history, while remaining committed to its mission to help individuals who are living on the margins of society. The first version of the organization started in 1888 as Travelers Aid, and since then has evolved into several different versions to provide social services. In 1908, the organization was called Immigrant Protective League, which reflected a time period in US history when millions of immigrants arrived in the United States. In 1929, the organization was called Great Depression Housing, which reflected the need for housing for individuals suffering during the Great Depression.

The organization was called Travelers Aid Society & Immigrations Protective League in 1968, which reflected the combining of different groups under one organization. This name was simplified to Travelers & Immigrant Aid (TIA) in 1980. The organization welcomed the Kovler Center in 1987, which is a mental health services organization, and partnered with HAH Food Program in 1988 and Uptown Health Center in 1993. Beginning in 1995, different versions of Heartland Alliance formed, leading to Heartland Human Care Services in 2024 (Heartland Human Care Services 2024a).

Heartland Human Care Services provides services in Chicago, along with fifteen other US states. The organization provides services for more than 200,000 individuals per year, including unaccompanied children. Services for unaccompanied children include residential care, case management, and support with accessing health, mental health, education, and legal supports. Heartland Human Care Services receives federal funding from the US Office of Refugee Resettlement and partners with a network of providers across the United States who provide case management services for unaccompanied children. Across its history, Heartland Human Care Services has responded to some of the most impactful challenges experienced in the United States, including arrivals of millions of immigrants, the deep poverty experienced during the Great Depression, the impact of the World Wars, and the pursuit of social justice during the Civil Rights era. Throughout each of these challenges, the organization has remained committed to upholding the dignity and worth of all people while also pursuing social justice for all.

International Rescue Committee

The International Rescue Committee (IRC) is a nonprofit organization based in New York City that provides humanitarian support for immigrants and displaced persons, focusing especially on the unique needs of women and girls. Formed in 1933 by Albert Einstein and a group of humanitarians, today IRC provides direct social services, including healthcare, education, and economic empowerment. In addition, IRC engages in advocacy to improve the lives and well-being of people experiencing forced displacement. The mission of IRC is "to help people whose lives and livelihoods are shattered by conflict and disaster, including the climate crisis, to survive, recover and gain control over their future" (International Rescue Committee 2025b).

IRC provides humanitarian relief services around the world, and areas of focus include economic well-being, education, empowerment, health, safety, and women and girls. These services are provided in refugee camps, low-income settings, and also in settings experiencing war, violence, and natural disasters. IRC's services range from providing food and basic human needs to empowering individuals in resettlement locations so they can continue flourishing after experiencing the trauma of displacement. Along with a focus on women and girls, IRC also provides services for unaccompanied children.

Similar to other organizations in the United States (e.g., United States Conference of Catholic Bishops), IRC provides home visit services that assess the safety of living settings that unaccompanied children move to after being placed with a sponsor. Home studies can be especially helpful for evaluating the relationship between an unaccompanied child and their sponsor, which is especially important for children who have never met their sponsor before or who have not lived with their sponsor in several years. For unaccompanied children who may struggle after placement with their sponsor, IRC also receives contracts from the Office of Refugee Resettlement (ORR) to provide post-release services (PRS). PRS are community-based services that focus on helping unaccompanied children adjust to their new neighborhoods. These services include helping children enroll in school, connecting them with health and mental health providers, and connecting them with legal services.

IRC is an organization that seeks out and supports individuals who are living on the margins of society, impacted by war, natural disaster, and at risk of forced displacement. The work of IRC manifests in education provided in a classroom in a refugee camp, or the food and water provided to people in the wake of a natural disaster, or the medicine and health care provided to people in a war zone. In all of these contexts, IRC is an organization committed to supporting those suffering on the margins of society, promoting their resilience, and recognizing their humanity.

Kids in Need of Defense

Kids in Need of Defense (KIND) is a nonprofit organization that provides social services, including legal services, for children who experience migration. With headquarters based in Washington, DC, KIND has additional offices throughout the United States, including in Georgia, Maryland, Massachusetts, California, New Jersey, and Washington. KIND also has offices in Northern and Southern Mexico (Kids in Need of Defense [KIND] 2025a).

Established in 2008 by Microsoft and actress Angelina Jolie, KIND has a clear vision that outlines the organization: "We envision a world in which children's rights and well-being are protected as they migrate alone in search of safety" (KIND 2025d). KIND was established in recognition that children experiencing migration lacked the necessary legal resources necessary to help them navigate the complexity of the US immigration system. The mission of KIND includes three separate components. First, KIND seeks to ensure that all children in need of legal representation in immigration court have access to an attorney. Second, KIND engages in advocacy to promote laws, policies, and regulations that recognize the human rights of children who experience migration. Finally, the organization seeks to find durable solutions that are focused on the best interests of children and strives to address the root causes of migration so no children are forced to migrate for their safety and well-being (KIND 2025d).

KIND's vision and mission are both guided by a set of core principles. The first emphasizes the organization's flexibility: "We will remain disciplined and nimble and adjust our programming to ensure delivery on our core mission of access to justice and protection of children's wellbeing and rights." The second explains how they organize an inclusive work setting: "We will develop and implement policies that promote a workplace experience in which people feel valued and heard and can thrive in support of our core mission." The third emphasizes the importance of a trauma-informed approach: "We will prioritize wellness and deploy trauma-informed strategies throughout the organization." Finally, the fourth principle describes the organization's commitment to sustainability: "We will maintain our commitment to long-term financial success and strengthening systems and capacity to ensure effective delivery of KIND's mission" (KIND 2025d).

A unique feature of KIND is the organization's commitment to a holistic approach to providing legal services for children experiencing migration. Child migrants, including unaccompanied children, can have complex health and mental health needs that can disrupt their ability to navigate legal systems. For example, the cognitive disruptions associated with trauma experienced during forced migration can impact the way a child focuses or concentrates, which are important cognitive skills in an immigration court. KIND uses a holistic approach to support the broad needs of children by providing an array of services, including legal services, social services, international programs, policy and advocacy, and a specific response for children who experience family separation.

The cornerstone of KIND's work is the legal services they provide immigrant children. With a firm commitment to work to ensure that no child is in immigration court alone, KIND provides direct legal representation for unaccompanied children and know-your-rights presentations that outline the rights unaccompanied children have in court. To date, KIND has represented more than 7,500 unaccompanied children, has provided more than 72,000 know-your-rights presentations, and has collaborated with 856 legal partners, including law firms, law schools, and bar association partners (KIND 2025b).

Kino Border Initiative

Among the most precarious moments that migrants experience in the middle of forced migration is arriving at an international border. This is especially the case at the US southern border, where each year tens of thousands of individuals arrive, seeking to escape violence, pursue opportunity, or reunite with family or loved ones. At official ports of entry, the border is an ominous wall of fortified steel, creating a stark barrier. Secured by militarized law enforcement officials who are trained to identify anyone approaching as a potential threat, border regions also experience high crime rates, leading to economic exploitation of vulnerable migrants, including unaccompanied children. The Kino Border Initiative is a nonprofit organization based in Nogales, Arizona, that aims to support migrants and promote a humane immigration system that recognizes the dignity of migrants who encounter borders (Kino Border Initiative 2023a).

The mission of the Kino Border Initiative is to "Promote humane, just, and workable migration" by providing humanitarian assistance to migrants, providing education opportunities for people to meet with migrants and enhance solidarity, and advocating for immigration policy reform in the United States and Mexico (Kino Border Initiative 2023a). The Kino Border Initiative was originally founded in 2009 as part of a collaboration between various Catholic organizations, including the Society of Jesus, Jesuit Refugee Services, Missionary Sister of the Eucharist, the Mexican Province of the Society of Jesus, the Diocese of Tucson, and the Archdiocese of Hermosillo. Since 2008, the Kino Border Initiative has focused efforts on accompanying vulnerable migrants as they encounter the US southern border.

The Kino Border Initiative focuses its work around three broad areas: humanitarian and holistic accompaniment, education, and advocacy. The Kino Border Initiative was originally organized to support migrants who were deported from the United States to Mexico. This work has evolved to include supporting migrants who arrive at the US border in Nogales, Mexico, but because of US asylum policy, are not able to immediately receive immigration relief. The Kino Border Initiative provides an array of humanitarian services, including health and mental health services, legal assistance in both Arizona and Mexico, food, clothing, and shelter.

The Kino Border Initiative engages in two main forms of education: presentations and immersion experiences. Presentations are provided to schools, churches, or other organizations that seek information about immigration policy and conditions at the border. Because Kino Border Initiative is a faith-based organization, the presentations also include elements of Catholic social teaching to explain how the church approaches the topic of migration. Since the founding of the organization, the Kino Border Initiative has also led immersion experiences for high schools, colleges, and churches in the United States that last three to six days and provide participants the opportunity to experience the border in person, to cross the border to Nogales, Mexico, and to meet with migrants who are experiencing the immigration system. The border immersion experiences allow participants to deepen their understanding of the complexities within the immigration system by directly experiencing it.

The Kino Border Initiative also engages in advocacy to promote policies that recognize the dignity and worth of all people who encounter the border. Along with advocacy, the Kino Border Initiative started the Border Action Team in 2017 to provide legal services for migrants at the US southern border. This was in response to more restrictive border policies that prevented asylum seekers from entering the United States.

The Kino Border Initiative seeks to support the rights and well-being of migrants at the US southern border. Guided by Catholic social teaching, the organization engages in direct humanitarian assistance by accompanying migrants and providing food, clothing, and shelter, as well as an array of health, mental health, and legal services. The organization also documents the experiences of migrants at the border and uses this research to promote policy reform (Kino Border Initiative 2023b).

Migration Policy Institute

Washington, DC, is the geographic focal point of policy development in the United States, with countless organizations working to develop and design policies that address a range of social issues, including immigration. Migration Policy Institute (MPI) is a think tank that is devoted to engaging in research that covers a wide range of topics related to immigration. Founded in 2001, "The Migration Policy Institute is an independent, nonpartisan think tank that seeks to improve immigration and integration policies through authoritative research and analysis, opportunities for learning and dialogue, and the development of new ideas to address complex policy questions" (Migration Policy Institute 2025b).

MPI seeks to harness the power of data to shed light on the ways migration shapes humanity and also use data to create policies that promote the successful integration of immigrants in communities throughout the world. With offices in the United States and in Brussels, Belgium, MPI examines the effects of migration from a global lens and seeks to enhance the capacity of immigrants and communities to facilitate integration. Recognizing the complexities of immigration, MPI is organized around three "program areas": the US

Immigration Policy Program, the National Center on Immigrant Integration Policy, and the International Program.

The US Immigration Policy Program at MPI examines and analyzes policies that shape a wide array of life experiences related to immigration in the United States. The program accomplishes this by applying a wide lens to policies, accounting for economic and political domains, and considering the effects of policies at the local, state, and federal levels. Some of the projects under this program include basic demographic data that documents the number of different types of immigrants in the United States, as well as the number of arrivals at US borders and through different visa programs. By examining the various contexts of immigration in the United States, the US Immigration Policy Program at MPI seeks to develop knowledge that will promote policies that aim to advance the well-being of citizens and immigrants throughout the country.

The National Center on Immigrant Integration Policy at MPI focuses on building knowledge that advances an understanding of how immigrant integration occurs throughout the United States. Furthermore, the center is described as "a crossroads for elected officials, grassroots and nonprofit leaders, educators, journalists, researchers, local service providers, state and local agency managers, and others who seek to understand and respond to the challenges and opportunities today's high rates of immigration create in local communities" (Migration Policy Institute 2025c). MPI started this center to highlight issues related to immigrant integration that have historically been overlooked, such as economic and education issues. In addition, the center strives to provide balanced and nuanced analysis of complex policies that shape integration at the local, state, and federal levels.

The International Program at MPI seeks to shape thinking related to global migration patterns and trends. The International Program pursues this goal in a variety of ways, including with policy analysis. In addition, the International Program at MPI consults with the European Union and the United Nations on ways to approach global migration that respects the rights and well-being of individuals and also enhances the capacity of resettlement nations. This work is organized in three different categories: "research and analysis, policy dialogue, and direct consultations with governments and government institutions" (Migration Policy Institute 2025a). These three categories further help organize five "pillars of work."

The first pillar of work of the International Program at MPI focuses on strengthening humanitarian protections for individuals experiencing forced migration. Second, MPI explores labor policies that respond to changing economic conditions associated with migration. Third, MPI examines how border policies changed during the Covid-19 pandemic and beyond the pandemic. Fourth, MPI explores how resettlement countries can promote cohesion as part of immigrant integration. Finally, MPI seeks to build resilience for individuals and communities who experience climate change and prevent conditions that lead to forced migration.

As one of the major nonpartisan and nonprofit policy organizations based in the United States, MPI strives to use knowledge and data to support individuals experiencing migration, enhance the capacity of states and governments that support immigrants, and reimagine ways for immigrants to thrive in the middle of global migration. As war, deep poverty, political instability, and climate change influence migration patterns, MPI continues to build the knowledge base that policymakers and government officials use to support people on the move.

Morrison Child and Family Services

Morrison Child and Family Services is a nonprofit organization based in Portland, Oregon, that provides behavioral health services for children and families. The organization's website explains that: "As a leader in Behavioral Healthcare in Oregon we believe it is our responsibility to meet the needs of as many children and families as possible. We are committed to providing services that are high-quality and effective and reflect the ever-evolving landscape of trauma-informed care. We actively promote environments of care, healing, and recovery" (Morrison Child and Family Services 2025b).

The organization was established in 1947 by a group of physicians and citizens who were concerned about the mental health of children. The organization provided behavioral health services for 216 children in the first year of operation. Across the next twenty-five years, the organization expanded its services to also include children in the juvenile justice system. The organization was renamed the Carl Morrison Center for Youth & Family Services to honor the legacy of Dr. Carl Morrison, who helped establish the organization. By the 1970s, the Morrison Center served on average 1,200 children per year. Growth continued through the 1980s, with 1,400 children supported. In the 1990s, the Morrison Center collaborated and merged with other organizations, including the Rosemont School for Girls and Edgefield Children's Center. This led to continued growth and 2,400 children served each year. The 2000s is when the organization changed its name to Morrison Child and Family Services. Additional programs were implemented across a variety of locations, including the Parent Mentor Program. During this time, the organization provided services for an average of 4,900 children per year. The organization started the Immigrant Youth Services Division in the 2010s and expanded beyond Oregon to Washington State in the 2020s. At this time, the organization provided services for more than 7,000 children per year.

Morrison Child and Family Services provides both Home Studies and Post-Release Services in their Immigrant Youth Services Division. These services are provided in three different locations: Portland, Oregon; Salem, Oregon; and Federal Way, Washington. In 2024, Morrison Child and Family Services provided services for 2,008 youth in their Immigrant Youth Services Division. These youth migrated from twenty-one different countries, and 89 percent of all youth migrated from El Salvador, Guatemala, Honduras, or Mexico. Data indicates that 92 percent of youth are placed with immediate or extended family members, and placements are in thirty-six different states. Most youth (55 percent) are between thirteen and seventeen years old (Morrison Child and Family Services 2025a).

Office of Refugee Resettlement

The Office of Refugee Resettlement (ORR) is an organization within the Administration for Children and Families (ACF), which is part of the US Department of Health and Human Services (DHHS). DHHS is one of the largest federal agencies, responsible for ensuring the health and well-being of individuals throughout the United States. During the 1970s, the US government experienced challenges with resettling thousands of Vietnamese refugees after the end of the Vietnam War in April 1975. In response to these challenges, the US Congress passed the Refugee Act in 1980. The Refugee Act of 1980 provided a legal framework for establishing ORR. Since 1980, ORR has partnered with state governments and nonprofit organizations to allocate resources and oversee services for various immigrant groups, including refugees and unaccompanied children.

The mission of ORR is "to promote the health, well-being, and stability of refugees, unaccompanied alien children, and other eligible individuals and families, through culturally responsive, trauma-informed, and strengths-based services" (Office of Refugee Resettlement 2024). ORR was originally organized to provide services for refugees, unaccompanied refugee minors, and Cuban and Haitian entrants, as reflected in the Refugee Act of 1980. However, ORR's scope of mission has expanded several times throughout its history, including asylees, survivors of torture, and victims of trafficking. Most recently, ORR's mission expanded in 2003 to include services for unaccompanied children. ORR services are delivered by two separate bureaus, the Unaccompanied Alien Children Bureau (i.e., Unaccompanied Children Bureau) and the Refugee Program Bureau.

The Unaccompanied Children Bureau was established on March 1, 2003. This bureau was established as part of the Homeland Security Act of 2002. More specifically, Section 462 of the Homeland Security Act transferred responsibility for caring for the health and well-being of unaccompanied children from the Commissioner of the Immigration and Naturalization Service to the Director of ORR. Because of this change, ORR recognized the need for a separate bureau to ensure the delivery of services for unaccompanied children who arrived in the United States. The service delivery by the Unaccompanied Children Bureau is informed by different laws and policies, including the Flores Settlement Agreement in 1997, the Trafficking Victims Protection Act of 2000 and its reauthorization acts, and the William Wilberforce Trafficking Victims Protection Reauthorization Act (TVPRA) of 2005 and 2008. Across these time frames, the Unaccompanied Children Bureau has adapted to changing political contexts at the federal level to strive for meeting the needs of unaccompanied children who arrive in the United States.

ORR is responsible for providing direct care to unaccompanied children who arrive in the United States, as well as coordinating the safe transfer of unaccompanied children to sponsors. This requires coordination with other government agencies, as well as collaboration with nonprofit organizations throughout the country. Unaccompanied children are typically transferred to ORR care after apprehension at the US border; however, ORR also receives referrals for children who are identified by immigration authorities after arriving in a community in the United States. ORR helps unaccompanied children connect with their sponsors as soon as they arrive at ORR care. While waiting for reunification, unaccompanied children remain in ORR custody, receiving services at one of the 240 facilities and programs located in twenty-seven states funded by ORR (Office of Refugee Resettlement 2005).

The Unaccompanied Children Bureau has an array of responsibilities related to the care of unaccompanied children. First, the bureau is responsible for ensuring unaccompanied children are placed in a safe and appropriate shelter setting. Unaccompanied children's best interests are always prioritized throughout their custody with ORR. The bureau is responsible for conducting home studies when indicated, as well as providing post-release services for eligible children. The bureau is responsible for managing facilities and staff who provide care for unaccompanied children. This requires periodic oversight visits to ensure all programs and facilities are in compliance with ORR regulations. The bureau provides training for program staff and also collects demographic data on unaccompanied children in ORR custody. The bureau coordinates with the US Department of Justice to ensure sponsors receive appropriate training prior to reunification. The bureau also ensures that unaccompanied children receive *pro bono* legal representation prior to reunification with their sponsor, as they will continue navigating immigration court after they leave ORR custody (Office of Refugee Resettlement 2005).

Refugee and Immigrant Center for Education and Legal Services

The Refugee and Immigrant Center for Education and Legal Services (RAICES) is a nonprofit organization that provides legal services for immigrants in the United States. Established in 1986, RAICES uses legal services and advocacy to help immigrants and families remain together and in the United States. RAICES recognizes the adversarial barriers inherent in the US immigration system and seeks to accompany individuals and families struggling with navigating the court system that is "a maze that was created to keep them out" (Refugee and Immigrant Center for Education and Legal Services [RAICES] 2025c). RAICES explains: "As the largest immigration legal services provider in Texas, RAICES believes in a country where everyone has access to legal and social services—no matter where you come from" (RAICES 2025a).

The history of RAICES includes many responses to changing contexts in the US immigration system. The organization was established in Texas in 1986 to help Central American refugees navigate immigration court. In 1990, RAICES opened its first office in San Antonio, Texas, and in 1993, it was accredited as a legal services agency by the US Department of Justice. Much of RAICES's history corresponds with major changes to US immigration law and policy, including the Illegal Immigration Reform and Immigrant Responsibility Act of 1996, which expanded immigrant detention, and the Flores Settlement Agreement of 1993, which established guidelines for detaining and releasing immigrant children (RAICES 2025b).

In 2009, RAICES established Unaccompanied Children's Services, which were implemented in over twelve government shelters in Texas. As part of this program, RAICES community advocates provide Know Your Rights Presentations for unaccompanied children who are detained in shelters (RAICES 2025a).

United States Conference of Catholic Bishops

The United States Conference of Catholic Bishops (USCCB) is a Catholic organization that seeks to promote the common good of humanity through advocacy, evangelization, and social services for vulnerable people in the United States and around the world. The mission of USCCB is "to support the ministry of bishops with an emphasis on evangelization, by which the bishops exercise in a communal and collegial manner certain pastoral functions entrusted to them by the Lord Jesus of sanctifying, teaching, and governing" (United States Conference of Catholic Bishops [USCCB] 2025a). Furthermore, USCCB serves multiple purposes, among them: "to unify, coordinate, encourage, promote and carry on Catholic activities in the United States; to organize and conduct religious, charitable and social welfare work at home and abroad; to aid in education; to care for immigrants; and generally to enter into and promote by education, publication and direction the objects of its being" (USCCB 2025a). The mission of USCCB, and the various purposes the organization serves, has evolved since its founding in 1917.

In 1917, in the middle of global turmoil caused by the First World War, bishops throughout the United States formed an organization called the National Catholic War Council (NCWC), which aimed to provide spiritual care for people directly and indirectly impacted by the First World War. The Council later formed the National Catholic Welfare Council in 1919, which focused on promoting social justice and peace. The organization's name underwent further revision in 1922, when it changed to the National Catholic Welfare Conference. The work of promoting peace and social justice continued until 1966, when two new organizations were formed: the National Conference of Catholic Bishops (NCCB) and the United States Catholic Conference (USCC). Advocacy and support for peace and social justice continued until 2001, when the organizations merged to form the USCCB. Among the many different issues USCCB focuses on is immigration, specifically care for unaccompanied children (USCCB 2025a).

The mission of the USCCB committee on migration is to create "a world where immigrants, refugees, migrants, and people on the move are treated with dignity, respect, welcome and belonging" (USCCB 2025e). Furthermore, USCCB's department of Migration and Refugee Services "serves as a leader in the protection of unaccompanied, refugee, and immigrant children by providing family reunification and foster care services" (USCCB 2025c). The USCCB Department of Migration and Refugee Services operates three different programs: the family reunification program, foster care for unaccompanied children, and Bridging Refugee Youth and Children's Services.

The family reunification program includes direct social services for unaccompanied children in the United States who are in immigration proceedings, meaning they do not have permanent legal status to remain in the United States. The family reunification program offers two distinct services for unaccompanied children: home study services and post-release services. Home study services are community-based and involve case workers visiting an unaccompanied child's home one to four times to assess strengths, potential risk factors in the home, provide sponsors with information on how to care for the mental health needs of the unaccompanied child, and collaborate with the family to build a plan for integration in the community. Post-release services, unlike home visits, offer extended community-based supports that help unaccompanied children navigate different parts of their environment, including support with enrolling in school, accessing legal services, and accessing health and mental health services (USCCB 2025d).

US Committee for Refugees and Immigrants

The US Committee for Refugees and Immigrants (USCRI) is an organization that provides an array of services for immigrants and newcomers in the United States. Formed in 1911, USCRI provides health care, legal services, and social services for refugees and immigrants, with the mission of addressing their needs and advocating for their rights. The mission of USCRI is "to protect the rights and address the needs of persons in forced or voluntary migration worldwide and support their transition to a dignified life" (US Committee for Refugees and Immigrants [USCRI] 2024d).

USCRI was formed at a time in the United States when three out of four people in New York City were either immigrants or first-generation Americans. In 1911, a young social worker named Edith Terry Bremmer established the

International Institute in New York City to support immigrant girls and women. The International Institute later changed to the Foreign Language Information Service, which provided information to legal service providers on changes to immigration laws. This was a timely endeavor, given the number of changes to immigration law happening at this time in the United States. The Foreign Language Information Service changed to the Common Council for American Unity in 1934. The Common Council for American Unity was later combined with the American Federation of International Institutes and became known as the American Council for Nationalities Services. This newly formed organization maintained a focus on supporting immigrants and newcomers to the United States. The American Council for Nationalities Services evolved into the Immigration and Refugee Services of America in 2004 and changed the name of the organization in 2011 to the US Committee for Refugees and Immigrants. Throughout the name changes and mergers with other organizations, one consistent part of the evolution across the twentieth century was a steadfast commitment to vulnerable people who experience forced displacement, including refugees (USCRI 2024c).

Services for unaccompanied children were first provided by USCRI in 2005. Similar to other organizations based in the United States (e.g., United States Conference of Catholic Bishops, International Rescue Committee), these services include home studies and post-release services for unaccompanied children who are placed with sponsors. A unique part of USCRI is the Unaccompanied Children Resource Center, which is "an online platform, operated by the US Committee for Refugees and Immigrants (USCRI), that offers information and resources to unaccompanied children, their families, and the providers who work with them" (USCRI 2024a). The Resource Center seeks to provide information that can help unaccompanied children adjust to their new communities. USCRI also provides trainings and online education opportunities to strengthen the capacity of service providers. Another unique part of USCRI is the Relationships, Education, Advancement, and Development for Youth for Life program (READY4Life).

READY4Life "aims to promote positive socioemotional development and healthy relationships amongst immigrant and refugee youth through three main components: 1. skills-based workshops, 2. case management, and 3. research" (USCRI 2024a). The READY4Life program serves immigrant and refugee youth, including unaccompanied children, who are between fourteen and twenty-four years old. Based on social and emotional learning values, the program covers twelve hours of content, based on "self-awareness, self-management, responsible decision-making, healthy relationships, and social awareness" (USCRI 2024a).

US Customs and Border Protection

Across the US southern border, specially trained law enforcement officials patrol border regions and monitor official ports of entry. These individuals are part of the US Customs and Border Protection (CBP), a law enforcement agency that is focused on preventing threats from entering the United States while also helping facilitate the safe and legal travel of individuals and trade. The mission of the CBP is "Protect the American people, safeguard our borders, and enhance the nation's economic prosperity" (US Customs and Border Protection 2024a). The mission of CBP frames additional priorities that help direct the activities and policies of the agency. These priorities include countering terrorism, combatting transnational crime, securing US borders, facilitating lawful trade, and facilitating lawful international travel arriving in or departing from the United States.

CBP has an extensive history. Starting in 1789, the agency was originally called the US Customs Service. Over decades, the agency introduced new officials who were tasked with protecting US borders, including Immigration Inspectors in 1891 and Agriculture Inspectors in 1912. Border Patrol Agents were first established as part of CBP in 1924. In 2006, CBP responded to a growing concern regarding protecting US borders from the air and sea by establishing the Office of Air and Marine. Also in 2006, CBP conducted a reorganization to consolidate all functions related to trade with the Office of International Trade (US Customs and Border Protection 2024b).

CBP agents are responsible for the initial apprehension and screening of unaccompanied children who arrive at the US border, either at or between official ports of entry. Research has revealed gaps in training for CBP officers who directly engage with unaccompanied children at the US border. According to research from the Appleseed Network, for example, CBP officers lack training on trauma-informed practices for meeting the unique needs of children who arrive at the border without caregivers or guardians. Furthermore, during the apprehension of unaccompanied children at the US southern border, it can be exceedingly difficult to evaluate the unique needs of unaccompanied children. After apprehension by CBP officers, unaccompanied children are transferred to temporary facilities for initial processing before transferring to the Office of Refugee Resettlement. Research from the Appleseed Network further explains that "CBP facilities will never be an appropriate environment for children—as CBP is a law enforcement agency and its mission is misaligned with the goal of protecting children" (Appleseed 2024, 66).

Young Center for Immigrant Children's Rights

The Young Center for Immigrant Children's Rights (Young Center) is a nonprofit organization based in Chicago, Illinois, that provides legal services for immigrant children and advocates for immigrant children's best interests. "The Young Center for Immigrant Children's Rights protects and advances the rights and best interests of immigrant children according to the Convention on the Rights of the Child and state and federal law" (Young Center 2025a). The Young Center is guided by a set of core values, including child-centeredness, courage, accompaniment, community, and equality and justice. The organization was established in 2004 in Chicago after providing legal services for a single unaccompanied child. Since then, the organization has grown, representing immigrant children in court, ensuring they remain out of government detention, and advocating for families to remain together. In 2009, the organization opened an office on the US-Mexico border in Harlingen, Texas. The US Congress amended a law in 2013 that expanded the Child Advocate Program for immigrant children in the United States, leading to the Young Center opening offices across the country in Houston, San Antonio, Phoenix, Los Angeles, Washington, DC, and New York (Young Center 2025c).

Throughout the United States, immigrant children, including unaccompanied children, struggle to navigate complex legal systems that can be adversarial and overlook the best interests of children. This can lead to child protection concerns, especially for vulnerable immigrants such as unaccompanied children. To address these concerns, the Young Center advocates for children's own wishes, as well as their best interests. The organization uses the legal system to advocate for children remaining with their families and out of government detention facilities. The Young Center provides legal services to ensure that all immigrant children have legal representation in court. The organization accomplishes these goals by providing direct services, as well as by engaging with community stakeholders and engaging with policymakers to advocate for systemic change (Young Center 2025d).

Among the direct services provided by the Young Center is the Child Advocate Program. This is an innovative and pathbreaking service, as "The Young Center has developed the only program in the nation that provides independent Child Advocates to unaccompanied immigrant children in government custody, whose job it is to advocate for the children's rights and best interests" (Young Center 2025b). Child advocates ensure unaccompanied children have access to legal services when they are in custody and separated from family or sponsors, as well as when unaccompanied children are released and still face potential deportation. Adults can volunteer to serve as a child advocate, which entails spending time with children and advocating for their best interests and rights when they are in detention as well as in court proceedings.

Child Advocates identify and advocate for children's best interests. The Young Center uses a paradigm approach to identify a child's best interests by accounting for a wide array of a child's life, as well as the Convention on the Rights of the Child. Specifically, the Young Center accounts for "the child's rights to health, family integrity, liberty, development, and identity" when determining their best interests (Young Center 2025b).

People

David Miliband (1965–)

David Miliband is the President and CEO of the International Rescue Committee (IRC), where he provides strategic and visionary leadership for the organization, which includes overseeing the emergency response programs around the world and the refugee resettlement programs in the United States and Europe. Among these services are post-release services for unaccompanied children. Prior to joining IRC, Miliband worked as a politician in the UK. Among his positions, Miliband served as the 74th Secretary of State for Foreign and Commonwealth Affairs from 2007 to 2010.

Growing up, Miliband's views were in part shaped by his parents' experiences. His father was a sociologist who specialized in Marxism, and his mother was a history teacher who later was a homemaker. His parents' own childhoods also deeply shaped Miliband's pursuit of politics and his later interest in serving vulnerable individuals around the world. Miliband's father escaped Nazi persecution when the Germans invaded Belgium in 1940. His mother arrived in the UK from Poland in 1946.

After studying politics at Oxford University and later at the Massachusetts Institute of Technology for his master's degree, Miliband entered politics. At twenty-nine years old, he served as an advisor for Prime Minister Tony Blair. His political career advanced when he served as Secretary of State from 2007 to 2010; however, he lost an election to lead the Labour Party to his brother in 2010. In 2013, Miliband joined IRC as president and CEO.

Miliband has both family experience and professional experience with people experiencing migration throughout the world. As IRC seeks to advance the health and well-being of immigrants and refugees around the world, including unaccompanied children, Miliband can use his own political acumen to advance the mission of the organization and position it for future success. The unique combination of his family background that includes parents who were refugees, and professional experience in political positions, affords Miliband a unique combination that informs his approach to leadership.

Eskinder Negash (1956–)

Eskinder Negash is the president and CEO of the US Committee for Refugees and Immigrants (USCRI). Throughout his nearly forty-year career working with immigrants and refugees, Negash has held positions in both governmental and nongovernmental agencies. Negash provides strategic leadership for USCRI to ensure services are delivered to a wide array of immigrants and refugees from around the world.

Prior to joining USCRI, Negash was the director of the Office of Refugee Resettlement (ORR) from 2009 to 2015. During this time, Negash was responsible for managing a budget over 1.5 billion dollars and coordinating services for refugees, victims of human trafficking, and unaccompanied children. Throughout his time at ORR, Negash oversaw the resettlement of over 850,000 people, including nearly 116,000 unaccompanied children.

Before joining ORR, Negash was vice president and Chief Administrative Officer at USCRI for seven years. Prior to that, Negash served in executive leadership at the International Institute of Los Angeles for fifteen years. Along with formal leadership positions, Negash has been part of various nonprofit boards in California, including the Joint Voluntary Agencies Committee of California. Throughout his career, Negash has strived to strengthen partnerships between government and nongovernmental organizations to ensure robust supports are provided for individuals experiencing migration. His work has been recognized by different organizations, including receiving the "Outstanding American by Choice" award from the US Citizenship and Immigration Services in the Department of Homeland Security.

Krish O'Mara Vignarajah (1979–)

Krish O'Mara Vignarajah is president and CEO of Global Refuge. O'Mara Vignarajah is a public servant who has served the United States in a variety of roles across her career. She has been at Global Refuge since 2019. In this role, she provides leadership and advocates for a wide range of programs, including services for unaccompanied children. O'Mara Vignarajah earned a bachelor's degree in Molecular, Cellular, and Developmental Biology from Yale, an M. Phil. degree in International Relations from the University of Oxford, and a JD from Yale Law School.

Prior to Global Refuge, O'Mara Vignarajah worked as director of policy development for First Lady Michelle Obama. In this position, O'Mara Vignarajah coordinated policy development across USAID, the US Department of Health and Human Services, and the US Department of Defense. O'Mara Vignarajah also worked at the law firm Jenner and Block and clerked for Chief Judge Michael Boudin on the US Court of Appeals for the First Circuit.

Richard Santos

Richard "Rick" Santos is the president and CEO of Church World Service. Santos has held this role since January 2021. In this role, Santos provides strategic leadership to enhance service delivery across all Church World Service programs, including programs that support unaccompanied children. Prior to joining Church World Service, Santos served as president and CEO of IMA World Health, which is an organization focused on public health initiatives.

Santos's work emphasizes collaboration across programs and between government and nonprofit organizations, and across regions. He has more than a decade of work experience in Asia, and holds a bachelor's degree in political science from the George Washington University and a Master of Business Administration degree from the Johns Hopkins University Carey School of Business.

Mark J. Seitz (1954–)

Most Reverend Mark J. Seitz, Bishop of El Paso, is Chairman of the Committee on Migration, US Conference of Catholic Bishops (USCCB). In this role, Bishop Seitz provides leadership that informs the strategic direction of the USCCB Committee on Migration. Bishop Seitz has been Bishop of El Paso since 2013.

Born in 1954 in Milwaukee, Wisconsin, Bishop Seitz is the oldest of ten children. He earned a BA in Philosophy in 1976, a Master of Divinity in 1980, and a Master of Arts in Theology in 1982, all from the University of Dallas.

Bishop Seitz was ordained to the Transitional Diaconate on April 7, 1979, and to the priesthood on May 17, 1980. Bishop Seitz has held a range appointments and assignments across his pastoral career, including Auxiliary Bishop of the Diocese of Dallas from 2010 to 2013, and pastor at various parishes, including All Saints and St. Rita in Dallas, Texas, and St. Joseph Catholic Church in Waxahachie, Texas.

Throughout his pastoral career, Bishop Seitz has been an outspoken advocate for migrants arriving in the United States. In his writing, Bishop Seitz has spoken against various federal policies addressing issues at the US border. In response to Executive Actions by President Trump's administration, Bishop Seitz wrote the following, as part of a statement released on January 22, 2025:

> The Catholic Church is committed to defending the sanctity of every human life and the God-given dignity of each person, regardless of nationality or immigration status. Church teaching recognizes a country's right and responsibility to promote public order, safety, and security through well-regulated borders and just limits on immigration. However, as shepherds, we cannot abide injustice, and we stress that national self-interest does not justify policies with consequences that are contrary to the moral law. The use of sweeping generalizations to denigrate any group, such as describing all undocumented immigrants as "criminals" or "invaders," to deprive them of protection under the law, is an affront to God, who has created each of us in his own image. (USCCB 2025b)

In addition to writing, Bishop Seitz has helped organize events to advocate for vulnerable immigrants. For example, he published an open letter on March 10, 2025, titled "An Open Letter to the Borderlands Community in El Paso." In this letter, Bishop Seitz wrote: "The heart wrenching pain coursing through our community is real. Indiscriminate immigration enforcement, the denial of due process and the pulling apart of families strike at our community and are grave attacks on human dignity. The threat of mass deportations is untenable and immoral and demands a credible response" (Seitz 2025). In this letter, Bishop Seitz also invited residents of El Paso to attend a march and vigil to pray for vulnerable migrants and to stand in solidarity with community members at risk of immigration enforcement. Throughout his writing and organizing, Bishop Seitz's pastoral ministry advocates for immigrants, promotes just border policies, and seeks to accompany individuals who face forced migration and exclusion. Much of this ministry is based on the broader efforts of the US Conference of Catholic Bishops.

Andrew Selee (1968–)

Andrew Selee is President of the Migration Policy Institute (MPI) and has been in the role since 2017. Andrew earned a bachelor's degree from Washington University in St. Louis, a Master of Arts degree in Latin American Studies from the University of California, San Diego, and a PhD in policy studies from the University of Maryland. Dr. Selee is a scholar whose career has focused on global migration, specifically in the United States, Latin America, and Caribbean. He has published several books and articles on these topics and has also taught as an adjunct instructor at Georgetown University, Johns Hopkins University, and George Washington University. Before joining MPI, Dr. Selee worked at the Woodrow Wilson Center and was a founder of the Center's Mexico Institute.

Throughout his career, Dr. Selee's scholarship has examined a variety of immigration policies, including in his most recent book *Vanishing Frontiers: The Forces Driving Mexico and the United States Together*. As a leader, Dr. Selee has provided strategic vision to ensure MPI engages in policy analysis that builds collaboration across communities and governments and promotes policy solutions to complex challenges in immigration systems. This includes focus on the policies that relate to the experiences of unaccompanied children who migrate to the United States.

Wendy Young

Wendy Young is President of Kids in Need of Defense (KIND). KIND is an organization that provides legal services for vulnerable immigrants, including unaccompanied children who need representation while navigating immigration court. Along with legal services, KIND also advocates for policy reform to promote a just legal system that recognizes children's rights and advances their health and well-being.

Young has been at KIND since 2009 and has a wide range of legal experience that informs her leadership. Prior to working at KIND, Young worked in government affairs as Chief Counsel on Immigration Policy in the Senate Judiciary Subcommittee on Immigration, Border Security, and Refugees for

Senator Edward Kennedy. In addition, she has work experience at other nonprofits that work with immigrants, including United Nations High Commissioner for Refugees and the US Conference of Catholic Bishops. Young earned a bachelor's degree from Williams College and a law and master's degree in international relations from American University in Washington, DC.

Further Reading

Appleseed. 2024. "Appleseed Mexico Report 2023: Children at the Border." https://www.texasappleseed.org/sites/default/files/2024-07/childrenattheborder-final-english-update-042024.pdf

Bethany Christian Services. 2025a. "Bethany's Beginnings." https://bethany.org/about-us/our-history

Bethany Christian Services. 2025b. "Family Changes Everything." https://bethany.org/about-us

Bethany Christian Services. 2025c. "Home Study and Post-release Services for Unaccompanied Children." https://bethany.org/service/home-study-and-post-release-services

Catholic Diocese of El Paso. 2025. "Most Reverend Mark J. Seitz, D.D. Sixth Bishop of El Paso." https://www.elpasodiocese.org/bishop-seitz.html

Center for Immigration and Child Welfare. n.d. "Research Statement." https://cimmcw.org/research-statement-affiliates/

Church World Service. n.d.a. "About CWS." https://cwsglobal.org/mission-vision-values/

Church World Service. n.d.b. "Children's Services." https://cwsglobal.org/our-work/united-states/children-services/

Church World Service. n.d.c. "CWS: A Brief History." https://cwsglobal.org/about/history/

Church World Service. n.d.d. "Rick Santos, President and CEO." https://cwsglobal.org/president-and-ceo/

Dorcas International Institute of Rhode Island (DIIRI). 2025a. "About Us." https://www.diiri.org/about-us/#history

Dorcas International Institute of Rhode Island (DIIRI). 2025b. "Unaccompanied Youth." https://www.diiri.org/what-we-do/unaccompanied-minors/

Endeavors. 2025a. "About Us." https://endeavors.org/about-us/

Endeavors. 2025b. "Migrant Children's Services." https://endeavors.org/test/

Endeavors. 2025c. "Our Story." https://endeavors.org/history/

Global Refugee. 2025a. "Meet Our President." https://www.globalrefuge.org/about-krish/

Global Refuge. 2025b. "Our History." https://www.globalrefuge.org/who-we-are/history/
Heartland Human Care Services. 2024a. "Our History." https://heartlandhumancareservices.org/about/history/
Heartland Human Care Services. 2024b. "Our Mission." https://heartlandhumancareservices.org/our-mission/
International Rescue Committee. 2025a. "Bio: IRC President and CEO David Miliband." https://www.rescue.org/page/bio-irc-president-and-ceo-david-miliband
International Rescue Committee. 2025b. "What We Do." https://www.rescue.org/what-we-do#main-content
Kids in Need of Defense (KIND). 2025a. "Contact Us." https://supportkind.org/who-we-are/contact-us/
Kids in Need of Defense (KIND). 2025b. "Legal Protection." https://supportkind.org/what-we-do/legal-services/
Kids in Need of Defense (KIND). 2025c. "Our Leadership." https://supportkind.org/who-we-are/our-people/leadership/
Kids in Need of Defense (KIND). 2025d. "Vision and Mission." https://supportkind.org/who-we-are/mission-vision/
Kino Border Initiative. 2023a. "Mission and Vision." https://www.kinoborderinitiative.org/mission-and-values/
Kino Border Initiative. 2023b. "What We Do." https://www.kinoborderinitiative.org/what-we-do/
Migration Policy Institute. 2025a. "About the International Program." https://www.migrationpolicy.org/programs/international-migration/about-international-program
Migration Policy Institute. 2025b. "About the Migration Policy Institute." https://www.migrationpolicy.org/about/about-migration-policy-institute
Migration Policy Institute. 2025c. "About the National Center on Immigrant Integration Policy." https://www.migrationpolicy.org/programs/national-center-immigrant-integration-policy/about-nciip
Migration Policy Institute. 2025d. "Experts & Staff, Andrew Selee." https://www.migrationpolicy.org/about/staff/andrew-selee
Morrison Child and Family Services. 2025a. "Home Study and Post Release Services." https://morrisonkids.org/what-we-do/home-study-and-post-release-services/
Morrison Child and Family Services. 2025b. "How We Work." https://morrisonkids.org/how-we-work/
Office of Refugee Resettlement. 2005. "Unaccompanied Alien Children Bureau Fact Sheet." https://acf.gov/orr/fact-sheet/programs/uc/fact-sheet
Office of Refugee Resettlement. 2024. "What We Do." https://www.acf.hhs.gov/orr/about/what-we-do
Refugee and Immigrant Center for Education and Legal Services (RAICES). 2025a. "Legal Services." https://raicestexas.org/legal

Refugee and Immigrant Center for Education and Legal Services (RAICES). 2025b. "Our History." https://raicestexas.org/history
Refugee and Immigrant Center for Education and Legal Services (RAICES). 2025c. "Rooted in Community." https://raicestexas.org/about
Seitz, Mark J. 2025. "An Open Letter to the Borderlands Community in El Paso." Catholic Diocese of El Paso. https://www.elpasodiocese.org/open-letter-from-bp-seitz.html
United States Conference of Catholic Bishops (USCCB). 2025a. "About USCCB." https://www.usccb.org/about
United States Conference of Catholic Bishops (USCCB). 2025b. "Executive Actions Will Subject Vulnerable Families and Children to Grave Danger, Says Bishop Seitz." https://www.usccb.org/news/2025/executive-actions-will-subject-vulnerable-families-and-children-grave-danger-says-bishop
United States Conference of Catholic Bishops (USCCB). 2025c. "Migration: Children and Migration." https://www.usccb.org/committees/migration/children-and-migration
United States Conference of Catholic Bishops (USCCB). 2025d. "Migration: Family Reunification Program." https://www.usccb.org/committees/migration/family-reunification-program
United States Conference of Catholic Bishops (USCCB). 2025e. "USCCB Committees: Migration." https://www.usccb.org/committees/migration
US Committee for Refugees and Immigrants (USCRI). 2024a. "Children's Services." https://refugees.org/childrens-services/
US Committee for Refugees and Immigrants (USCRI). 2024b. "Eskinder Negash." https://refugees.org/leaderships/eskinder-negash/
US Committee for Refugees and Immigrants (USCRI). 2024c. "100 Years of USCRI." https://refugees.org/history/
US Committee for Refugees and Immigrants (USCRI). 2024d. "Who We Are." https://refugees.org/who-we-are/
US Customs and Border Protection. 2024a. "About CBP." https://www.cbp.gov/about
US Customs and Border Protection. 2024b. "CBP History through the Years." https://www.cbp.gov/about/history
The Young Center for Immigrant Children's Rights. 2025a. "About the Young Center." https://www.theyoungcenter.org/about/mission-and-values/
The Young Center for Immigrant Children's Rights. 2025b. "Direct Services." https://www.theyoungcenter.org/what-we-do/direct-servcices/
The Young Center for Immigrant Children's Rights. 2025c. "Our History." https://www.theyoungcenter.org/about/our-history/
The Young Center for Immigrant Children's Rights. 2025d. "What We Do." https://www.theyoungcenter.org/what-we-do/

5

Documents

In 2023, the US Senate Committee on the Judiciary held a full committee hearing titled "Ensuring the Safety and Well-Being of Unaccompanied Children." The hearing was held in two parts, on June 14, 2023, and October 25, 2023, and was intended to closely examine concerns related to the safety and well-being of unaccompanied children, with special focus on the risk of human trafficking for unaccompanied children who are placed with sponsors in the United States. At the time of the hearing, the Democratic Party held control of the US Senate. Along with statements from both Democratic and Republican members of the committee, the committee heard prepared statements from several expert witnesses, as well as officials from the Office of Refugee Resettlement, the US Department of State, and the US Department of Homeland Security. This chapter includes eight of these statements: two from sitting senators on the committee, three from expert witnesses, and three from officials from federal agencies. Together, the statements communicate the many considerations and viewpoints related to the topic of unaccompanied children and incorporate diverse political and professional perspectives. Before each statement is a brief introduction that highlights the main topics of the statement and the significance of the statement.

Part of a group of ninety-two Guatemalan migrant minors arrive back in their country after being stopped at the border between Mexico and the United States and deported, February 7, 2023. Citing a drastic increase in arrivals of unaccompanied children to the US border, some conservatives advocate for deporting unaccompanied children back to their country of origin. (Johan Ordonez/AFP via Getty Images)

Opening Statement of Hon. Richard J. Durbin, US Senator from Illinois (June 14, 2023)

The opening statement from Senator Richard Durbin provides a brief background into how the US Senate has tried to address the topic of unaccompanied children in the United States. Senator Durbin also argues that previous bipartisan support for legislation has faded, and now the topic of unaccompanied children, like many other immigration-related topics, is a partisan issue. Senator Durbin centers the role of the Trafficking Victims Protection Reauthorization Act of 2008 and the importance of strengthening, rather than weakening, this legislation. Senator Durbin's concern is that Republican politicians will seek to increase the ways in which unaccompanied children can be deported from the United States, rather than supported in their resettlement communities.

Chair DURBIN. This hearing of the Senate Judiciary Committee will come to order. I want to start with a little history. Back in 2002, over 20 years ago, this Committee held a hearing on bipartisan legislation entitled the Unaccompanied Alien Children Protection Act. It was introduced by our colleague, Senator Dianne Feinstein, along with Republican Senator from Kansas Sam Brownback. The bill was a response to a bipartisan concern that unaccompanied children seeking safe haven in the United States were being deported back to countries where they were not safe and where they might be persecuted.

Six years of debate followed on this issue and in 2008, listen carefully, the Senate unanimously passed the Trafficking Victims Protection Reauthorization Act, TVPRA. That bill included the Unaccompanied Alien Child Protection Act. It was signed into law, listen again, by President George W. Bush. Sadly, since then, the immigration debate has devolved into a much more partisan issue, and often then vulnerable children are the victims of that political battle. During the Obama administration, some Republicans falsely claimed that the DACA program, which the President initiated at my urging to protect Dreamers from deportation was the reason that unaccompanied children were fleeing to our border.

I've heard that argument made by one Senator on the floor repeatedly. When the Trump administration began and unaccompanied children were still coming, some Republicans claimed the TVPRA of 2008 was really to blame. They're ignoring the obvious. The world was and still is in the middle of the worst refugee crisis in modern history. And we used to believe a bipartisan approach to this would have a moral and legal responsibility created to protect vulnerable children who are fleeing persecution. We've received about 10,000 or 12,000 migrant children in the City of Chicago sent to us from the Governor of Texas and other Republican leaders in States. I've made a point of trying to meet some of these people and understand what led them to this desperate situation.

It's heartbreaking. It was less than 2 weeks ago that I was at a Piotrowski Park shelter in the City of Chicago and met with 50 or 60 of these mothers and their kids. The kids are little kids who have made this death-defying journey to the United States. And you think to yourself, "Who in their right mind—what parent in their right mind would subject their kids to the danger of that journey? How desperate they would be to have that happen." You see it over and over again. They felt that they couldn't feed their children, or the children couldn't exist in a safe way in their countries any longer, and they were prepared to risk their lives and the lives of their children to make the journey.

This is an issue that should transcend politics. So I tried to be consistent in my oversight efforts, whether the President was Republican or Democrat. I vigorously opposed President Trump's inhumane family separation policy, and I immediately raised concerns following recent reports that unaccompanied children were being exploited. Ranking Member Graham and Immigration Subcommittee Ranking Member Cornyn, along with other Republican Members of the Committee, sent a letter asking me to hold this hearing. As I told them in response, I would accommodate this request because I was already working with Immigration Sub-committee Chair Padilla on today's hearing.

I also asked Senators Padilla, Graham, and Cornyn to join me in a document request to the Department of Health and Human Services to learn more about what went wrong and how to fix it. What we must not do is weaken the TVPRA and make it easier to deport unaccompanied children back into harm's way. Our laws require that these children are screened for human trafficking, housed in child-appropriate settings, reunified with any family in the United States while they await their immigration proceedings. But the tragedy is that these children are still at risk. Migrant children have been forced to work long hours in extremely dangerous conditions, from meatpacking plants and slaughterhouses, for example.

Well, many, many years ago when I was in college, I worked my way through college four straight summers in a slaughterhouse in East St. Louis, Illinois. I can tell you from my personal observation it is no place for a child. They could easily lose a limb or their life in this dangerous environment. Since 2018, our Nation has seen a nearly 70 percent increase in illegally employed children. Earlier this year, I demanded the Departments of Labor and Health and Human Services do more to protect these kids. Both have made some progress, but not enough. And let's not forget our responsibility on this side of the table. It's no secret that employers throughout our country are struggling to find workers.

Some States like Arkansas, actually loosen child labor laws in the hopes of addressing workforce needs. Let's consider another approach. Let's reform our immigration laws and allow adults to meet workforce needs instead of exploiting children fleeing abuse. I hope today's hearing will be an opportunity to revive the bipartisan spirit of many years ago and discuss how to protect unaccompanied children who are frightened and traumatized.

With that, I hand off to the Ranking Member, Senator Graham.

Source: US Senate Committee on the Judiciary. 2023. "Ensuring the Safety and Well-being of Unaccompanied Children." Part 1 of hearing, June 14, 2023. https://www.judiciary.senate.gov/ensuring-the-safety-and-well-being-of-unaccompanied-children

Opening Statement of Hon. Lindsey O. Graham, US Senator from South Carolina (June 14, 2023)

Senator Lindsey Graham's opening statement offers a conservative perspective of unaccompanied children in the United States. Senator Graham centers his statement on the increased arrivals of unaccompanied children to the US border, from 33,329 arrivals in 2020 to 152,057 arrivals in 2022. Senator Graham's statement focuses on an argument against policies from President Biden. More specifically, Senator Graham advocates for deporting unaccompanied children who arrive in the United States back to their country of origin. This argument appears to disregard the conditions of many countries that unaccompanied children migrate from, as well as the US government's responsibility of processing individuals who seek asylum, in accordance with international law and the concept of non-refoulement, or not deporting someone to conditions that place their lives at risk. In regard to policy changes, along with expanding pathways for deporting unaccompanied children, Senator Graham also advocates for changing the Flores Settlement Agreement, which he argues incentivizes human smuggling. Overall, Senator Graham expresses concern for unaccompanied children being victims of human trafficking. However, he seems to believe that the best way to prevent human smuggling of unaccompanied children is to not allow them in the United States at all, even if they are seeking to escape legitimate human rights abuses in their home countries.

Senator GRAHAM. Thank you, Mr. Chairman. I appreciate you having the hearing. I think this hearing will illustrate the differences between our side and yours about a problem we have in common. Nobody wants unaccompanied children to be abused, to be put in labor environments that are unhealthy. Bottom line is, the policies of this administration, Mr. Chairman, are not working. In FY 2020, there were 33,239 unaccompanied minor encounters at our border. In FY 2022, 2 years later, it's 152,057. There's been a 357 percent increase regarding unaccompanied minors at our border.

Have you ever asked, "What happened?" You should. We all want children to be well taken care of. But have you ever asked the question, "What is it in the last 2 years that's driven the numbers up 357 percent?" It's policy. The Biden administration has a policy that if you're an unaccompanied child not from Canada or Mexico, you will not be sent back to the country of origin. In FY 2022, the average age of an unaccompanied minor was around 14, 64 percent were boys.

The countries of origin: 47 percent from Honduras, 29 percent from El Salvador, and others 11 percent. Honduras, Guatemala—excuse me: Guatemala, 47 percent; Honduras, 29; El Salvador, 13. These three countries make up the bulk of unaccompanied minor encounters at the border.

Now, why is that? If you're an unaccompanied minor from that country, you're not sent back, and people know it. You're located in the United States at taxpayer expense. You're enticing more, not less. Here's a solution. Have a consistent policy. Send children back to their home country even if they're not from Mexico or Canada. This will stop overnight. The journey to get here is hell on earth. Only God knows what happens to young girls in particular.

So the reason we wanted this hearing is to highlight the problem and ask the Biden administration to consider changing policy. They have changed policy regarding post-Title 42. We're down to 3,500 a day, and we're celebrating that. But that's better than 10,000 a day. So, Mr. Chairman, the answer to why there's been a 357 percent increase in unaccompanied minors is policy. I'd love to work with you, but there's nothing we can do until you change your policy.

The three countries I just named have figured out that if you can get an unaccompanied minor here in the United States they never leave. Bottom line is, the Flores decision has also incentivized the use of children. If you come as a family unit, we can't detain a child. Then, the family most likely is released in the United States. We've created a demand for human smugglers to get children involved in the smuggling process. Because if you can get a child, whether it's a family member or not, you claim it to be a family, then the chance of you being deported has gone way down.

So we have incentivized the use of children in illegal immigration, and nothing will change until we change our policy. This idea of a family unit, it's obvious to me that more and more people in the human trafficking business, smuggling, have figured out that if you can get a minor child, not an unaccompanied adult male in the mix, the chance of the unit staying in the United States goes exponentially up. So, as we talk about the abuse, we all agree is bad, we'd like it to stop in terms of hiring children illegally. Count me in in stopping that.

But the reason we wanted this hearing is to try to persuade our friends on the other side that the policy choices of the Biden administration are creating an unending flow of children to this country. The idea of having a child in a family unit, whether they're family or not, the incentives for the smugglers to use children is through the roof. And we're now seeing children be recycled that came here, released in the United States, sent back to the country of origin, and the smugglers use them yet again. You're never going to break this cycle until you change policy. And there'll never be an immigration deal that codifies this strategy.

So a good-faith step in fixing our immigration problems is to change policy regarding unaccompanied minors. It's in the minor child's interest and it's in our national security interest and it's in our interests as a nation. This needs to change and stop. And a 357 percent increase in the last 2 years is going to continue in perpetuity until we change policy.

Source: US Senate Committee on the Judiciary. 2023. "Ensuring the Safety and Well-being of Unaccompanied Children." Part 1 of hearing, June 14, 2023. https://www.judiciary.senate.gov/ensuring-the-safety-and-well-being-of-unaccompanied-children

Testimony of Venus Bradley, Foster Parent, Durham, North Carolina (June 14, 2023)

Venus Bradley, a foster parent from North Carolina, offers a compelling depiction of the lived experiences of unaccompanied children who arrive in the United States, including the trauma they experience before they migrate to the United

States, the struggle they encounter at the US border during immigration processing, and the ongoing challenges with navigating the immigration system after their arrival. Bradley's statement is based on her own experiences as a foster parent for unaccompanied children and centers on the important observation that these are children who are vulnerable and in need of support. The statement provides important context to the overall political arguments made about immigration policy during the hearing, reinforcing the notion that behind vague policies are children who have hopes, dreams, strengths, and areas for need.

Ms. BRADLEY. Thank you. My name is Venus Bradley. My husband and I have been foster parents in Durham, North Carolina, for the past 7 years. In that time, we have taken in 25 children ranging in age from 2 to 17. Five of them have been immigrant children. In March 2020, we were placed with two sisters who were 15 and 17 at the time. I would like to share a little bit about their story and with their permission, of course. When they were 11 and 13, it was decided that they were going to be sent to America to come live with their father.

Their mother was a palm oil plantation worker. She worked long days, and she had her first baby at 14 years old. She knew the life that her children were going to have, and she was worried about their future. Their uncle was in the military, and he was beheaded. They knew who did it, and they were told that if they went to the police they would be killed, too. So their mom made the difficult decision to have a trusted relative take them on the long journey to the Mexican border. There they were taken into custody.

They were first taken to a detention center. They were immediately separated because one was a teenager, so she was put in a different room. And the younger one describes how she just cried for hours, along with a lot of other kids who cried long into the night. She says it was really cold. They were just given these little aluminum blankets and not much information. They didn't know what was going on, and they were there for 2 weeks. Eventually, they were moved to a children's home which was a little better. There were other kids there. There was school. They got to watch movies.

But there were also a lot of rumors. And the girls met kids who had been there for 2 or 3 years. And so they were very concerned about what was going to happen. They were very scared, and they also were still separated. They weren't allowed to, you know, sleep in the same room or anything like that. So there was still a lot of fears there. After 6 weeks, which was a short time, they were eventually moved to their father. And that relationship was fine for a while, but eventually turned sour and they reported abuse, and they were taken into foster care.

And when no safe relatives could be found, they were moved to us in foster care. When they came to us, they were very traumatized. They didn't trust adults. They had a lot of fear. The youngest had nightmares nightly. She had to take sleep aids to go to sleep. The oldest was very parentified, which means that she tried to be a mom to her little sister but didn't have any of the emotional skills to do it. And they really struggled in the beginning. And we tried to help them as much as we could with therapy, but it took a while before they were willing to trust and start dreaming of a future for themselves.

We're going to fast forward now. My oldest is 20. She just graduated with a cosmetology degree. She's passed her State boards. She's already got two job offers. My youngest just graduated high school on Monday. She's been accepted into a 4-year college. She's going to major in business, and she wants to go into real estate, I think. And before you think that that's a happy ending, my girls still have a lot of obstacles that are in their way besides the employment authorization documents that we have struggled to get and maintain. And we also have a huge visa backlog.

I was told it would take 3 to 8 years for my girls to get their green cards and that's after they've applied, which they did a year and a half ago. And so we are waiting, and they are eligible for nothing. They are not eligible for FAFSA. They're not eligible for student loans, scholarships, or even foster care finances. And that's been a real struggle for us trying to find them services and ways for them to grow and for them to actually be, you know, proud members of society, to be able to work, and eventually they hope to have their citizenships. They want to be American citizens.

They are lucky they have us, but there's a lot of kids in the system who just—they don't get anything. And then, they have people who aren't supporting them and they're not getting any services to help provide for them and they're struggling. So my takeaway is that these are kids. They're just kids. They have dreams and hopes for the future, and like my daughters they deserve and need support and care in order to achieve their dreams. Thank you.

Source: US Senate Committee on the Judiciary. 2023. "Ensuring the Safety and Well-being of Unaccompanied Children." Part 1 of hearing, June 14, 2023. https://www.judiciary.senate.gov/ensuring-the-safety-and-well-being-of-unaccompanied-children

Testimony of Lorie Davidson, LCSW-C, Vice President, Children and Family Services, Lutheran Immigration and Refugee Service, Baltimore, Maryland (June 14, 2023)

Lorie Davidson's statement provides an overview of the challenges unaccompanied children experience during the resettlement process as well as the need for policy reform to address ongoing risk factors. Davidson acknowledges the increased risk of labor exploitation that unaccompanied children face and also advocates for more resources to ensure all children have a home study prior to their placement with a sponsor. Due to increasing numbers of unaccompanied children in 2020 and 2021, the Office of Refugee Resettlement changed policy regarding the need for background checks for potential sponsors. Davidson argues that with increased resources, appropriate background checks can occur to ensure unaccompanied children are not exposed to exploitation in resettlement communities.

Ms. DAVIDSON. Thank you, Chairman Durbin and Ranking Member Graham and Members of the Committee for the opportunity to appear——

Chair DURBIN. If you——

Ms. DAVIDSON [continuing]. Before you today.

Chair DURBIN [continuing]. Pull the microphone just a little bit closer. Appreciate it.

Ms. DAVIDSON. My name is Lorie Davidson, and I'm a licensed clinical social worker and the vice president for Children and Family Services at Lutheran Immigration and Refugee Service. LIRS is a faith-based organization that has been serving refugees and immigrants for over 80 years, including unaccompanied children from all over the world.

Chair DURBIN. I'm sorry. You've got to use the microphone directly in front of you there.

Ms. DAVIDSON. Okay. Sorry about that. Is that better?

Chair DURBIN. Yes.

Ms. DAVIDSON. There we go. Okay.

Chair DURBIN. There we go.

Ms. DAVIDSON. Excellent. Children separated from their parents are among the most vulnerable populations. And when they arrive in the U.S., they frequently have limited support and significant difficulty accessing services in their communities. This is a result of language and cultural barriers and unfamiliarity with U.S. laws designed to protect children, such as labor laws and mandatory schooling. While considerable progress to safeguard UC has been made through legislation such as TVPRA, it is imperative that we provide additional safety measures both prior to and following the release of unaccompanied children to a sponsor.

The custody of unaccompanied children falls within the purview of the Office of Refugee Resettlement which is a part of Health and Human Services. ORR is required to care for unaccompanied children until they are reunified with the sponsor. Prior to the release of unaccompanied children, ORR requires that potential sponsors complete a family reunification process which includes various types of background checks depending on the relationship of the minor and the proposed sponsor.

Over the last decade, ORR has frequently changed the requirements for complying with background checks. Following the influx of 2014, where images of children under Mylar blankets flooded the news, ORR rolled back policies around background checks. The following year, Senators Portman and McCaskill held a hearing very similar to the one we are here today. By 2017, ORR stated that all required—ORR started requiring all categories of sponsors and household members to undergo extensive background checks.

But, when the census became too high and children were being held in military bases, ORR began rolling back background check protections; 2021 brought additional changes in ORR's policies related to background checks. With the intention of releasing children to sponsors quickly, ORR adopted Field Guidance, which expedited releases and removed some background checks for certain categories of sponsors. During this period, cases of child labor exploitation were exposed in meatpacking plants. The recent cases of child labor highlighted by The New York Times echo the 2014 Ohio egg farm case.

We must learn from our past mistakes. Rolling back background checks in times of influx cannot continue to be the solution to move children out of influx care facilities. ORR must consistently and appropriately vet sponsors based on their relationship to the child 100 percent of the time. LIRS recognizes that even when sponsors are thoroughly vetted, children may still find themselves in unsafe and exploitative situations. To mitigate these concerns, all children must be provided with access to in-person post-release services immediately following their unification with a sponsor.

LIRS applauds ORR's efforts to expand the home study in post-release program. Unfortunately, there are over 18,000 children who are waiting for home study post-release services. Some of whom have been on the waitlist since 2021. Post-release services are a highly effective way to mitigate the risk of exploitation and ensure the safety of children. But to do so, they must be implemented immediately following release and they must involve in-person visits. Additionally, UC need access to ongoing legal services post release. All unaccompanied children are in removal proceedings, yet most do not have access to legal counsel. This makes it very difficult for them to comply with their immigration case. Attorneys are also often the only trusted adult relationship that an unaccompanied child has and the only individual to help them understand their rights and to really understand if they are being exploited. Not only do attorneys screen children for protection cases, but they also assist in creating a repatriation plan if it's determined that it's safe for the child to return to their country.

I believe that all children have a right to protection and that they're best cared for by their families. To ensure the safety and well-being of unaccompanied children in our communities, Congress must focus on improving protections and ensuring adequate resources to make sure that all unaccompanied children receive in-person post-release services immediately following their release, and that they have access to ongoing legal representation to safeguard against labor and other types of exploitation. Thank you.

Source: US Senate Committee on the Judiciary. 2023. "Ensuring the Safety and Well-being of Unaccompanied Children." Part 1 of hearing, June 14, 2023. https://www.judiciary.senate.gov/ensuring-the-safety-and-well-being-of-unaccompanied-children

Testimony of Lora Ries, Director, Border Security and Immigration Center, Heritage Foundation, Washington, DC (June 14, 2023)

Lora Ries's statement offers another conservative view of immigration policies related to unaccompanied children. Similar to Senator Graham, Ries critiques the Trafficking Victims Protection Reauthorization Act (TVPRA), as well as the Flores Settlement Agreement, as an incentive for unaccompanied children to migrate to the United States. Ries argues that these policies encourage human trafficking, which places unaccompanied children at further risk. This argument disregards the legitimate reasons unaccompanied children migrate to the United States, including well-founded fear of violence and persecution. Ries's statement argues that the US government should replace laws such as TVPRA with laws that prevent unaccompanied children from entering the United States. However, this overlooks legitimate human rights concerns that unaccompanied children have that could warrant asylum status.

Ms. RIES. Chairman Durbin, Ranking Member Cornyn, Senators——

Chair DURBIN. Sorry, we can't hear you.

Ms. RIES [continuing]. Thank you for inviting me to testify today on how we can ensure the safety and well-being of unaccompanied children. The historic border crisis our country is currently facing isn't only harming American communities and the integrity of our system, but migrants themselves, especially children many of whom arrive unaccompanied. Let's face it, this is a crisis within a crisis, and it began in 2008 with passage of the Trafficking Victims Protection Reauthorization Act or TVPRA, a law that hasn't lived up to its name.

If we really want to ensure the safety and well-being of these vulnerable children, we must be honest about what caused the crisis and how to end it. What started in the mid-1980s as the Flores class action lawsuit about immigration detention conditions for alien minors and to whom such minors may be released has turned into a multibillion-dollar legal regime that encourages unaccompanied minors to come on a treacherous journey to the U.S., requires the Federal Government to release them into the custody of sponsors who too often end up abusing or trafficking them, and according to DHS's Enforcement Lifecycle Report, results in 94 percent of them remaining in the U.S.

Alejandro Mayorkas said repeatedly at the beginning and throughout his tenure as Secretary of Homeland Security that he would not send back unaccompanied minors. What did that tell parents, teenagers, and smugglers seeking to line their pockets? That this administration was opening the door wide open for unaccompanied minors to enter and stay in the U.S. And the parents, teens, and smugglers around the world heard it loud and clear. A historic 366,000 unaccompanied minors have been encountered just on the southwest border so far under the Biden administration.

For those who closely follow border security, border data is tracked month by month. Yet after 28 months of record entry of unaccompanied minors, the Biden administration has not changed its policies to prevent such minors from coming here. Instead, the administration's response has been, "Get them in faster." HHS Secretary Xavier Becerra was quoted by The New York Times complaining to staff about delays in releasing unaccompanied minors into the country, saying, quote, "If Henry Ford had seen this in his plants, he would have never become famous and rich. This is not the way you do an assembly line," unquote.

Secretary Mayorkas has likewise pushed for speedier processing of illegal aliens, including minors, into the U.S. In his joint proposed rule, Circumvention of Lawful Pathways, Secretary Mayorkas admits that the objective of the CBP One mobile application appointment scheme is for CBP, quote, "to process more individuals than would otherwise be possible," unquote. Like the border crisis itself, this administration's handling of unaccompanied minors is intentional. And beyond the historically high numbers, the results have been disastrous for the children involved and for Americans.

Unaccompanied children are regularly raped and exploited on their journey to the U.S. and their lives, sadly, do not improve once they enter the U.S. They are turned over to questionable, if not dangerous, sponsors, forced to work in unsafe conditions that violate child labor laws, go missing by HHS, and are sex trafficked. Furthermore, MS-13 and other gang members, who are often teenagers, easily enter the U.S. as unaccompanied minors. Too many Americans and migrants have needlessly died at the hands of vicious gang members who were released into our communities.

The Biden administration has also recently made the nonsensical decision to stop using DNA testing of suspected fake families at the border. The results are very predictable, a return to more child smuggling, child recycling, and trafficking. Say you're a family and we'll take your word for it. Both the title and intent of Section 235 of the TVPRA is, quote, "enhancing efforts to combat the trafficking of children," unquote.

And yet, from the historic volume of unaccompanied minors enticed by the law, the careless release of these minors to inadequately vetted sponsors, and the multibillion-dollar windfall in profits this administration's open border policies have given the cartels, it is clear this administration is only creating more abuse, exploitation, and human trafficking. Section 235 of the TVPRA and the Flores court interpretation are abject failures. Instead of exploring ways to accommodate the current flow of unaccompanied children, Congress should accept that laws and judicial orders have resulted in terrible consequences, and it should replace them with a rational and effective system to prevent the unlawful and dangerous flow of unaccompanied minors into the U.S. Thank you.

Source: US Senate Committee on the Judiciary. 2023. "Ensuring the Safety and Well-being of Unaccompanied Children." Part 1 of hearing, June 14, 2023.

https://www.judiciary.senate.gov/ensuring-the-safety-and-well-being-of-unaccompanied-children

Testimony of Robin Dunn Marcos, Director, Office of Refugee Resettlement, Administration for Children and Families, US Department of Health and Human Services (October 25, 2023)

Rob Dunn Marcos was director of the Office of Refugee Resettlement from September 2022 to January 2025. As part of her role, Marcos was responsible for the Unaccompanied Children Program. During her testimony, Marcos provides an overview of the Unaccompanied Children Program, including background and the current state of the program with relevant statistics. The testimony then describes the sponsor vetting process, which explains how the Unaccompanied Children Program ensures unaccompanied children are safely placed with a caring and supportive sponsor. Marcos then outlines the services available for unaccompanied children after their placement with sponsors. She then explains how the Unaccompanied Children Program partners with other federal agencies to address the risk of exploitation and trafficking of unaccompanied children. The testimony concludes with a request for additional support of the Unaccompanied Children Program.

Introduction

Chairman Durbin, Ranking Member Graham, and distinguished Members of the Committee, thank you for the opportunity to appear before you today on behalf of the U.S. Department of Health and Human Services (HHS or Department) along with my esteemed colleagues. I am the Director of the Office of Refugee Resettlement (ORR) within the Administration for Children and Families (ACF), which includes the Unaccompanied Children (UC) Program that is responsible for the care and placement of unaccompanied children in HHS custody. Since assuming my position as ORR Director in September 2022, I have led a dedicated team of career federal staff, contractors, and grantees who are committed to ensuring the safety and well-being of every child in our care. I have met some of the children we serve and many of the dedicated professionals who serve them, and I have witnessed the commitment and devotion of our staff. Providing for the safety and well-being of children in our care is not only our mandate, it is also our guiding principle. This goal is reflected in our policies, our people, and our efforts to strengthen the program every day.

In my testimony today, I will describe the work we are doing to implement ORR's UC Program, the policies that ORR has in place to promote the safety and well-being of unaccompanied children in our care, and the steps we are taking—consistent with our authorities and mission—to support and promote their well-being following their release from ORR.

Responsibility for Unaccompanied Children

Under the Homeland Security Act of 2002 (6 U.S.C. 279(b)(1)) and the Trafficking Victims Protection Reauthorization Act of 2008 (TVPRA) (8 U.S.C. 1232(b)(1)), ORR is required to assume custody of and provide care for all unaccompanied children from the time they are transferred to ORR from the Department of Homeland Security (DHS) or other federal entity until they are released to a vetted sponsor, typically a parent or other family member. Further, the 1997 Flores Settlement Agreement establishes minimum standards for specific services for unaccompanied children under ORR-funded programs.[1]

To fulfill ORR's statutory and court-ordered obligations, ORR funds nearly 300 programs in 27 states for different levels of care such as shelter programs, transitional foster care, long-term foster care, group homes, staff secure facilities, and residential treatment centers as well as two operational and active Influx Care Facilities (ICF) in Pecos, Texas and Dimmit County, Texas. Additionally, ORR maintains a preparedness posture by ensuring the Office can quickly scale-up capacity if needed to provide safe facilities appropriate for the care for children. In fact, ORR now has the ability to award new Indefinite Delivery, Indefinite Quantity task orders for scalable ICF capacity and services in a timely manner. At all of its facilities, ORR provides child-focused services, including education, health care and counseling services, case management services, recreation, access to legal services, access to religious services, and access to child advocates where applicable. These services are delivered according to child welfare best practices in a manner that is appropriate to the age, culture, preferred language, and needs of each child.

In every aspect of our mission, we recognize the importance of our work in caring for children, many of whom come to our care during extremely difficult periods in their life. The work is not easy, and ORR staff performs this critical work with the utmost care and dedication.

Current State of the Unaccompanied Children Program

As of September 30, 2023, ORR had 11,064 children in ORR care and had received 118,798 referrals from federal entities in Fiscal Year (FY) 2023. ORR continues working with DHS to minimize the time an unaccompanied child spends in a border processing facility or port of entry, neither of which are equipped for extended stays for children. Through flexible capacity, improved case management processes, and coordination with inter-agency partners, ORR can efficiently and consistently accept DHS referrals. The average amount of time an unaccompanied child spends in DHS border facilities is now well under the 72-hour maximum time within which children must be transferred from DHS to HHS care under the TVPRA, absent exceptional circumstances.

In FY2023, ORR placed more than 113,602 children with vetted sponsors. The average length of time a child spent in ORR care over this period was less than one month. Given ORR's UC Program's child welfare mission, we know that the best place for a child is with a family in a community, not in a congregate care setting. In FY2022 and FY2023, the vast majority of children—more than 85 percent—were placed with a parent, legal guardian, or other close family member.

Sponsor Vetting Process

In fulfilling its sponsor placement responsibilities, ORR employs thorough sponsor screening and vetting processes for each category of sponsor that are based on child-welfare principles. To that end, ORR has implemented and funded seven-day-a-week case management—specifically for family unification services, which ensures comprehensive staff support so that every child's case is worked on even after normal business hours and on weekends. Additionally, ORR has implemented significant updates to the UC Portal (the UC Program technology system) to increase usability and search functionality to build in safeguards, streamline processes, and make it easier to identify potential child welfare concerns during sponsor suitability assessments.

ORR identifies potential sponsors for unaccompanied children in different categories of cases: parents or legal guardians as Category 1; brothers, sisters, grandparents, or other immediate relatives as Category 2; distant relatives or unrelated individuals as Category 3; and unaccompanied children with a sponsor yet to be identified as Category 4. ORR's sponsor suitability assessment process includes verifying the sponsor's relationship to the child; speaking with the child's parents when possible; conducting separate interviews with the child and sponsor; collecting supporting documentation to verify the sponsor's information; and administering background and address verification checks—which include public records and sex offender registry checks, as well as FBI fingerprint checks in certain cases.

Prior to release of a child and placement with a vetted sponsor, ORR also carries out home studies in certain circumstances, as required by the TVPRA and ORR policy. Home studies further investigate a potential sponsor's ability to ensure the child's safety and well-being, which include home visits, sponsor interviews, background checks of additional adult household members, and, if necessary, interviews with other household members.

Home studies are required under circumstances specified by the TVPRA, including when a child has previously been a victim of trafficking or has a disability; and, per ORR policy, in instances when a potential sponsor is a non-relative and the child is 12-years-old or younger or the sponsor has previously sponsored or sought to sponsor a child or is seeking to sponsor multiple children.

Additionally, to provide additional safeguards, home studies may also be conducted at ORR's discretion if the ORR Federal Field Specialist, Case Manager, or Case Coordinator determine that additional information is needed regarding the sponsor's ability to care for the health, safety, and well-being of the child. All releases following home studies require post-release services.

Services Following Unaccompanied Children's Release to Sponsors

ORR recognizes that many children released from our care may benefit from ongoing assistance by a social services agency. Further, even though sponsors are thoroughly vetted, we recognize that some children may still find themselves in unsafe situations or otherwise in need of support after they are released from our care. ORR has policies in place, beyond when our custodial responsibilities legally end, to promote children's well-being after they have been released from our custody and transition into a new community.

These policies include Safety and Well-being calls to children and sponsors after ORR releases a child from its care. Per ORR policies, ORR care providers are required to make a minimum of three attempts for every case to reach and speak with the child and the sponsor. Children and sponsors are not required to participate in Safety and Well-being calls and may choose not to answer a call for a variety of reasons, including fear or distrust of government, hesitation to answer an unknown number, or simply missing the call. Nevertheless, ORR made contact with either the child, the sponsor, or both in more than 81 percent of households since FY2022.

When a care provider identifies a child who may benefit from additional resources through a Safety and Well-being call, the child is referred to ORR's National Call Center (ORRNCC), which is staffed 24 hours a day, seven-days-a-week. This helpline connects children and sponsors with resources within their local community to help address their individual needs. Children receive information about the ORRNCC while in ORR's care, and upon release they and their sponsor are provided a card with the ORRNCC information, which also includes additional resources.

Children, family members, sponsors, legal service providers, child advocates, and other members of the community can request assistance or report concerns to the ORRNCC. The ORRNCC is required to document any safety concerns and report such concerns to ORR, as well as to appropriate local law enforcement agencies and state and local child protective services as appropriate, in accordance with mandatory reporting laws, state licensing requirements, federal laws and regulations, and ORR policies and procedures. Additionally, ORR requires the ORRNCC to provide children who call the helpline and express safety concerns with information regarding the authorities to which their safety concerns will be reported. The ORRNCC connects children directly with the appropriate authorities, when possible, and places a follow-up call to the child to confirm if any further actions are needed.

ORR also provides post-release services (PRS) to unaccompanied children who receive TVPRA-mandated home studies, which includes all children who are victims of trafficking and to children who, in the determination of a care provider, would benefit from ongoing assistance. PRS includes referrals and connection to community resources as well as intensive case management services in cases where additional support is necessary to address a child's specific needs or challenges. These referral and case management services are offered by a network of ORR-funded grant recipients across the United States. PRS can include help with school enrollment, support in finding and accessing health and mental health care, connections with local organizations, and other supports to ensure children's well-being.

Further, if at any point during an interaction with an unaccompanied child, either while in ORR's care or post-release such as through a Safety and Well-being call, ORR care provider staff identifies or suspects any safety concerns, they are required to issue a Notification of Concern to ORR and notify appropriate investigative agencies, including local law enforcement and child protective services. This includes any suspicion that the child has run away, is at risk of or posing a danger to themselves or others, or is at risk of human trafficking, exploitation, or other abuse. ORR then conducts further review and determines what actions should be taken, which may include additional reporting and engagement with local law enforcement, state child welfare authorities, and/or referral to PRS.

While ORR does not have authority to remove a child from a home—that authority resides with state child welfare and law enforcement agencies—ORR recognizes the critical importance of its notification and coordination processes to ensure that local authorities can respond appropriately to any allegations of abuse or neglect. For this reason, we have engaged multiple child welfare agencies on the needs of unaccompanied children. However, state child welfare agencies vary in capabilities and these local and state entities also need robust resources to help ensure their ability to review or investigate such allegations.

If ORR care provider staff, such as a case manager or clinician, suspect that a child is a victim of trafficking or is at risk of trafficking at any point during their interaction with an unaccompanied child, they must make a referral to HHS's ACF Office on Trafficking in Persons (OTIP) and to DHS's Homeland Security Investigations Division and DHS's Center for Countering Human Trafficking for further investigation. OTIP provides further assessment assistance to ensure that victims can access appropriate care and services. Such care is then coordinated with ORR to provide direct referrals for grant-funded comprehensive case management services, medical services, food assistance, cash assistance, and health insurance tailored to the child's individual needs. HHS engages in constant efforts to improve care and information-sharing efforts for better human trafficking prevention. For example, in February 2023, ORR entered into a data sharing Memorandum of Agreement (MOA) with OTIP and the National Center for Missing and Exploited Children (NCMEC) to increase information sharing and visibility on unaccompanied children who are referred to NCMEC and who may be at risk of trafficking or exploitation. Additionally, ORR works regularly with OTIP to further coordinate their efforts to align care and services for victims.

Continuing Progress and the Path Forward

ORR is continually assessing, identifying, and implementing improvements to the UC Program to ensure the highest level of care and support for children.

While unlawful child labor is not limited to migrant children, ORR recognizes that unaccompanied children released from ORR custody are often particularly vulnerable. Thus, consistent with our statutory authorities, ORR is working closely in partnership with the Department of Labor (DOL) to advance federal efforts to protect children against labor exploitation. Our joint efforts to address child labor exploitation have been ongoing and, as of March 23, 2023, have also been formalized in an MOA between DOL's Wage and Hour Division and HHS's ACF, which oversees ORR. The MOA expands the agencies' collaboration, including information-sharing to aid investigations and to help identify communities in which and employers for whom children may be at risk of child labor exploitation; coordination to ensure that child labor victims or potential victims have access to critical services; and cross-training of staff. Thus, we are actively engaged with DOL to ensure we are finding and addressing the needs of children who may face exploitation.

The MOA has also resulted in joint public education efforts. In April 2023, ACF and DOL developed and distributed new materials and trainings to provide information to children about child labor laws in the United States so that they understand the laws on labor rights and restrictions to working in the United States, which may differ from many labor laws in their country of origin. The cross-training efforts of DOL and ACF staff have been successful and robustly attended, with approximately 800 ACF staff, including more than 600 ORR staff, trained by DOL and 250 DOL managers trained by ACF. In an effort to further educate and engage impacted communities, ACF led two roundtable sessions with educators on the issue of unlawful child labor in collaboration with the US Department of Education and DOL in August 2023.

Additionally, ORR launched an audit of individuals who have sponsored multiple unrelated unaccompanied children, to ensure all necessary safeguards were followed. On June 2, 2023, ORR released the results of its audit, which found that ORR adhered to its program policies and procedures designed to meet or exceed statutory requirements in the placement of unaccompanied children with a vetted sponsor. The audit also identified areas for continued improvement. ORR announced additional efforts to protect the safety and well-being of unaccompanied children, including a new Program Accountability team in ORR that is responsible for assessing and addressing potential exploitation risks faced by unaccompanied children. Further, ORR and the Administration is committed to expanding PRS tailored to the unique needs of each child. In FY 2022, ORR more than doubled the rate of children offered PRS, providing access to more than 40 percent of children compared to just over 20 percent in FY2021. This past fiscal year, we continued to expand PRS access, offering more than 50 percent of discharged children access to these services. We are offering services to all children with known vulnerabilities and to children released to unrelated sponsors. With continued funding from Congress, we can continue to advance toward our goal of providing all children access to PRS.

In fact, earlier this month, ORR published the proposed UC Program Foundational Rule, which would establish a comprehensive framework for placement and care, and would formalize and expand services for unaccompanied children, including legal services, Child Advocate access, language access, and post-release services—all critical tools to help prevent and respond to child labor exploitation. As always, this is contingent on robust funding to fulfill the goal of expanding these services.

Conclusion

We appreciate Congress' prior support of ORR programs, including the contingency funding in the FY2023 omnibus. However, ORR still faces a significant overall budgetary shortfall in FY2024 and has requested supplemental appropriations. Without this funding, there could be a significant impact on ORR's ability to timely accept referrals and it could lead to a curtailing of timely or expanded post-release services and legal services, beyond what is minimally required. These services play a critical role in ORR's ability to promote the safety and well-being of children—including combating the risk of child labor exploitation—but are only possible with continued investment and support from Congress to build on ORR's efforts to further strengthen and improve the UC Program. We would also welcome more resources from Congress in order for ORR to expand not just access to, but the nature of services to all children following release.

Thank you for the opportunity to provide an update on ORR's UC Program. We are committed to caring for and protecting children in HHS custody and continue to do all we can to promote their well-being following their release. Children who come into ORR care face unique challenges that require a whole of government approach—including our partners in Congress, fellow federal agencies as well as state and local agencies, and national and community partners. At ORR, we are proud to do our part in this critical work.

Note

1. Stipulated Settlement Agreement, *Flores v. Reno*, No. CV 85-4544-RJK (Px) (C.D. Cal. January 17, 1997, as amended December 7, 2001).

Source: US Senate Committee on the Judiciary. 2023. "Ensuring the Safety and Well-being of Unaccompanied Children." Part 2 of hearing, October 25, 2023. https://www.judiciary.senate.gov/committee-activity/hearings/ensuring-the-safety-and-well-being-of-unaccompanied-children-part-ii

Testimony of Joseph Salazar, Office Director, Office of Central American Affairs, Bureau of Western Hemisphere Affairs (October 25, 2023)

Joseph Salazar provided testimony to the US Senate Committee on the Judiciary hearing that provided important geopolitical context to understand the topic of unaccompanied children. As the Office Director of the Office of Central American Affairs in the Bureau of Western Affairs, Salazar's statement offers unique expertise on this topic. He offers important information regarding the economic conditions in Central America, such as employment rates, as well as social conditions, such as crime rates. His statement provides an overview of initiatives organized by President Biden's administration that seek to stabilize conditions in Central America, including investment in humanitarian aid, such as food and education support, for individuals who may be at risk of forced migration.

Thank you, Chairman Durbin and Ranking Member Graham, for holding this important hearing. I am honored to be joined by my colleagues here who are the true experts in the fight against trafficking and what happens once Central

Americans make the difficult choice to leave their countries. I'm grateful for the opportunity to talk to you more about the complex conditions that drive them to migrate from northern Central America, as well as important progress on our efforts to address them.

Northern Central America faces several serious challenges. Democratic backsliding in the region affects peoples' trust in institutions and perception of how freely they can exercise their rights. Victims of corruption are more likely to express intentions to migrate. High youth unemployment rates, numerous barriers inadequate access to education, and vast economic inequality spur migration. Coupled with high levels of informality, low wages that do not cover basic needs, and a vicious cycle of reliance on debt to meet those basic needs, the lack of decent jobs in all three countries contributes to the migratory wave. Despite decreased homicide rates, other types of crime and violence—including rampant gender-based violence—cause insecurity. Many individuals and families see migration as their only alternative to escape poverty, instability, narcotics violence, and climate-related catastrophes.

In 2021, the Biden-Harris Administration launched the Strategy to Address the Root Causes of Irregular Migration from Central America. The Root Causes Strategy focuses on creating good jobs, promoting democratic governance, protecting human rights, improving security, and countering gender-based violence to help Central Americans build better futures at home. The strategy addresses the factors that drive irregular migration and forced displacement from northern Central America, including food insecurity, chronic structural challenges, extreme poverty, citizen insecurity, poor governance, and endemic corruption.

First and foremost, we need strong governance in the region. Without it, we cannot achieve sustainable, equitable progress across all strategic areas, including economic prosperity and security.

We partner with civil society, the private sector, labor unions, regional governments, and international actors to advance U.S. policy goals.

In the last year, the State Department and U.S. Agency for International Development (USAID) supported more than 1,500 human rights defenders and trained more than 300 independent journalists. This support provides quick help to embattled human rights defenders and civil society organizations through emergency assistance, supporting human rights actors and media practitioners to remain resilient, mitigate risks, overcome threats, and continue their important work as safely as possible.

Through the Voices Initiative, we bring together U.S. resources—public and private diplomacy, foreign assistance programming, and enforcement authorities—to protect, defend, and promote civic space in Central America. The initiative focuses on promoting digital democracy and countering digital authoritarianism, promoting freedom of expression, strengthening independent media, countering criminalization, and providing protections for those who are targeted.

We are also taking actions to promote accountability for corrupt and undemocratic actors, as well as human rights abusers. On July 19, the U.S. government issued our most recent public list, consistent with Section 353 of the United States–Northern Triangle Enhanced Engagement Act, of individuals who knowingly engaged in acts that undermine democratic processes or institutions, engaged in significant corruption, or obstructed investigations into such acts of corruption in El Salvador, Guatemala, Honduras, or Nicaragua. This critical tool promotes accountability, and we appreciate bipartisan support for it.

In Fiscal Year 2022, the State Department trained over nine thousand civil police officers in the region. Our vetted units supported over four thousand arrests in the region.

On economic growth, Vice President Harris leads "Central America Forward," an innovative public-private partnership to create good jobs in the region. Under Central America Forward, companies have committed to invest over $4.2 billion in El Salvador, Guatemala, and Honduras. These investments have created thousands of good jobs, connected four million people to the internet, brought more than one million people into the formal financial economy, and trained almost 500,000 people to enhance workforce abilities, including digital and language skills. This is key to ending irregular migration. But this is not just about investment. Our private sector engagement reinforces the rule of law, good governance, and human rights. USAID supported more than 465,000 students through primary and secondary education programs in fiscal year 2022, far exceeding annual targets. Over 300,000 students received USDA nutrition assistance.

We certainly are not naïve about the challenges we face. It will take time to address many of these long-term, structural issues. My team works on these issues day in and day out, and we are grateful for continued, bipartisan support to ultimately help the people in the region maintain their futures in their home countries. Thank you for the opportunity to testify before this committee today. I look forward to working with Congress to strengthen our approach.

Source: US Senate Committee on the Judiciary. 2023. "Ensuring the Safety and Well-being of Unaccompanied Children." Part 2 of hearing, October 25, 2023. https://www.judiciary.senate.gov/committee-activity/hearings/ensuring-the-safety-and-well-being-of-unaccompanied-children-part-ii

Testimony of Cardell T. Morant, Assistant Director, Homeland Security Investigations, Center for Countering Human Trafficking, US Department of Homeland Security (October 25, 2023)

Cardell T. Morant's testimony provides an overview of Home Security Investigations (HIS) and how the agency investigates an array of federal crimes related to the trafficking and exploitation of unaccompanied children. The testimony provides important context into the different functions of the agency, including data and statistics on the number of investigations conducted by HSI. Morant's testimony then explains important differences between human trafficking and human smuggling, human trafficking and child sex abuse material, and human trafficking and labor exploitation. Morant also describes how HIS supports unaccompanied children and concludes with a description of the agency's "victim first" approach to investigations, which centers the needs of individuals who are victims of crime throughout the course of investigations.

Chairman Durbin, Ranking Member Graham, and distinguished members of the Committee, thank you for the opportunity to testify regarding the role of U.S. Immigration and Customs Enforcement Homeland Security Investigations (HSI) in investigating federal crimes relating to the trafficking and exploitation of unaccompanied children. I am honored to be here today with my esteemed colleagues on this panel.

Introduction

This month marks my 30-year anniversary as a career federal law enforcement official. I have served as a Special Agent investigating a wide variety of crimes, a supervisor of teams of agents, and later as the Special Agent in Charge of an HSI field office. In my current role, I serve as the Director of the Department of

Homeland Security (DHS) Center for Countering Human Trafficking (CCHT), which is located within HSI.

The CCHT's mission is to advance counter human trafficking law enforcement operations, protect victims, and enhance prevention efforts by aligning DHS's capabilities and expertise. Essentially, we are building capacity across DHS and supporting HSI criminal investigations of human trafficking worldwide, whether sex trafficking or labor trafficking, including forced labor in the supply chain. We do this through training and providing multi-disciplinary operational and strategic guidance from subject matter experts throughout DHS. We greatly appreciate that Congress codified the CCHT just last year, recognizing the promise and the need driving the creation of a cross-cutting coordination center.

The CCHT celebrated its third anniversary five days ago on October 20th. In this brief time, we have supported more than 400 significant and large-scale criminal human trafficking investigations with technical assistance, enhanced intelligence, and funding. The CCHT is equipped and positioned to support investigations that are sophisticated, complex, or novel, including traffickers who use opioids to control victims, exploit temporary worker visas or unaccompanied children, or conduct their illicit activities using social media.

The scope of my testimony today is related to criminal human trafficking investigations once an agency of first contact for unaccompanied children notifies HSI. The two primary agencies of first contact that provide referrals are U.S. Customs and Border Protection (CBP) and the U.S. Department of Health and Human Services (HHS). While HSI executes a robust and comprehensive response to human smuggling, my remarks are focused on today's hearing topic, the exploitation of unaccompanied children after their arrival in the United States.

Please note that I use the term "victim" throughout as a defined law enforcement term given the scope of my testimony. However, I personally recognize—as does HSI—that victims transition to become survivors and persons with lived experience. We see it every day.

HSI's Counter Human Trafficking Mission

Human trafficking impacts national security, public safety, public health, and the U.S. economy, with human traffickers inflicting lasting and devastating physical, psychological, and financial harm on victims. HSI conducts approximately 1,000 human trafficking investigations annually; identifies and assists hundreds of victims; and performs extensive outreach and trainings about human trafficking to law enforcement, nongovernmental organizations (NGOs), and the public. HSI informs noncitizen victims about the resources and immigration options available to them, such as Continued Presence, T visas and U visas.

With approximately 6,800 HSI special agents assigned to 237 U.S. cities and 93 offices in 56 countries, HSI has one of the largest international footprints in U.S. law enforcement. We have dedicated human trafficking investigative groups in each primary office across the United States. These agents participate in human trafficking task forces nationwide consisting of federal, state, and local law enforcement, as well as victim service providers, so that there is a cohesive approach to human trafficking within local areas of responsibility. The CCHT works to ensure all aspects of human trafficking investigations are fully pursued through the close coordination of all HSI Divisions.

HSI also employs specialized victim assistance personnel to assist with all victim-based HSI investigations, including human trafficking, child sexual exploitation, human rights violations, financial crimes, and identity and benefit fraud. These personnel—including forensic interviewers and victim assistance specialists—support victims using age and developmentally appropriate interviews and comprehensive referrals to social services.

The mission of HSI's human trafficking investigations is two-fold. First, to proactively identify, disrupt, and dismantle domestic and transnational human trafficking organizations and minimize the risk they pose to national security and public safety. Second, to employ a victim-centered approach, whereby equal value is placed on the identification and stabilization of victims and the investigation and prosecution of traffickers. Over the past five years, HSI assisted more than 3,000 victims and arrested more than 8,000 subjects in connection with investigations involving human trafficking. These actions have led to more than 2,500 convictions for local, state, and federal violations. These are the most difficult, time-consuming, and heart-breaking cases that our personnel pursue, and I am grateful every day for their dedication and unwavering faith in justice.

Human Trafficking versus Human Smuggling: Distinct Crimes

The terms "human trafficking" and "human smuggling" are often used interchangeably; however, they are distinct crimes. Human trafficking is the crime of compelling another person into labor or commercial sex through force, fraud, or coercion, or inducing a minor under the age of 18 into commercial sex. It is an exploitation-based crime against a person that does not need to involve travel or border crossings but can. Global estimates indicate that human traffickers victimize a staggering 27.6 million people worldwide, with an estimated 77 percent in forced labor and 23 percent in sex trafficking. Children represent 27 percent of forced labor and 8 percent of sex trafficking worldwide, though victims can be any age, race, gender, nationality, or immigration status.[1] HSI investigations show that traffickers operate within agriculture, landscaping, construction, hospitality, manufacturing, in private homes with nannies and domestic workers, restaurants, elder care, massage parlors—essentially, in jobs with low pay and few legal protections, in the underground economy, and in the service industry.

By contrast, human smugglers engage in the crime of bringing people into the United States, or unlawfully transporting and harboring people already in the United States, in deliberate evasion of immigration law. Human smuggling is inherently travel-based and requires a border crossing. It may involve elements of violence such as hostage taking, kidnapping, extortion, physical assault, and sexual assault, however these aggravating factors and additional crimes do not constitute human trafficking, absent exploitation of another person for labor, services, or commercial sex.

Human smuggling can leave smuggled migrants at risk of human trafficking, either by persons associated with their smugglers, or by others they may later encounter. Human trafficking occurs when prohibited means of force, fraud, or coercion are used to compel labor, services, or commercial sex, or when a minor is exploited for commercial sex. HSI special agents, through experience, have learned that it is highly unlikely that an individual knows during their smuggling that they are destined for either forced labor or sex trafficking once they reach their destination in the United States.

HSI conducts extensive local community outreach to places where victims may turn to for help—organizations that advocate for worker rights, assist crime victims, or are faith-based to name a few. HSI relies on referrals from partnering federal, state, and local agencies which can include criminal law enforcement as well as civil law enforcement such as labor inspectors, health and safety inspectors, and fair housing and workplace investigators. Only once HSI starts a trafficking investigation, do we learn about the deception, debts, threats, and other coercive means used to exploit the victims for forced labor or sex trafficking, and whether an individual may also have been smuggled. Only then can we seek justice against the traffickers, who may or may not be associated with the smugglers who unlawfully and perhaps dangerously brought the individual into the country.

Human Trafficking versus Child Sexual Abuse Material

HSI personnel around the world work tirelessly to protect children from exploitation by predators who are involved in the production, distribution, or possession of child sexual abuse material or who travel internationally to engage in illicit sexual conduct with minors. HSI employs the latest technology to collect evidence and track the activities of individuals and organized groups who sexually exploit children using the dark web, chat rooms, peer-to-peer networks, and other internet-based platforms.

These crimes may transition to human trafficking if a commercial sex act is introduced or filmed and distributed. From HSI's perspective, we are primarily identifying unaccompanied child victims in forced labor, not in child sexual abuse material.

Human Trafficking versus Labor Exploitation

HSI has authorities to investigate forced labor. Therefore, when appropriate, HSI makes referrals to the U.S. Department of Labor (DOL) for violations of labor laws that do not rise to the level of human trafficking under federal criminal statutes. HSI routinely works with DOL, most often through human trafficking task forces comprised of federal, state, and local law enforcement and victim service providers. Within these task forces, law enforcement entities can jointly work cases and refer cases to one another.

Referrals to HSI for Criminal Investigation Involving Potential Unaccompanied Child Victims

HSI is not an agency of first contact for unaccompanied children. HSI may receive referrals regarding unaccompanied child victims as we do for any other human trafficking case. These referrals may come from CBP and HHS, but generally come from human trafficking task forces, trusted NGOs, community-based partners locally, the National Human Trafficking Hotline, or anyone who has called the HSI hotline in response to the DHS Blue Campaign's national public awareness.

One of those first contact agencies is CBP, which refers all instances where human trafficking is suspected to HSI. In Fiscal Year (FY) 2022, HSI initiated 24 human trafficking investigations originating from CBP information. This referral process is generally conducted at the local level whereby the CBP sector, port of entry, or field office coordinates with the HSI field office. CBP does not contact the CCHT. It is more common that CBP transfers the child to HHS custody, then HHS identifies potential human trafficking through its extensive screening, and then notifies a local HSI office.

HHS is another first contact agency. HSI and HHS coordinate in two ways regarding unaccompanied noncitizen children who may be human trafficking victims. First, if HHS suspects potential criminal activity involving an unaccompanied noncitizen child, they contact the nearest HSI office. Provided HSI has jurisdiction, we will investigate.

Second, per the Trafficking Victims Protection Reauthorization Act of 2008, HHS is required to consult the U.S. Department of Justice (DOJ), DHS, and NGOs before they provide an unaccompanied child identified as a trafficking victim with federal benefits entitled as "interim relief." The HHS Office on Trafficking in Persons and the CCHT have an established process for these consultations. If there is a nexus to the United States and the child is willing to be interviewed, the CCHT forwards the summary information to a local HSI office for investigation. However, most consultations are related to claims of trafficking in the child's country of origin, not in the United States, and therefore HSI has no jurisdiction to investigate. In the last year, HSI provided hundreds of consultations and did not find federal criminal jurisdiction warranting a referral for investigations in any of the consultations. HSI remains available to anyone and any agency that wants to report human trafficking.

HSI Criminal Investigations & Initiatives

From its criminal investigations, HSI sees that traffickers use the same tactics against unaccompanied children as they do for any other victim. They make false promises of school and good jobs to earn money to send home to family. They force them into long hours of work for little or no pay. They make victims work in conditions that are often poor, dangerous, or inhumane. They threaten victims with arrest, deportation, physical harm, and/or harm to family in their home country. They create or build upon debt so that their work becomes never-ending. This is why the CCHT and HSI invest so much into seeking justice for the victims we encounter. In FY 2022, HSI assisted 765 human trafficking victims: 459 adults and 306 children.

Over the last three fiscal years, HSI has opened more than 3,000 investigations into human trafficking and related federal, state, or local violations. Statistically, there are fewer labor trafficking than sex trafficking investigations because labor trafficking can be especially difficult to detect, investigate, and prosecute. This is for several reasons, including isolation of the victims, limited sources of corroborating evidence, and challenges in earning the trust of victims to elicit their statements. As a result, HSI fully supports the National Action Plan to Combat Human Trafficking that calls for an increased focus on forced labor and, over the next year, the CCHT is establishing an entire unit of 15 personnel dedicated to supporting forced labor investigations.

The CCHT is also part of an interagency Forced Labor Initiative with the goal to increase federal prosecutions of criminal forced labor violations. Under this initiative, the CCHT coordinates with DOJ's Human Trafficking Prosecution Unit, the Federal Bureau of Investigation, the Executive Office for United States Attorneys, the Department of State's Bureau of Diplomatic Security, and DOL's Office of Inspector General, Occupational Safety and Health Administration, and Wage and Hour Division. Members meet monthly to identify significant investigations to support through specialized expertise and strategic guidance. The initiative has a substantial focus on forced child labor and, for example, has been analyzing reports, complaints, and other indicators of potential trafficking of unaccompanied children to initiate and advance federal investigations. The initiative has yielded U.S. Attorney's Offices' support for specific HSI investigations, for which we are grateful.

Victim-Centered Approach

HSI is first and foremost about the people it is here to protect and serve, therefore, identifying and assisting victims is paramount. The CCHT includes the words "Victims First" in its logo as a reminder of why we do this work.

At HSI, a victim-centered investigation and prosecution means focusing the investigation and prosecution around the victim while minimizing any undue stress, harm, and trauma to the victim. Using this approach prioritizes victims' rights, safety, and interests. It is key to successful trafficking investigations.

Being victim-centered is a responsibility of all personnel in accordance with federal law, including the Victims' Rights and Restitution Act, 34 U.S.C. § 20141, and the Crime Victims' Rights Act, 18 U.S.C. § 3771. Special agents conducting trafficking investigations receive specific training on victims' needs and trauma so that they can best work with them. HSI forensic interview specialists conduct fact finding interviews that are designed to elicit accurate and complete information in an investigation and are developmentally appropriate for children. HSI Victim Assistance Program Specialists make sure that victims receive referrals for any services they may need in the aftermath of the crime. Such referrals are based on the unique needs of the victim and can be comprehensive to include case management, shelter, clothing, food, medical and mental health care, legal assistance, immigration assistance, employment placement, and education. We offer age-appropriate services to children and referrals for community-based services to parents and guardians. HSI immediately refers unaccompanied children to HHS to take custody and to provide assistance through its programs.

Challenges

Our Victim Assistance Program serves to provide the necessary and legally mandated victim services that help to ensure victims are put on a path to recovery. Currently we do not have enough victim assistance specialists for every office participating in a human trafficking or child exploitation task force, where there is a consistent demand for services. This puts an undue burden on our special agents who must take on that role while also conducting their criminal investigations.

Just as victim assistance is so very important, HSI personnel hear victim accounts and seek evidence about the worst of humanity, and they carry that with them the rest of their lives. They need professional and peer support to maintain their mental health. HSI needs a permanent peer and clinician support program that addresses the secondary trauma HSI personnel experience from working human trafficking cases.

Additionally, I bring your attention to an Office of Management and Budget-approved DHS legislative proposal transmitted to this Congress regarding statutory improvements for Continued Presence (CP). The proposal would bring much needed clarifications and reduce barriers to ultimately ensure that the currently underutilized CP is fully available, accessible, and used.

These improvements would likely increase the number of noncitizen victims who receive CP and greatly aid them in their recovery. Simultaneously, it would strengthen human trafficking investigations at the federal, state, and local level because more noncitizen victims would achieve greater stability that would allow them to better cooperate with law enforcement.

Conclusion

HSI is committed to using every authority and resource available to make federal criminal arrests of human traffickers and to identify and assist the victims. We remain available for reports, referrals and tips of human trafficking from our federal interagency partners here today; other federal, state, local, tribal, and territorial law enforcement; and victim service providers and NGOs. We will continue to focus on increasing forced labor investigations, including forced child labor investigations, through strong existing partnerships.

Thank you again for the opportunity to appear before you today and for your continued support of HSI and its law enforcement mission. I look forward to your questions.

Note

1. International Labour Organization, Walk Free, and International Organization for Migration, Global Estimates of Modern Day Slavery: Forced Labour and Forced Marriage, Geneva 2022.

Source: US Senate Committee on the Judiciary. 2023. "Ensuring the Safety and Well-being of Unaccompanied Children." Part 2 of hearing, October 25, 2023. https://www.judiciary.senate.gov/committee-activity/hearings/ensuring-the-safety-and-well-being-of-unaccompanied-children-part-ii

6

Resources

This chapter provides an overview of key documents, including articles, reports, books, and media, that cover unaccompanied children. Each citation is accompanied by a brief annotation that outlines the main components of the document. The resources in this chapter help explain pre-migration, migration, and post-migration contexts that unaccompanied children experience. In addition, the resources describe different supports and policies that are in place to support unaccompanied children who arrive to the United States.

Articles

Amuedo-Dorantes, Catalina, and Thitima Puttitanun. "DACA and the Surge in Unaccompanied Minors at the US-Mexico Border." *International Migration* 54, no. 4 (2016): 102–17.

Policymakers and researchers have long tried to understand what explains the increased numbers of unaccompanied children who have migrated to the United States. One theory that has been raised is that US immigration policy itself has created incentives for unaccompanied children to migrate to the United States. For example, some politicians raised concern that the Deferred Action for Childhood Arrivals (DACA) incentivized children to migrate to the United States by presenting an impression that children would be shielded

---

An unaccompanied Guatemalan twelve-year-old arrives via an illegal boat crossing of the Rio Grande River from Mexico near the US border city of Roma on March 27, 2021. In addition to threats to their physical safety, unaccompanied migrant youth face emotional trauma, putting them at higher risk for mental health disorders and substance abuse, often with little support for their integration into US society. (Ed Jones/AFP via Getty Images)

from deportation. Economists Amuedo-Dorantes and Puttitanun explored this question by analyzing data from US Customs and Border Protection that documents apprehensions of unaccompanied children at the US border. Results indicate that increased number of unaccompanied children migrating to the United States was not associated with DACA. Rather, economic conditions in countries of origin, as well as in the United States, along with violence in countries of origin, are more accurate explanations of why unaccompanied children migrate to the United States.

Berger Cardoso, Jodi. "Running to Stand Still: Trauma Symptoms, Coping Strategies, and Substance Use Behaviors in Unaccompanied Migrant Youth." *Children and Youth Services Review* 92 (2018): 143–52.

Social work scholar Berger Cardoso conducted one of the first studies that focused on mental health outcomes for unaccompanied children in the United States. The study used a mixed-method design to analyze data collected from thirty unaccompanied children who migrated from Honduras, Guatemala, Mexico, and El Salvador and were resettled in the United States. The study analyzed qualitative data collected by focus groups, and the participants also completed a survey. Results showed that more than half of the children met criteria for a diagnosis of posttraumatic stress disorder, 30 percent presented symptoms aligned with a diagnosis of major depressive disorder, and 30 percent reported experiencing suicidal ideation in the past year. Results from focus groups showed that children struggled with stress related to family separation and migration-related trauma such as community violence. Adaptive coping skills, such as spirituality, hobbies, or sports, helped mitigate substance use behavior. The study highlighted important considerations for clinicians working with unaccompanied children and also emphasized the importance of future studies, including larger sample sizes.

Berger Cardoso, Jodi, Kalina Brabeck, Dennis Stinchcomb, Lauren Heidbrink, Olga Acosta Price, Óscar F. Gil-García, Thomas M. Crea, and Luis H. Zayas. "Integration of Unaccompanied Migrant Youth in the United States: A Call for Research." *Journal of Ethnic and Migration Studies* 45, no. 2 (2019): 273–92.

Social work scholar Berger Cardoso and colleagues wrote an article that argued for an increase in research on unaccompanied children in the United States. This article, published in 2019, frames the argument as necessary due to the increased numbers of unaccompanied children migrating to the United States, and necessary due to the humanitarian needs of unaccompanied children. The paper frames the argument using the social ecological theoretical model, which emphasizes unique strengths and needs that are part of an individual's life, as well as their broader environment. When applied to the context of migration, this theory posits that unaccompanied children experience risks before, during, and after their migration to the United States that warrant attention. The article also suggests key areas for future research that relate to unaccompanied children's lives, including education, health and mental health, and legal services.

Canizales, Stephanie L. "Work Primacy and the Social Incorporation of Unaccompanied, Undocumented Latinx Youth in the United States." *Social Forces* 101, no. 3 (2023): 1372–95.

Sociologist Canizales conducted a study that explored the experiences of unaccompanied children who transitioned to young adulthood and navigated work environments in Los Angeles, California. As unaccompanied children grow up, along with experiencing biological and psychological developmental changes, they also must navigate added stressors related to the immigration system. This study unearthed important insights into the experiences of young adults who were formerly unaccompanied children. The results show that young adults in the study managed pressure to financially support family members in their country of origin and also struggled with limited financial independence and limited job mobility. This created conditions where participants struggled to engage with their broader community because of constricted employment opportunities. Rather than engines for social mobility, the challenges of immigration status constrained young adults' ability to grow in both social settings and employment settings. Adding to a growing literature on undocumented young adults, this study contributes an important perspective by including the voices and experiences of unaccompanied children, who are a uniquely vulnerable group of immigrants, especially as they transition to young adulthood.

Castañeda, Ernesto, Daniel Jenks, Jessica Chaikof, Carina Cione, SteVon Felton, Isabella Goris, Lesley Buck, and Eric Hershberg. "Symptoms of PTSD and Depression among Central American Immigrant Youth." *Trauma Care* 1, no. 2 (2021): 99–118.

Sociologist Castañeda and colleagues conducted a study that explored mental health symptoms, as well as exposure to trauma, that unaccompanied children and other immigrant children experience. The study used a mixed-method design, where quantitative data was collected with a survey and qualitative data was collected with in-depth interviews. Participants were asked to respond about their experiences before and after migration to the United States. The sample included thirty-four unaccompanied and twenty-four accompanied children. Participants in the study migrated from El Salvador, Guatemala, and Honduras. The results show that both unaccompanied and accompanied immigrant children experience heightened traumatic experiences before and during migration to the United States. Results also show that mental health symptoms did not increase after migration to the United States and that symptoms of posttraumatic stress disorder and depression improved after resettlement in the United States. The results of the study align with existing research on unaccompanied children's mental health and support the expansion of social services for unaccompanied children and other vulnerable immigrant children who are navigating acculturation in the United States.

Crea, Thomas M., Anayeli Lopez, Robert G. Hasson, Kerri Evans, Caroline Palleschi, and Dawnya Underwood. "Unaccompanied Immigrant Children in Long Term Foster Care: Identifying Needs and Best Practices from a Child Welfare Perspective." *Children and Youth Services Review* 92 (2018): 56–64.

Some unaccompanied children who migrate to the United States are not able to be placed with a sponsor, so they are instead placed in long-term foster care. However, there is limited research on the unique needs, as well as best practices for care, for unaccompanied children in the United States. Social work professor Crea and colleagues examined this topic by analyzing qualitative data that was collected with focus groups with seventy-nine long-term foster care providers and foster parents in the United States. Results reveal a series of challenges unaccompanied children experience, including securing appropriate and stable foster placements; promoting connections in the community; accessing education and independent living skills; and difficulties with acculturation, trauma and mental health issues, and challenges with legal status. Strategies to address these issues include supporting culturally competent foster placements, providing English-language training, and connecting unaccompanied children with relational supports in the community, such as mentors and mental health professionals.

Creswell Báez, Johanna, Padma Swamy, Adriana Gutierrez, Ana Ortiz-Mejias, Jacquelyn Othon, Nohemi Garcia Roberts, and Sanghamitra Misra. "Insights for Clinical Providers and Community Leaders: Unaccompanied Immigrant Children's Mental Health Includes Caregiver Support." *Child and Adolescent Social Work Journal* 42 (2024): 675–89.

Social work scholar Creswell Báez and colleagues conducted a study that explores the perspectives of caregivers who support unaccompanied children in the United States. This study was unique in that it focused on caregivers, whereas previous research has often focused on unaccompanied children's experiences. This qualitative study analyzed data that was collected with in-depth interviews with thirty-six participants, including unaccompanied children, their caregivers, health and mental health clinicians, and community members in Houston, Texas. Along with identifying themes related to unaccompanied children's experiences in resettlement, the study also revealed notable experiences of caregivers. For example, financial challenges, feelings of guilt, and ongoing difficulty with securing stable and supportive environments in resettlement communities are all experiences reported by caregivers. The results of the study offer important considerations for policymakers who will lead future efforts to reform the immigration system and align policies and laws with the best interests of children and the unique needs of their caregivers.

Doering-White, John. "The Shifting Boundaries of 'Best Interest': Sheltering Unaccompanied Central American Minors in Transit through Mexico." *Children and Youth Services Review* 92 (2018): 39–47.

As unaccompanied children migrate to the United States, they are subject to a variety of conditions that may threaten their health or well-being. Some threats to well-being include dangerous modes of transportation, such as on the tops of trains. Other threats relate to economic and sexual exploitation from human traffickers. Social work scholar and anthropologist Doering-White conducted an ethnographic study that explored how perceptions of a child's "best interest" shift depending on the context of their migration to the United States. By observing conditions in migrant shelters in Mexico, Doering-White adds important context to the lived experiences of unaccompanied children who receive services at shelters in Mexico. Some observations include nuanced intersections of humanitarianism and human smuggling and a tension between nonprofit shelters and government agencies in Mexico.

Doering-White, John, Jessica Darrow, Breanne Grace, Benjamin Roth, Aimee Herring, and Stefan Liew. "Care under Pressure: Policy Contradictions of Speedy Release, Safety, and Placement Suitability in ORR-contracted Programs for Unaccompanied Migrant Children." *Children and Youth Services Review* 169 (2025): 108093.

This article from social work scholar Doering-White and colleagues explores the perspectives of social service providers who work with unaccompanied children in the United States. The article analyzes qualitative data collected with in-depth interviews with sixty-five professionals, including case managers, social workers, and educators, who provide Office of Refugee Resettlement contracted services in four different states. The authors' analysis reveals how policy frameworks, including the 1997 Flores Settlement Agreement and the Trafficking Victims Protection Reauthorization Act of 2008, inform the way social service providers work with unaccompanied children. In the middle of politicized environments that surround the topic of immigration, the researchers of this article suggest that a tension emerges between pressure to place unaccompanied children with a sponsor and the child's best interests. This tension and subsequent pressure can lead to "compromising care" for unaccompanied children.

Evans, Kerri. "Policy and Legal Implications for Working with Unaccompanied Immigrant Children in Foster Care in the United States." *Laws* 12, no. 2 (2023): 31.

In this article, social work professor Evans provides a broad overview of unaccompanied children's experience migrating to the United States. She offers background information and data and also describes the process of apprehension and care of unaccompanied children when they arrive at a US border. The article includes a visual depiction of the number of unaccompanied child arrivals to the United States between 2003 and 2021. Evans describes the legal process unaccompanied children must navigate in the United States and also explains the long-term foster care program.

Evans, Kerri, Thomas M. Crea, and Ximena Soto. "A Human Rights Approach to Macro Social Work Field Education with Unaccompanied Immigrant Children." *Journal of Human Rights and Social Work* 6, no. 1 (2021): 67–77.

This article includes a thoughtful application of a human rights lens to understand the needs of unaccompanied children. Drawing on the Universal Declaration of Human Rights and the National Association of Social Workers (NASW) Code of Ethics, the authors provide a background of unaccompanied children and analyze how macro social work can address their unique needs and support their adjustment in the United States. Both the Universal Declaration of Human Rights and the NASW Code of Ethics emphasize the importance of social justice to ensure basic human needs are met. Macro social work, including advocacy, community organizing, and policy development, can help address myriad human rights violations that unaccompanied children experience, including violence and poverty. Evans and colleagues suggest there are multiple ways that schools and social work educators can build training and curriculum to include content on unaccompanied children. For example, trainings can include content on the specific mental health needs of unaccompanied children and how to use culturally informed assessments and intervention. Social work curriculum can include content on the theories of human rights and social work ethical principles, and how they apply to the needs of unaccompanied children. The authors argue that awareness of the unique needs of unaccompanied children can help practitioners serve unaccompanied children in different settings.

Evans, Kerri, Dominique Culley, and Thomas M. Crea. "The Role of the Foster Care Agency and Foster Parents in the Lives of Children Who Are Unaccompanied Immigrants from Central America." *Child Welfare* 100, no. 4 (2022): 67–88.

After unaccompanied children migrate to the United States and are processed by Customs and Border Protection officials, their care is transferred to the Office of Refugee Resettlement, which is responsible for placing children with a sponsor in the community. Some unaccompanied children are unable to be placed with a sponsor because one is not identified or officials determine an available sponsor is not a safe or appropriate placement. Evans and colleagues explored the features that create positive foster care placements for unaccompanied children who are placed in long-term foster care. They specifically explored the role of foster parents and the ways that programming and policies in foster care programs help unaccompanied children. The researchers analyzed qualitative data collected with focus groups with seventy-nine different foster care service providers. The analysis depicted key roles that foster parents play when caring for unaccompanied children, including the importance of supportive and stable relationships between foster parent and child, a welcoming home environment, having access to culturally appropriate food, and having space in the community to develop a clear sense of self. The results showed that foster care programs supported unaccompanied children by offering community-based services that support acculturation, offering programming focused on cultural orientation, teaching unaccompanied children independent living skills, employing bilingual and bicultural staff, and having clear safety protocols to ensure unaccompanied children are safe at home and in the community. The study adds important knowledge that can guide foster care service providers and programs.

Evans, Kerri, Kylie Diebold, and Rocío Calvo. "A Call to Action: Re-imagining Social Work Practice with Unaccompanied Minors." *Advances in Social Work* 18, no. 3 (2018): 788–807.

In this article, social work professor Evans and colleagues provide a broad overview of unaccompanied children in the United States, including relevant data and statistics and a review of services, supports, and policies related to their care. The article includes nuanced analysis of gaps between services designed for supporting unaccompanied children and the limited resources available to support those services. Analysis also explains important themes such as health, mental health, and education supports. Evans and colleagues offer insightful recommendations for social workers who support unaccompanied children, including building partnerships with community-based mental health providers and advocating for education services for unaccompanied children. By building partnerships and creating culturally relevant services, Evans and colleagues suggest that unaccompanied children will be better served in communities as they navigate resettlement and adjust to life in the United States.

Evans, Kerri, Robert G. Hasson III, Samantha Teixeira, Virginia Fitchett, and Thomas M. Crea. "Unaccompanied Immigrant Children in ORR Foster Care: Community Level Facilitators of Adjustment Identified by Service Providers." *Child and Adolescent Social Work Journal* 41, no. 1 (2024): 125–38.

One gap in research on unaccompanied children is how aspects of the community are related to unaccompanied children's adjustment in resettlement communities. Evans and colleagues explored this topic by focusing on the facilitators of prevention and intervention that support unaccompanied children who are living in foster care in the United States. The study aimed to better understand how parts of the community can inform positive youth development for unaccompanied children living in foster care. The authors analyzed qualitative data collected with focus groups with seventy-nine foster care service providers and foster parents. The study identified two prevention strategies for positive youth development: welcoming communities and inter-agency collaborations. Unaccompanied children are better supported in communities that are welcoming, both in terms of interest about unaccompanied children that is expressed by community members, as well as welcoming immigration policies. In addition, results unearthed how partnerships that advance education opportunities and that foster connection with legal service providers are important prevention strategies for unaccompanied children. For intervention strategies, the results showed that community relationships with mentors, as well as access to health care services and engaging with church communities, are all important interventions within the community that help unaccompanied children. This study added important knowledge to a growing area of research on the various ways communities can support unaccompanied children in the United States.

Evans, Kerri, Gabrielle Oliveira, Robert G. Hason III, Thomas M. Crea, Sarah E. Neville, and Virgginia Fitchett. "Unaccompanied Children's Education in the United States: Service Provider's Perspective on Challenges and Support Strategies." *Cultura Educación Sociedad* 13, no. 1 (2022): 193–218.

Schools are often a location where newcomer students can receive an array of supports, and research shows these supports can lead to academic achievement and language skills. However, there is limited research on the role of school settings for unaccompanied children, who are a unique population of immigrant students who often do not have parents in the home to provide extra support with academics. Evans and colleagues applied a human rights lens to explore how schools support unaccompanied children. They examined qualitative data that was collected using focus groups with seventy-nine service providers who work with unaccompanied children. The results revealed that there are a variety of school-related supports, including academic and language services, collaboration among service providers and school personnel, and programming that addresses emotional and behavioral issues. Among the challenges schools experience are limited resources to fund programming, limited English-language skills among unaccompanied children, cultural differences that impede adjustment to the school environment, and unaccompanied children's mental health issues. The article concludes by offering a variety of recommendations for schools. For example, the authors suggest that schools could support unaccompanied children by building partnerships with community-based organizations and implementing policies that welcome unaccompanied children, such as streamlining paperwork requirements.

Grace, Breanne Leigh, and Benjamin J. Roth. "Bureaucratic Neglect: The Paradoxical Mistreatment of Unaccompanied Migrant Children in the US Immigration System." *Journal of Ethnic and Migration Studies* 47, no. 15 (2021): 3455–72.

In this article, social work scholars Grace and Roth examine Post-Release Services (PRS) from multiple perspectives. PRS are community-based case management services that help unaccompanied children in the United States navigate resettlement communities and access a variety of supports, including legal services, education services, and health and mental health services. This study analyzes a wide range of data, including document analysis of all publicly available documents on PRS in the United States, ethnographic observations at four different agencies providing PRS in the United States, and interviews with twenty unaccompanied children, seventeen sponsors, and thirteen employees of an agency providing PRS. Despite its name, the authors emphasize that PRS does not deliver services for unaccompanied children; rather, PRS provides referrals for services in the community. Along with this structural reality of PRS, the article describes how cultural and linguistic barriers inhibit unaccompanied children's access to services. For children trying to navigate the complexity of immigration court systems, the authors refocus on the structural barriers that can lead to heightened risk for unaccompanied children: "PRS exists as a series of paradoxes. The aim of PRS is to identify the children who are most 'at risk' to help them adjust once they are placed with their sponsors and access basic rights; instead, it actually compounds risks and legal vulnerability as poverty, language, immigration status, and trauma undermine children's access to services."

Hasson, Robert G., III, Caitlin Corbett, Antonia Diaz-Valdés, Kerri Evans, Thomas M. Crea, and Dawnya Underwood. "Educational Services for Unaccompanied Immigrant Children in the United States." *Journal of Social Service Research* 48, no. 5 (2022): 606–16.

This study was conducted by social work scholar Hasson III and colleagues and explored the factors that are related to unaccompanied children reporting education services as their primary need upon arriving to the United States. Research shows education is one of the main reasons unaccompanied children migrate to the United States. This study examined administrative data that was shared by a national nonprofit organization that helps facilitate Post-Release Services, or case management services, for unaccompanied children in the United States. A total of 851 unaccompanied children were part of the dataset, and 219 children reported education services as their primary need. The results show that older unaccompanied children were more likely to report education services as their primary need. This suggests that older unaccompanied children may be migrating to the United States to pursue education opportunities that are not available in their country of origin. The results also show that unaccompanied children who are placed with their mothers, compared to other sponsor types, are less likely to report education services as their primary need. This finding suggests that mothers have a high level of involvement in their child's life, which can manifest as helping them with school-related activities. The results also show that male unaccompanied children, compared to female unaccompanied children, are more likely to report education services as their primary need. One interpretation of this finding is that unaccompanied male children, who research shows are more likely to migrate due to violence, may perceive education as a means to escape violence. Collectively, the findings can help inform service providers as they seek to help unaccompanied children connect with schools. In addition, the results can inform policy developments to enhance education access for unaccompanied children and other vulnerable immigrant groups.

Hasson, Robert G., III, Thomas M. Crea, Scott D. Easton, and Dawnya Underwood. "Child Maltreatment and Substance Abuse: Unaccompanied

Children and Adverse Outcomes in Long-Term Foster Care in the United States." *Child & Family Social Work* 27, no. 3 (2022): 435–43.

A large body of research in the child welfare field has analyzed child maltreatment, substance abuse, and outcomes for children in foster care. However, little research has examined these topics as they relate to unaccompanied children in the United States. Hasson III and colleagues analyzed survey data that was shared by a nonprofit organization in the United States that provides long-term foster care for unaccompanied children. When unaccompanied children are in long-term foster care, they sometimes have adverse experiences, such as mental health emergencies, self-harm, physical or verbal aggression, or runaway behavior. This study explored how a history of child maltreatment (verbal, physical, and sexual abuse, as well as neglect) or substance use behavior is associated with adverse experiences for 204 unaccompanied children in long-term foster care. Results show that a history of sexual abuse and a history of neglect are associated with increased risk of adverse outcomes for unaccompanied children at their time of discharge from long-term foster care. The study results align with a large and extensive body of research on child welfare in the United States. The results confirm the toxic outcomes that can occur when children experience maltreatment and help inform treatment planning and intervention steps that clinicians can take when working with unaccompanied children.

Hasson, Robert G., III, Thomas M. Crea, Ruth G. McRoy, and Ân H. Lê. "Patchwork of Promises: A Critical Analysis of Immigration Policies for Unaccompanied Undocumented Children in the United States." *Child & Family Social Work* 24, no. 2 (2019): 275–82.

Hasson III and colleagues conducted a policy analysis of immigration policies that relate to the experiences of unaccompanied children in the United States. Many immigration policies in the United States are focused on security and identifying and managing potential threats at US borders. However, many such laws conflict with the best interests of children, as well as with best practices in child welfare. Hasson III and colleagues argue that the vast assortment of immigration policies focused on children create a "patchwork of promises" that fail to center unaccompanied children's health and well-being, as well as their best interests. Practices of family separation, child detention, and limited legal representation in immigration court are examples of how US immigration policies fail to meet the needs of unaccompanied children. The article offers insights for future policy reform that seeks to recognize and meet the best interests of unaccompanied children who are resettled in the United States.

Hasson, Robert G., III, Antonia Diaz-Valdez, and Dawnya Underwood. "Mental Health Services for Unaccompanied Children in the United States." *Journal of Loss and Trauma* 28, no. 7 (2023): 599–615.

This study, conducted by social work scholar Hasson III and colleagues, explored the factors that are associated with unaccompanied children reporting mental health services as their primary need. While research shows many unaccompanied children experience migration-related trauma and struggle with mental health symptoms, this is one of the first known studies to explore what aspects of a child's life are related to their need for mental health services, rather than other services in their resettlement community. The quantitative study analyzed data that was shared by a national nonprofit that provides case management services for unaccompanied children in the United States. The dataset included 851 unaccompanied children, and 200 children reported mental health services as their primary need. The researchers found that older unaccompanied children and children from Honduras, compared to other countries of origin, were more likely to report mental health services as their primary need. Unaccompanied males were less likely to report mental health services as their primary need. The results reveal the importance of country-specific stressors that may influence the need for mental health services. In addition, the study can inform the way case management services are delivered for unaccompanied male and female children.

Hasson, Robert G., III, Scott D. Easton, Antonia Díaz-Valdés Iriarte, Laura M. O'Dwyer, Dawnya Underwood, and Thomas M. Crea. "Examining the Psychometric Properties of the Child PTSD Symptom Scale within a Sample of Unaccompanied Immigrant Children in the United States." *Journal of Loss and Trauma* 26, no. 4 (2021): 323–35.

Research shows unaccompanied children, like other groups of immigrants who experience forced migration, have high risk of exposure to trauma at various parts of the migration journey. This includes trauma in home countries, such as violence in the community or maltreatment at home. It also includes trauma during migration journeys, such as economic and sexual exploitation by smugglers. Unaccompanied children may experience trauma at the US border, as well as after resettlement in the United States. However, a challenge for clinicians in the United States is assessing trauma symptoms that unaccompanied children experience due to cultural variations in mental health symptomology. Many mental health measures have been designed in the context of Western, English-speaking populations. This study by Hasson III and colleagues explored rates of trauma, as well as the extent to which one trauma measure, the Child PTSD Symptom Scale (CPSS), accurately assesses trauma symptoms in a sample of unaccompanied children. The CPSS was completed by 149 unaccompanied children who were resettled in the United States. Results showed that 8.1 percent of the sample met criteria for PTSD. The results also showed nuanced expressions of trauma symptoms that unaccompanied children experience, such that reactivity symptoms (e.g., feelings of anger and having difficulty paying attention) cluster together in a way that suggests the challenges with immigrant integration, like language barriers, may complicate underlying symptoms of trauma. The results highlight important considerations for future research to help strengthen assessment techniques and tools when working with unaccompanied children and other vulnerable immigrants.

Hasson, Robert G., III, Kerri Evans, and Thomas M. Crea. "Foster Care for Unaccompanied Immigrant and Refugee Children and Youth." In *Encyclopedia of Social Work*. National Association of Social Workers Press and Oxford University Press, 2024. https://doi.org/10.1093/acrefore/9780199975839.013.1293

Social work professor Hasson III and colleagues provide an overview of the foster care system for unaccompanied children in the United States. The article includes key facts and data related to the number of unaccompanied children arriving in the United States, and the location of placements in the country. The article offers an analysis of key features of the long-term foster care system for unaccompanied children, including aspects of the system that align with child welfare best practices. Unaccompanied children are similar in some ways to children in domestic foster care programs, such as the need for a primary caregiver to provide support. However, there are key differences, including language barriers, the stress involved with immigration court, and mental health challenges that are specific to migration-related trauma. These unique differences require the long-term foster care system to offer special programming and support to ensure unaccompanied children get their basic human needs met and are also able to navigate resettlement communities during their acculturation.

Hasson, Robert G., III, Bianca LaBella, Antonia Díaz-Valdés, and Dawnya Underwood. "Family Stabilization Services for Unaccompanied Children in the United States." *Families in Society* 105, no. 4 (2024): 507–19.

During initial processing by the Office of Refugee Resettlement that facilitates placement with a sponsor, unaccompanied children identify their primary need to help guide future services. Social work scholar Hasson III and colleagues examined the factors that are related to unaccompanied children, identifying family stabilization services as their primary need. These are services that help children who may have difficulty navigating relational dynamics in a family setting. The study analyzed administrative data that was shared by a national nonprofit that provides post-release services for unaccompanied children. The sample included a total of 851 unaccompanied children, and 162 children identified family-stabilization services as their primary need upon arrival to the United States. Children from Honduras and children placed with their fathers, compared to other sponsor types, had greater odds of needing family-stabilization services. The results also showed that older unaccompanied children exhibited lower odds of needing family-stabilization services. The findings suggest that placement with the father may present unique challenges for unaccompanied children in a family setting. One possibility is that fathers, compared to mothers, may work more hours outside of the home, which could limit the time spent with the family. The study offers insightful considerations for clinicians working with unaccompanied children who may be struggling in their sponsor placement.

Hasson, Robert G., III, Clara A. Oliva, Bianca LaBella, and Dahiana Rodriguez. "'Little by Little, I Go': Multiple Dimensions of Distress and Support for Unaccompanied Children in the United States." *Children and Youth Services Review* 160 (2024): 107541.

Existing scholarship shows that unaccompanied children experience various traumatic events before, during, and after their migration to the United States. This includes violence in their home country, exploitation during their migration journey, and detention at the US border. However, much less is known about how different experiences lead to distress. Furthermore, there is limited scholarship on what unaccompanied children describe as most supportive after their arrival in the United States. Hasson III and colleagues explored these topics in a qualitative study that analyzed data collected by in-depth interviews with sixteen unaccompanied children. For challenges and mental distress, unaccompanied children reported that language barriers complicate their ability to develop social connections. In addition, family separation is a unique and universal distress that complicates existing trauma symptoms. Unaccompanied children also struggle with family reunification, specifically navigating new family relationships. Unaccompanied children reported that material supports, such as school supplies and coats, are important for meeting their immediate needs. Family support helps facilitate resilience for unaccompanied children. Similar to previous research, in this study, unaccompanied children identified education as an important gateway for developing relationships and adjusting to the United States. Finally, unaccompanied children identified nonprofit staff relationships as integral for integration. The study offers important insights for clinicians and practitioners working with unaccompanied children in the United States. Specifically, the study helps identify specific stressors that treatment plans and interventions can address. The study can also inform policy development that focuses on enhancing integration for unaccompanied children and other vulnerable immigrants in the United States.

Patel, Sita G., Vicky Bouche, William Martinez, Karla Barajas, Alex Garcia, Maya Sztainer, and Kathleen Hawkins. "'Se extraña todo': Family Separation and Reunification Experiences among Unaccompanied Adolescent Migrants from Central America." *New Directions for Child and Adolescent Development* 2021, no. 176 (2021): 227–44.

Psychologist Patel and colleagues conducted a study that explored the experiences of unaccompanied children from Central America who experienced family separation and later reunification with family in the United States. The qualitative study analyzed data collected with in-depth interviews with forty-two unaccompanied children who were resettled in the western United States. The results show that family separation is distressing and complex. Rather than only parents, participants reported experiencing distress when separated from a sibling or other extended family member. Family reunification was associated with positive emotional experiences, as well as negative emotional experiences. For example, some unaccompanied children reported feeling disconnected from family members, feelings of sadness, and confusion regarding unfamiliar family dynamics. The study adds insights into the importance of attachment with caregivers, the vital role of family units for child well-being, and how migration can stress family relationships that are vital for adaptive child development.

Roth, Benjamin J., Thomas M. Crea, Jayshree Jani, Dawnya Underwood, Robert G. Hasson, Kerri Evans, Michael Zuch, and Emily Hornung. "Detached and Afraid." *Child Welfare* 96, no. 5 (2019): 29–50.

One unique challenge during President Trump's first administration was an immigration policy called "Zero Tolerance" that included criminally prosecuting all adults who cross the US border without documentation. This resulted in forcibly separating children from their parents, and immigrant children becoming unaccompanied while in US custody. Social work professor Roth and colleagues conducted a study to explore the various outcomes of this policy. The study analyzed qualitative data collected from twenty in-depth interviews with foster care professionals who worked directly with children who were separated from their caregivers. Results indicate that children forcibly separated from their parents exhibited trauma-related symptoms that disrupted their functioning. Foster care professionals also reported having difficulty building trust with some of the children, especially tender-aged children (e.g., less than five years old), due to language and cultural barriers. Programs adapt to this unique population of immigrant children by providing more time-intensive one-on-one care for children separated from their parents, as well as investing more time into tracking information about family relationships.

Roth, Benjamin J., and Breanne L. Grace. "Falling through the Cracks: The Paradox of Post-release Services for Unaccompanied Child Migrants." *Children and Youth Services Review* 58 (2015): 244–52.

The gap in post-release services was the subject of a study conducted by Roth and Grace, who used qualitative methods in a cross-sectional study to examine how post-release services help unaccompanied children adapt to new environments post-migration. As stipulated in the Trafficking Victims Protection Reauthorization Act (TVPRA), unaccompanied children in the custody of the Office of Refugee Resettlement (ORR) receive a risk assessment prior to release to a sponsor to determine if the unaccompanied child has any notable risks or needs to be addressed. If the risk assessment identifies areas of need or high risk, the unaccompanied child and their sponsor receive a home study. Unaccompanied children who receive a home study are eligible for six months of post-release services. Importantly, language in the TVPRA indicates unaccompanied children who do not receive a home study but exhibit mental health needs and could benefit from ongoing support from a community-based agency are also eligible for post-release services.

Roth, Benjamin J., and Caroline S. Hartnett. "Creating Reasons to Stay? Unaccompanied Youth Migration, Community-Based Programs, and the Power of 'Push' Factors in El Salvador." *Children and Youth Services Review* 92 (2018): 48–55.

Unaccompanied children migrate to the United States for various reasons. Social work scholar Roth conducted a study with scholar Hartnett to explore the contexts that influence unaccompanied children migrating to the United States. The study analyzed survey data from 445 youth in El Salvador who engaged with community-based social service agencies throughout El Salvador. Results from this study reveal that violence is a common factor that influences migration. In fact, 61 percent of participants reported that at least one homicide occurred in their neighborhood the previous year. Although many participants reported that the community agencies helped them with academic success and employment outcomes, 42 percent confirmed that they planned to migrate to the United States in the next three years. The results from this study suggest that robust investment in community-based social services in El Salvador can lead to tangible benefits for adolescents. However, pervasive violence, as seen across different historical and geographic contexts, remains a strong influence of migration to the United States.

Schmidt, Susan. "'They Need to Give Us a Voice': Lessons from Listening to Unaccompanied Central American and Mexican Children on Helping Children Like Themselves." *Journal on Migration and Human Security* 5, no. 1 (2017): 57–81.

Social work scholar Schmidt conducted a study that analyzed qualitative data from a sample of unaccompanied children who migrated to the United States from Central America and Mexico. The study focused on the following research question: "What can we learn from the observations and recommendations of Central American and Mexican unaccompanied migrant children for helping children like themselves?" The study analyzed a secondary dataset from a previous study conducted by the United Nations High Commissioner for Refugees. The sample included a total of 404 children. Results from the study revealed several themes that answer the main research question. Addressing conditions of poverty, security, and violence; government instability; limited education opportunities; support during migration journeys; and family support are all areas that unaccompanied children identified as important areas of concern. Furthermore, some of these themes interact in dynamic ways, such as poverty and violence, violence and education, and education and poverty. Overall, this article unpacks the complex reasons that explain why unaccompanied children migrate to the United States.

Szlyk, Hannah Selene, Jodi Berger Cardoso, Liza Barros Lane, and Kerri Evans. "'Me perdía en la escuela': Latino Newcomer Youths in the US School System." *Social Work* 65, no. 2 (2020): 131–9.

Research shows that one of the primary reasons that unaccompanied children migrate to the United States is to pursue education. An important area of research is exploring the experiences of unaccompanied children who access schools after resettlement in the United States. Social work scholar Szlyk and colleagues explored this topic in a qualitative study that analyzed data collected by in-depth interviews with thirty unaccompanied children and ten other informants. The results of the study reveal six key themes that describe the experiences unaccompanied children have in schools in the United States. First, respondents described the importance of getting along with other students. Analysis shows that there is limited trust in school staff and students in the new school. Respondents in the study also described language barriers as a distinct challenge when trying to adjust to the new school. Given the substantial cultural differences, school staff described unaccompanied children as experiencing a "hard landing" when arriving to the school. The very process of migration to the United States, and the time it takes to navigate the immigration system and arrive to a resettlement community, results in an interrupted education experience. Finally, participants expressed gratitude for being able to pursue education in the United States. This study provides school officials, including teachers and administrators, important considerations when designing school policies and practices to welcome unaccompanied children.

Reports

Evans, Kerri, and Tatiana Londoño. "Post-release Services for Unaccompanied Children: Current Gaps and Needed Improvements." The Center on Immigration and Child Welfare, 2022. https://cimmcw.org/Post-Release-Services-for-UC_Research-Brief.pdf

This report by social work scholar Evans and colleague describes key challenges with the Post-Release Services (PRS) program for unaccompanied children and offers suggestions for improving the services for unaccompanied children in the United States. Among the key challenges, the report describes how some unaccompanied children do not receive PRS because of inadequate assessment processes when unaccompanied children are in ORR care. Another major challenge is limited community-based services due to geographic barriers and limited providers. The report offers recommendations, including expanding PRS, addressing mental health needs by improving assessment practices, expanding training opportunities for local providers who work with unaccompanied children, adapting practices to improve cultural adaptation, engaging with local schools, and pursuing more research.

Hasson, Robert G., III, A. Díaz-Valdés, and C. Corbett. "Primary Needs for Unaccompanied Children Receiving Post Release Services in the United States."

Providence, RI: Providence College, 2020. Available from https://social-work.providence.edu/researchspotlight-hasson/

Hasson III and colleagues published a report that explores the primary needs of unaccompanied children who migrated to the United States. As part of the processing by the Office of Refugee Resettlement, unaccompanied children identify what they perceive is their primary need. Specific needs include education services, family-stabilization services, legal services, mental health services, substance use services, and gang-prevention services. This report explores the three most commonly identified primary needs in 2019 among a sample of 851 unaccompanied children: education services, mental health services, and family stabilization services. Most unaccompanied children identified education services as their primary need (25.74 percent). This includes support with enrolling in school and navigating new education systems. The next most reported primary need was mental health services (23.50 percent). These services are designed to support unaccompanied children who are struggling with symptoms related to family separation or other migration-related trauma. The third most reported need was family-stabilization services (19.04 percent). These services are intended to support children who may experience distress when adjusting to a new family setting, such as living with a parent they have not seen in several years. The report also describes different patterns and trends among the three different primary needs.

Kennedy, Elizabeth. "No Childhood Here." *Perspectives* (2014).

Kennedy is a scholar who completed a report that explored the reasons why unaccompanied children migrated from El Salvador to the United States. As part of this project, Kennedy interviewed 322 minors in El Salvador to understand the reasons that motivated their migration to the United States. At the time of this project, results showed that crime and violence were primary factors that motivated migration to the United States. Kennedy found that 59 percent of Salvadoran boys and 61 percent of Salvadoran girls reported crime and threats from gangs as reasons for their migration to the United States. The study also unearthed notable differences between urban and rural regions. Specifically, children from rural regions cited poverty as a reason for migrating to the United States, so they could find work. In this study, the results showed that only 35 percent reported family reunification as their primary reason for migrating to the United States, even though more than 50 percent of children reported a parent or both parents lived in the United States. This finding sheds light on the stress related to violence in the community, and poverty in rural areas, as more pressing concerns that motivated children to migrate to the United States. This report provides readers important context for understanding the complex reasons that motivate children to migrate to the United States without parents or caregivers. Rather than one single reason, the motivation to undertake a dangerous journey to the United States with limited resources or support is multifaceted.

Kids in Need of Defense. *CARE: Connect, Assess, Respond, and Educate Intervention Toolkit.* 2025. https://supportkind.org/resources/care-connect-assess-respond-and-educate-intervention-toolkit/

Kids in Need of Defense (KIND) created a toolkit to support professionals who work with unaccompanied children who are at risk of labor exploitation. The toolkit is based on the principles of psychological first aid and covers four main areas: Connect, Assess, Respond, and Education. Connect refers to the importance of building a relationship with unaccompanied children. Assess refers to meeting with the child to learn about their background, their needs, and their strengths. After learning about the child's background, respond refers to helping the child access services that build on their strengths and address their needs. Finally, education refers to providing the child and their sponsor information to continue meeting future needs.

Lutheran Immigration and Refugee Services. "At the Crossroads for Unaccompanied Migrant Children: Policy, Practice, and Protection." 2015.

This report describes various policy and practice recommendations that are based on a series of three roundtables that Lutheran Immigration and Refugee Service organized in 2014. LIRS, which is now known as Global Refuge, is a national nonprofit based in the United States that is one of the main providers of services for unaccompanied children who are resettled in the United States. This report was published in response to large numbers of unaccompanied children migrating to the United States from Central America. The authors recommend that the process of apprehension, initial screening, and referral to the Office of Refugee Resettlement should prioritize the best interests of children, which includes placement in the least restrictive environment possible. Unaccompanied children are uniquely vulnerable because they lack the presence of a supportive and caring adult. The report recommends that unaccompanied children have access to legal counsel when navigating the immigration system. The report also recommends improvements in the family reunification process, including revising assessment tools to ensure placements are safe settings for children. Furthermore, the report recommends that the US Congress authorize funding for all unaccompanied children to receive Post-Release Services to further support their adjustment to life in the United States. The report also recommends improved coordination between governmental and nongovernmental organizations to streamline services for unaccompanied children. Finally, the report recommends that government agencies use existing laws, such as the Trafficking Victims Protection Reauthorization Act, to provide oversight of organizations serving unaccompanied children in the United States.

United Nations High Commissioner for Refugees. "Children on the Run: Unaccompanied Children Leaving Central America and Mexico and the Need for International Protection." 2016. http://www.unhcr.org/en-us/children-on-the-run.html

In 2016, the United Nations High Commissioner for Refugees published a landmark report that explored the experiences of unaccompanied children migrating to the United States, as well as their reasons for leaving their country of origin. This report was one of the first large-scale investigations of the experiences of unaccompanied children in the United States since the increased numbers of arrivals started in 2012. In addition, this report is notable because it included a total of 404 unaccompanied children, all of whom migrated to the United States from El Salvador, Guatemala, Honduras, or Mexico. In-depth interviews with participants in the study showed that 72 percent of children from El Salvador, 38 percent of children from Guatemala, 57 percent of children from Honduras, and 64 percent of children from Mexico demonstrated potential international protection needs, such as protection from persecution or violence in their home country. The most common reasons for migrating to the United States included escaping violence, abuse in the home, deprivation (i.e. poverty), and to pursue family reunification in the United States, or another opportunity, such as education. The reasons for migrating to the United States differed by country of origin. For example, unaccompanied children from El Salvador were more likely to report family reunification as their reason for leaving, followed by escaping violence in El Salvador. Children from Guatemala were most likely to report family reunification as their reason for migrating to the United States. Children from Honduras, as well as from Mexico, were most likely to report family reunification as their reason for leaving, followed by escaping violence. The report outlines a series of recommendations to ensure that unaccompanied children's human rights are respected and that their best interests are met. These include enhancing training for immigration officials, enhancing assessment and intervention tools, and strengthening collaboration among agencies and organizations that work with unaccompanied children.

Book

Nazario, Sonia. *Enrique's Journey: The Story of a Boy's Dangerous Odyssey to Reunite with His Mother*. Random House Trade Paperbacks, 2007.

Enrique's Journey is a book that tells the story of Enrique, a young boy from El Salvador, whose mother migrates to the United States to search for work. The book follows different parts of the migration journey, beginning with Enrique making the decision to leave his country of origin and migrate to the United States to search for his mother. The book offers readers an in-depth look at the deeply emotional struggle of family separation that is a universal experience of unaccompanied children. Readers learn about the complex feelings that inform Enrique's attachment with his mother. The book also portrays the challenges Enrique encountered during his migration to the United States, including violence and threats of exploitation. The book pays particular attention to the complex emotional experience involved with family reunification and how the distress that can accompany reconnection is processed across borders and cultures.

Media

Finno-Velasquez, Megan, Kristina Lovato, and Rachel Prandini. "The U.S. Must Adopt Child Welfare Strategies for Unaccompanied Minors." The Hill, June 30, 2021. https://thehill.com/opinion/immigration/560981-the-us-must-adopt-child-welfarestrategies-for-unaccompanied-minors#bottom-story-socials

This op-ed, by social work scholar Finno-Velasquez and colleagues, argues that the US government should use child welfare principles when meeting the needs of unaccompanied children. In the op-ed, the authors outline the reasons why unaccompanied children are among the most vulnerable immigrants who arrive in the United States. They recommend that the Office of Refugee Resettlement expand capacity for unaccompanied children, rather than rely on emergency intake settings that do not address child welfare needs.

2

7

Chronology

This chapter offers a chronology of major laws and policies that relate to immigration in the United States, with a focus on unaccompanied children. Beginning with a description of major immigration laws that shaped demographic trends in the early twentieth century, the chronology also covers major bills that aim to address the needs of people forcibly displaced, particularly after World War II. Next, the chapter describes policies that address individuals and families displaced due to the Vietnam War and reviews laws in the early twenty-first century that address the needs of vulnerable immigrants, including victims of human trafficking and unaccompanied children. Finally, the chronology describes laws, policies, and lawsuits that relate to immigration actions by President Trump in his first and second administrations.

1924: The Immigration Act of 1924 is signed by President Calvin Coolidge. It is a restrictive immigration bill, which limits the number of visas for lawful entry to the United States and uses a quota system that is based on an immigrant's national origin. The law allocates visas for 2 percent of individuals from each country as identified in the 1890 US Census. Furthermore, the law excludes all immigrants from Asia.

1939: The Wagner-Rogers Children's Bill is an attempt by the US Congress to implement a policy to help secure the evacuation and resettlement of children from Germany, mainly Jewish children,

---

A temporary processing facility in Donna, Texas, for family units and unaccompanied children in the custody of the US Border Patrol, March 17, 2021. The facility was built to bolster processing capacity while the permanent Centralized Processing Center in McAllen was renovated. (US Customs and Border Patrol photo by Jaime Rodriguez Sr.)

who are at risk of persecution from the Nazi government. The bill ultimately fails to pass due to concerns that German children would eventually take American jobs, as well as anti-Semitism that fuels political opposition.

1945: The Truman Directive is an effort to support resettling unaccompanied children from Europe. The Directive is part of President Truman's attempt to address the United States' failure to support migrant children during the First and Second World Wars. The directive results in approximately 1,300 children arriving in the United States from Poland, Czechoslovakia, Hungary, Germany, Rumania, Lithuania, and Estonia.

1948: The Displaced Persons Act of 1948 facilitates the resettlement of more than 400,000 people, including close to 3,000 unaccompanied children, mainly from Europe. A continued response to the massive displacement that resulted from the Second World War, the Displaced Persons Act provides children nonquota visas if they were under age sixteen, and quota-based visas for young people between sixteen and twenty-four years old. Under the Displaced Persons Act, unaccompanied children arrive in the United States from Germany, Greece, Poland, Italy, Yugoslavia, and Austria.

1950–1951: The 1951 Convention Relating to the Status of Refugees is a major United Nations document that specifies the shared efforts that the United Nations takes to ensure the health and well-being of refugees. Along with specifying the definition of a refugee, the document outlines the rights refugees have when experiencing displacement. The United States does not sign the 1951 Convention Relating to the Status of Refugees; however, it does sign the 1967 Protocol Relating to the Status of Refugees, which includes content specific to the needs of unaccompanied children.

1952: The Immigration and Nationality Act of 1952 increases the quota of visas available for immigrants from Eastern Europe and authorizes the Department of State to deny entry to immigrants who would lower wages of US citizen workers. The law also establishes a minimum of 100 visas for every country. The

Immigration and Nationality Act promotes family reunification, as children and spouses of US citizens are excluded from any caps on visas. Among the preferences for legal pathways in the bill, 20 percent of visas are allocated for children of legal residents.

1953: The Refugee Relief Act of 1953 is legislation that provides pathways for refugees to resettle in the United States. The legislation allocates nonquota immigrant visas for individuals from certain countries (e.g., West Germany or Austria, Italy, and Greece) and allocates 4,000 visas for "orphans" (i.e., unaccompanied children) under age ten. This includes children whose parents are deceased or who are otherwise separated from their parents, children who were adopted abroad by a US citizen, and children who do not qualify for other visas due to quotas.

1960–1962: Operation Pedro Pan is an initiative by the US federal government that facilitates the transfer of 14,048 Cuban children to the United States in the early 1960s. This operation is a response to the growth of communism and deteriorating conditions in Cuba. This operation differs from previous efforts by the US government to resettle unaccompanied children in that the operation does not experience widespread resistance.

1965: The Immigration and Nationality Act is signed into law by President Lyndon Johnson. The law is a major departure from previous immigration law in the United States that included quotas for immigrants from different parts of the world. The new law abolishes the use of national-origin quotas and instead prioritizes an immigrant's relationship with US citizen family or, secondarily, an immigrant's skills. The law caps available visas from the Eastern Hemisphere at 170,000 and caps visas from the Western Hemisphere at 120,000. The law also reserves 75 percent of visas for immigrants in family categories. The bill results in large increases in the number of immigrants living in the United States, rising from 9.6 million in 1965 to 45 million in 2015.

1967: The Protocol Relating to the Status of Refugees is an amendment to the 1951 United Nations Convention relating to the Status of Refugees. The 1967 Protocol removes geographic limits that were specified in the 1951 Convention, which was intended to meet the needs of refugees who were displaced during the Second World War. The Protocol of 1967 also includes specific content related to unaccompanied children. The Protocol explains that an integral component of the "principle of unity of the family" is the protection of unaccompanied children, with special focus on guardianship and adoption.

1975: Operation Babylift is an effort to resettle 3,000 Vietnamese children displaced because of the Vietnam War. The operation occurs at a time when the Vietnam War is viewed negatively by many in the United States and is seen by some as an effort to build support for the war. Later efforts to reunify children with their parents fail, and the majority of children who resettle during Operation Babylift are not reunified with family due to challenges with record keeping.

The Indochinese Refugee Program is an initiative to resettle children displaced during the Vietnam War. During the program, 8,000 children are resettled in the United States.

1980: The US Refugee Act of 1980 is landmark legislation that codifies critical parts of the refugee resettlement program in the United States. The legislation passed in the wake of the Vietnam War, after previous efforts to resettle refugees failed or encountered difficulty. The US Refugee Act is also the first piece of legislation that specifies procedures for the care, custody, and protection of unaccompanied children. A major part of the Act is formalizing the provision of funds for foster care services for unaccompanied children in the United States. The law also gives authority to the Office of Refugee Resettlement (ORR), under the auspices of the US Department of Health and Human Services, to coordinate the care of unaccompanied children. The legislation specifies the ways the ORR coordinates with state child welfare offices and also specifies that unaccompanied children can receive care until one month after they turn eighteen.

1990: The Immigration Act of 1990 is a major restructuring of immigration policy in the United States that includes new visa classifications that allow expanded legal pathways for immigrants. The law is a shift away from emphasizing family-based migration and prioritizes skills-based migration to address needs in the US economy. The Immigration Act also establishes special visas for children who are dependent on juvenile court, including children who are survivors of child maltreatment or are otherwise eligible for long-term foster care. These visas are also a form of relief for unaccompanied children who may be survivors of child maltreatment in their home country.

1997: The Flores Settlement Agreement is the outcome of a class action lawsuit filed in 1985, *Flores v. Reno*, that attempts to address concerns regarding the detention of immigrant children and families. The Flores Settlement Agreement results in guidelines that Immigration and Naturalization Services are required to follow when an immigrant child is held in detention. These guidelines include ensuring children are aware of their rights and have access to basic human needs, including toilets, sinks, drinking water, and food; access to medical care if needed; adequate supervision; and contact with any family members who were apprehended with the child. The Flores Settlement Agreement stipulates that children are to be detained in the least restrictive setting possible, children cannot be detained with a nonrelative adult for more than twenty-four hours, and children generally cannot be held in detention for more than twenty days before their transition to a less restrictive setting.

2000: The Victims of Trafficking and Violence Prevention Act is a law that seeks to prevent human trafficking, protect survivors of human trafficking, and prosecute individuals who engage in human trafficking. Within the law are protections for immigrants in the United States who are not citizens, including children, who are survivors of human trafficking. One protection is a "T-visa," which provides relief from deportation for adults and children who experience human trafficking. A T visa is granted for four years, during which time a child can receive services from the ORR and also apply for a Green Card after three years of continuous residence in the United States.

2002: The Homeland Security Act of 2002 marks a major change in immigration policy in the United States. In the wake of the September 11 terrorist attacks, the Homeland Security Act establishes the Department of Homeland Security (DHS). Part of DHS includes expanded immigration enforcement efforts. The Homeland Security Act of 2002 transfers all immigration matters to DHS, closes Immigration and Naturalization Services, and establishes US Citizenship and Immigration Services as a department in DHS. The Homeland Security Act also specifies that all unaccompanied children apprehended by Customs and Border Protection should be transferred to the ORR, which is part of the Department of Health and Human Services. This policy aligns with the best interests of children.

2005: The Unaccompanied Alien Child Protection Act of 2005 is a piece of legislation that is focused solely on the needs of unaccompanied children. The bill specifies that unaccompanied children cannot be detained in adult facilities and prioritizes family reunification. The bill intersects the fields of child welfare and immigration. For example, it prohibits US officials from deporting unaccompanied children to their country of origin if there is credible fear for their safety. The bill also authorizes unaccompanied children to have access to legal counsel during immigration proceedings.

2008: The Trafficking Victims Protection Reauthorization Act (TVPRA) of 2008 is legislation that protects individuals from human trafficking. The bill requires coordination between the Secretary of Homeland Security, the Secretary of State, the Attorney General, and the Secretary of Health and Human Services in the course of caring for unaccompanied children. TVPRA specifies the conditions where an unaccompanied child is not admissible to the United States, including if there is no known fear of trafficking if the child is returned to their country of origin. Countries contiguous with the United States (i.e., Canada or Mexico) have separate agreements with the United States to ensure unaccompanied children are safely returned to their country of origin. The bill requires that unaccompanied children be screened for risk of human trafficking within forty-eight hours of apprehension and also requires annual reporting to Congress to ensure oversight of all agency activities related to the bill.

2017: The Executive Office for Immigration Review, under President Trump's administration, redefines the criteria that help define when a child is "unaccompanied." This redefinition informs the way immigration judges determine a child's status during immigration proceedings. With new criteria for determining a child's status, children are at risk of not having protections that are available to unaccompanied children.

The federal government requires the director of the ORR to review the release of any unaccompanied children in ORR custody. The previous practice involved the assessment of experts in the field. Requiring the approval of administration within ORR slows the release of unaccompanied children, resulting in increased detention times.

2018: The Zero Tolerance Policy is a set of immigration policies that attempt to restrict migration across the US southern border. Among the policies is the criminal prosecution of all individuals who attempt to cross the border, even when crossing to apply for asylum. This results in family units being separated, with adults and children being detained separately. Attorney General Jeff Sessions announces the Zero Tolerance Policy in April 2018. The Zero Tolerance Policy results in children being detained, and many are unable to be reunified with family members. Children who are unable to reunify with family are "unaccompanied" and are subsequently placed in shelter or foster care placements.

In April 2018, the ORR signs a memorandum of understanding with Immigration and Customs Enforcement (ICE) that includes the policy that ORR officials will share the personal information of potential sponsors for unaccompanied children with ICE officials. This increases the risk of immigration enforcement, including detention and deportation, of potential sponsors for unaccompanied children. Potential sponsors are less likely to apply to sponsor a child due to this fear, resulting in unaccompanied children being detained. This is an example of immigration enforcement efforts being prioritized over child welfare practices.

Attorney General Jeff Sessions changes the performance criteria of immigration judges, requiring that judges close 700 cases per year to receive a satisfactory evaluation. This change adds pressure to an already stressed immigration court system and leads to fewer protections for unaccompanied children who are navigating immigration court and seeking relief from deportation.

The class action lawsuit *Ms. L v. U.S. Immigration and Customs Enforcement* is in litigation in response to President Trump's practice of family separation, which is part of the Zero Tolerance Policy. Ms. L. was separated from her daughter as part of the Zero Tolerance Policy. The lawsuit alleges violations of the US Constitution's due process clause, federal law protecting asylum seekers, and President Trump's own administrative directive to keep families intact. Ms. L. and her daughter are reunified in March 2018, and the class action suit continued.

2022: The Children's Safe Welcome Act is legislation that seeks to protect the health and well-being of children who are in immigration detention. The bill seeks to prioritize placing unaccompanied children in family-like settings and limiting the time unaccompanied children spend in detention facilities. In addition, the bill's provisions include prohibiting family separation and family detention, requiring that unaccompanied children be placed in the least restrictive setting possible, enhancing standards of care for Customs and Border Protection facilities, guaranteeing unaccompanied children have legal representation for immigration court, and establishing an ombudsperson to ensure there is oversight of the bill.

2023: A settlement is reached in the class action lawsuit *Ms. L v. U.S. Immigration and Customs Enforcement*. The lawsuit limits the use of family separation in immigration enforcement actions. The settlement also extends the period of parole for individuals part of the class action, to provide time for their reunification with their children. The settlement also provides an array of services for individuals and children who were injured as part of the

Zero Tolerance Policy. These services include health and mental health services, housing support for a twelve-month period, legal services to support families in immigration court, and specified processes to receive relief from deportation for three years, with work authorization for adults during those three years. The settlement also specifies how the government is to report ongoing compliance with the parts of the settlement.

The Protecting Unaccompanied Children Act is a bill that seeks to establish mechanisms for reporting violations against immigrant children in detention facilities, establishing protections for unaccompanied children, and supporting the safe release of unaccompanied children to sponsors. Among the provisions in the bill are expanding access to post-release services and ensuring unaccompanied children receive home studies when there is risk of human trafficking or child maltreatment.

2025: *Community Legal Services in East Palo Alto et al. v. United States Department of Health and Human Services et al.* is a class action lawsuit in response to President Trump cancelling a program that provided legal service providers for unaccompanied children in immigration court. The lawsuit argues that this violates the TVPRA 2008. The lawsuit argues that US Congress already allocated funds for legal services for unaccompanied children through 2027. Cancelling these services leaves more than 27,000 unaccompanied children without legal representation in court and places them further at risk of deportation without due process.

Angelica v. U.S. Department of Health and Human Services is a lawsuit filed by the National Center for Youth Law and Democracy Forward, which argues that President Trump's administration is violating the rights of unaccompanied children by prolonged immigration detention and separating children from their families during immigration enforcement actions. Furthermore, the lawsuit argues that new criteria for sponsor documentation violate existing policy at the ORR that aims to facilitate the placement of unaccompanied children.

Glossary

Family Reunification: Family reunification is the process where unaccompanied children, typically with the support of the Office of Refugee Resettlement (ORR), are reunified with family or a sponsor in the United States.

Home Study: A home study is an evaluation that assesses the appropriateness of an unaccompanied child's potential placement with a sponsor. Along with evaluating the physical safety of the living conditions, a home study also includes interviews with sponsors and other members of the household.

Influx Care Facility: An Influx Care Facility, also known as an Emergency Influx Facility, is a facility that opens when large numbers of unaccompanied children arrive at the US border and ORR shelters no longer have space for children. Influx Care Facilities may be unlicensed or exempt from state or federal licensing requirements due to the emergency response to housing unaccompanied children.

Know-Your-Rights (KYR) Presentations: Know-Your-Rights Presentations are presentations provided by legal service providers, to inform unaccompanied children of their basic rights and also provide an overview of the immigration court system. This includes a review of the types of immigration relief that may be available to unaccompanied children, as well as the importance of attending all scheduled immigration court hearings.

Legal Service Provider (LSP): A legal service provider is an individual or an organization that provides unaccompanied children with legal services. The legal services are provided on a *pro bono* basis or may be funded by ORR. Along with providing KYR presentations, LSPs also provide direct legal representation for unaccompanied children who are navigating immigration court.

Long-term Foster Care: Some unaccompanied children are unable to reunify with a sponsor because one is not available or appropriate. In these circumstances, unaccompanied children are placed in long-term foster care. These are placements in communities throughout the United States that are funded by ORR. While in long-term foster care, unaccompanied children access services in the community, including public school.

Office of Refugee Resettlement (ORR): The Office of Refugee Resettlement is a federal agency that is part of the US Department of Health and Human Services and is responsible for supporting immigrants and refugees who arrive in the United States. ORR is the agency responsible for helping unaccompanied children reunify with family or be placed with a sponsor or in long-term foster care in the United States. ORR operates a network of shelters where unaccompanied children reside after apprehension at the US border and while they wait for placement with a sponsor or in long-term foster care.

ORR/Federal Field Specialist (FFS): An ORR/FFS is a staff person who acts as a liaison in the community between ORR and ORR care providers, such as programs that provide home studies and post-release services.

ORR/Project Officer (PO): ORR/PO are staff who supervise ORR care providers, home study providers, and post-release services providers.

Post-Release Services (PRS): Post-Release Services are case management services that some unaccompanied children receive after they are placed in the United States with a sponsor. PRS are intended to help unaccompanied children connect with supports in the community, such as education services, health or mental health services, and legal services. PRS are offered at three different levels, which differ by length of service and amount of service delivery. Level 1 PRS lasts for 30 days and includes virtual check-ins with the unaccompanied child at 7, 14, and 30 days after the child is placed with a sponsor. Level 2 PRS lasts six months and includes case management services to help unaccompanied children adjust to their new community. Level 3 PRS provides intensive case management, including weekly visits to ensure complex mental health needs are met.

Post-Release Services Case Manager: Post-Release Services Case Managers are professionals who provide Level 2 PRS. Case managers may also provide Level 1 or Level 3 PRS.

Post-Release Services Case Worker: Post-Release Services Case Workers are professionals who provide Level 1 PRS.

Post-Release Services Clinician: Post-Release Services Clinicians are professionals who provide Level 3 PRS.

Post-Release Services Provider: PRS providers are organizations that receive funding from ORR to provide community-based services for unaccompanied children, including home studies and PRS, after a child leaves ORR custody and is placed with a sponsor or in long-term foster care.

Residential Treatment Center (RCT): The ORR defines a Residential Treatment Center as "A sub-acute, time limited, interdisciplinary, psycho-educational, and therapeutic 24-hour-a-day structured program with community linkages, provided through non-coercive, coordinated, individualized care, specialized services, and interventions" (Office of Refugee Resettlement 2025). RCTs are designed to provide intensive therapeutic services for unaccompanied children with complex needs, with a goal of helping children transition to community-based placements with sponsors or foster care providers.

Significant Incidents: Significant incidents are nonemergency events that may pose a threat to the health and well-being of an unaccompanied child. Significant incidents are documented and shared with ORR using a "Non-Emergency Significant Incident Report."

Therapeutic Foster Care: Therapeutic foster care is a placement for unaccompanied children who do not have an identified sponsor in the United States and also have demonstrated complex health or mental health needs. Therapeutic foster care placements are funded by ORR, and programs partner with foster parents, as well as community-based services, to ensure unaccompanied children's needs are met.

Unaccompanied Alien Children: Unaccompanied Alien Children, or unaccompanied children, are individuals apprehended at or near the US border, are under eighteen years old when they are apprehended, and are without parents or caregivers at the time of their apprehension, or a parent or caregiver is unavailable at the time of their apprehension.

Unaccompanied Alien Children Bureau: The Unaccompanied Alien Children Bureau is the organization within ORR that is directly responsible for providing care to unaccompanied children who are in the federal government's custody.

US Customs and Border Protection (USCBP): US Customs and Border Protection is a federal agency that is part of the Department of Homeland Security and is responsible for securing US borders and official ports of entry. USCBP agents evaluate terrorism threats, combat transnational crime, and facilitate the lawful flow of commercial goods across US borders. USCBP agents are also among the first individuals who encounter and apprehend unaccompanied children who arrive at US borders.

Further Reading

Office of Refugee Resettlement. 2025. "ORR Unaccompanied Alien Children Bureau Policy Guide: Guide to Terms." https://acf.gov/orr/policy-guidance/unaccompanied-children-program-policy-guide-guide-terms

Index

About the Author

Robert G. Hasson III, PhD, LICSW, is an associate professor of social work at Providence College, where he is a member of the Department of Social Work. His research focuses on the intersection of mental health and forced migration. His teaching focuses on human behavior through the lifespan, research methods, and foundational social work practice skills. Rob also maintains a small private practice where he provides clinical social work services for adolescents and young adults. Rob lives in New England with his wife, Caitlin, and they divide their time between Rhode Island and Maine.